PUBLIC SPENDING AND THE ROLE OF THE STATE

Given high government spending, debt and the new challenges on the horizon, the themes of this work are more relevant than ever: the essential tool of spending by the state, its 'value for money', likely risks in the future, and the remedies to create lean, efficient and sustainable government. This book takes a holistic and international approach, covering most advanced countries, and discusses a historical overview of public expenditure, from the nineteenth century to the modern day, as well as future challenges. It sees the government's role as providing sound rules of the game and essential public goods and services. In presenting the relevant arguments, information and policy recommendations through comprehensive tables, charts and historical facts, the book addresses a broad readership, including students, professionals and interested members of the public.

LUDGER SCHUKNECHT is co-author of *Public Spending in the 20th Century* (2000), previously working as Deputy Secretary General of the OECD and Chief Economist of the German Federal Ministry of Finance.

Public Spending and the Role of the State

History, Performance, Risk and Remedies

LUDGER SCHUKNECHT

CAMBRIDGE
UNIVERSITY PRESS

University Printing House, Cambridge CB2 8BS, United Kingdom

One Liberty Plaza, 20th Floor, New York, NY 10006, USA

477 Williamstown Road, Port Melbourne, VIC 3207, Australia

314–321, 3rd Floor, Plot 3, Splendor Forum, Jasola District Centre, New Delhi – 110025, India

79 Anson Road, #06–04/06, Singapore 079906

Cambridge University Press is part of the University of Cambridge.

It furthers the University's mission by disseminating knowledge in the pursuit of education, learning, and research at the highest international levels of excellence.

www.cambridge.org
Information on this title: www.cambridge.org/9781108496230
DOI: 10.1017/9781108496230

© Cambridge University Press 2021

First published 2021

A catalogue record for this publication is available from the British Library.

ISBN 978-1-108-49623-0 Hardback
ISBN 978-1-108-79170-0 Paperback

Cambridge University Press has no responsibility for the persistence or accuracy of URLs for external or third-party internet websites referred to in this publication and does not guarantee that any content on such websites is, or will remain, accurate or appropriate.

To my wife Jyoti

Contents

Figures

Tables

Preface

Nothing in life is to be feared, it is only to be understood. Now is the time to understand more so that we fear less.

Marie Curie

The curious task of economics is to demonstrate to 'men' how little they really know about what they imagine they can design.

Friedrich August von Hayek

Much of what makes today's advanced economies work well requires government and government spending: the rule of law and effective regulation, security, modern infrastructure, good education and basic social safety nets. Vito Tanzi and I called these the 'core tasks of government' in our book *Public Spending in the 20th Century* twenty years ago. Governments that do well on these core tasks build trust in them and amongst their citizens. Markets then function well and people are likely to prosper in freedom with little regard to their economic and social background.

We also argued in our book that governments do not need to be very big to perform these tasks: government spending of 30–35% of gross domestic product (GDP) is enough, perhaps 40% in some cases. Government expenditure reforms are a good way for governments to stay lean, efficient and sustainable, and there was much optimism about 'limited government' at the time.

In the current situation, with a global financial crisis behind and 'new' challenges from the COVID19 pandemic, the environment to cybersecurity, we are experiencing an unprecedented sense of unease about the role of government and public expenditure and a decline in trust that governments still can and will deliver on their core tasks. We are witnessing very vocal calls for more public spending by some and for less government spending by others. Some have voiced concerns about too much austerity and too little redistribution, while others have deplored falling productive spending and too much debt.

It seems, therefore, timely to revisit the role of the state and public expenditure, to look at the strengths and weaknesses of the 'spending state' and the challenges for the future across a broad range of advanced countries. There are four main themes and findings:

- First, government is essential for a well-functioning market economy. Governments delivering on their core tasks – not just spending more money – are trusted more to deliver. Government has grown enormously over the past 150 years, building up the administration, infrastructure and education systems and, in recent decades, the welfare state. Social spending has grown to over half of total spending, while the share of other spending has declined. However, revenue has often not been keeping up, and public debt has reached record levels in a number of countries.

- Second, there are huge differences in the performance and efficiency of governments, with smaller governments tending to do better in many cases. Three reform waves in the 1980s, 1990s and 2010s show that lower spending can reinvigorate both governments and economies. Experience shows that public spending of 30–35% of GDP, perhaps 40%, suffices to do well for core tasks. One could call this a pragmatic 'optimum' – without being dogmatic about it for every country case.

- Third, there are dark clouds caused by the ever-increasing insurance role of government, notably in the social and financial sphere. If social expenditure trends continue or if a financial crisis leads to major spending obligations and debt increases again, public finances may not be sustainable in many countries and may put domestic economies, central banks and international stability at risk.

- Fourth, many governments need to strengthen their rules and institutions to deliver better on their core tasks, adjust the size of the state, shrink their debt and limit future fiscal and financial risks. Economists can contribute to this by advising on stronger governance and better policies, and they can help in building realistic expectations of what governments can, and should, do.

Acknowledgements

My biggest gratitude of course goes to my family and to my wife Jyoti. She bore with me through the many years of gestation and production of this book and its underlying papers. My wife always gave me good advice and constructive criticism on what I wrote.

I am also very grateful to Vito Tanzi, with whom I wrote *Public Spending in the 20th Century* twenty years ago and many follow-up papers on the role of the state thereafter. He has been a mentor to me for many years and extensively commented on the manuscript.

I also owe much gratitude to many former colleagues at the European Central Bank. Otmar Issing and Jürgen Stark, with whom I wrote several papers and articles, provided great encouragement and comments. My many co-authors on topics of government performance and efficiency, reform experiences and fiscal rules and institutions that have influenced the book deserve my sincere thanks. These include Antonio Afonso, Luca Agnelli, Kerstin Bernoth, Sebastian Hauptmeier, Martin Heipertz, Albert Jaeger, Ana Lamo, Richard Morris, Rainer Martin, Philippe Moutot, Xavier Perez, Huw Pill, Philipp Rother, Jesus Sanchez-Fuentes, Mika Tujula, Jürgen von Hagen and Guido Wolswijk.

The majority of the work on this book was done after I joined the German Ministry of Finance as its Chief Economist and advisor to Minister Wolfgang Schäuble in 2011. It was an exciting but also a difficult time, with many intellectual and political challenges, and the Ministry provided an open and vibrant atmosphere for airing them. I enjoyed many discussions with the Minister, and my colleagues Thomas Steffen, Johannes Geismann, Michael Meister, Jens Spahn, Werner Gatzer, Thomas Westphal, Levin Holle, Matthias Hass, Martin Jaeger, Bruno Kahl, Friederike von Tiesenhausen, Helmut Herres, Wilfried Steinheuer, Rita Schutt and Marianne Kothe. Papers with my co-authors Florian Buck, Matthias Dauns,

Elmar Doennebrink, Werner Ebert, the late Norbert Hoekstra, Nadja König (Boehme), Andrea Rieck and Holger Zemanek contributed to the discussion on trust, public insurance, social dominance and fiscal financial risks. Sonia Polczyk and Andy Wetzke were the best assistants one could have.

From my inspiring and rewarding time at the Organisation for Economic Co-operation and Development (OECD), I would like to highlight the collaboration with Jon Blondal on budgetary institutions, Roberto Patalano, Serdat Çelik on bond markets, Peter Hoeller and Boris Cournede on government efficiency, and Andreas Schleicher on education. I am also very thankful for the discussions with Masamichi Kono and Laurence Boone, and especially to Elizabeth Morgan and Vincent Siegerink for their wonderful support.

I must also praise the colleagues and friends that I relied on when writing this book: my friends of many years Jörg Stephan, Peter Doyle and Gerd Schwarz for exciting discussions and much advice, Silvia Ardagna, Mark Bowman, Claudio Borio, Dave Coady, Clemens Fuest, Vitor Gaspar, Harold James, Andrea Maechler, Niklas Potrafke, Hans Werner Sinn, Ramin Toloui and Frity Zurbruegg for excellent exchanges and comments. Alberto Alesina has been a great inspiration through his work and in my collaboration with him; he died much too young. Finally, I would also like to thank three anonymous referees for their valuable suggestions and apologise to those that I forgot to mention here.

All remaining errors are naturally my responsibility.

Acronyms and Abbreviations

BIS   Bank for International Settlements
CBA   cost-benefit analysis
CCP   centralised trading platform
CEE   Central and Eastern Europe
CGFS   Committee on the Global Financial System
DEA   data envelope analysis
ECB   European Central Bank
EEAG   European Economic Advisory Group
EFB   European Fiscal Board
EFSM   European Financial Stability Mechanism
EMU   European Monetary Union
ERM   European Exchange Rate Mechanism
ESM   European Stability Mechanism
ESRB   European Systemic Risk Board
ETF   exchange-traded fund
FSB   Financial Stability Board
G7   Group of Seven: Canada, France, Germany, Italy, Japan, United Kingdom, United States
G20   group of 19 largest economies + the EU
GDP   gross domestic product
GFSR   Global Financial Stability Report (IMF)
GNP   gross national product
IFS   Institute for Fiscal Studies
IMF   International Monetary Fund
IOSCO International Organization of Securities Commissions
NATO   North Atlantic Treaty Organization

NPL   non-performing loan
OBR   Office for Budget Responsibility (UK)
OECD   Organisation for Economic Co-operation and Development
PIMA   Public Investment Management Assessment (IMF)
PISA   Programme for International Student Assessment
PPF   production possibility frontier
PPP   public–private partnership
SDR   Special Drawing Right (IMF)
SFT   security financing transaction
SGP   Stability and Growth Pact
SOE   state-owned enterprise
VAT   value added tax
WEO   World Economic Outlook
WTO   World Trade Organization

Introduction

What Should Governments Do?

> *Government is a contrivance of human wisdom to provide for human
> wants. 'Men' have a right that these wants should be provided for by
> this wisdom.*
>
> Edmund Burke

> *What we have ignored is what citizens can do and the importance of real
> involvement of the people involved.*
>
> Elinor Ostrom

Highlights

Well-functioning governments are at the basis of a modern, democratic society,
the rule of law and a market process that generates trust, opportunities, prosperity
and freedom.

To maintain the economic success of advanced economies and the trust of our
citizens, governments need to do well on their core tasks: setting sound rules of the
game in the market economy and providing high-quality, essential public goods and
services. These include security, education, infrastructure, basic social safety nets, the
environment and sound public finances. Public expenditure is an important tool in
this regard, but more spending is not correlated with more trust – 'better' spending
and better performance on core tasks is (Figure I.1).

This introduction also sets out the map of the book: How public spending has
evolved over time and how it has been financed in Part I; government performance
and efficiency, the role of expenditure reforms and the 'optimal' size of government in
Part II; the main fiscal risks in the social and financial sphere in Part III; and the case
for strong rules and institutions to govern public spending and limit fiscal risks in the
concluding Part IV.

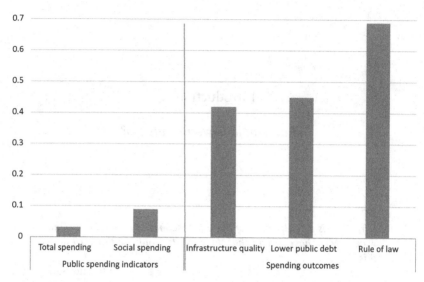

Source: Koenig and Schuknecht (2019). Correlation coefficient on Y-axis

Figure I.1 Correlation between trust in government, public spending and performance on core tasks.

I.1 Public Expenditure as a Key Tool of Government

Without government, life would be 'miserable, brutish and short'. We would be stuck in anarchy, without freedom and security, with hunger, disease and ignorance, as stressed by Thomas Hobbes over 350 years ago (Hobbes, 1651).

From that vantage point, governments have been stunningly successful. The world has never been more peaceful, secure and prosperous than today. Never has poverty been so limited and never have people had so many opportunities to better their lives. We have never been so free to pursue happiness. Collaboration between people and trust in our governments help the smooth functioning of our societies and economies. This success story holds in particular for advanced economies, but also increasingly for emerging markets and government expenditure has played a key role in it.

But many advanced country governments seem to be in crisis today. Many people are unhappy about what governments do despite the obvious successes. This is confusing at first sight and it is definitely a wake-up call to ask what is going wrong and what needs to change.

When analysing the crisis of Western government, we can learn much from looking at the private sector. When companies are in trouble, we often hear that they have neglected their core business, that they allowed spending to get out of control, that they have too much debt and that they missed the boat on important, emerging challenges. We expect them to become more focussed, lean, resilient and forward looking. In our own private lives, it is not that much different, and we often have to adjust and reform our ways of doing things.

This should also hold for government, and we should ask similar questions. Government should provide core goods and services via spending and regulation and financed by taxes. It should react to new challenges while 'living within its means'. But with governments, we often hear a different tune. Many people see them as a 'Wunschkonzert', a kind of 'Father Christmas' responsible for fulfilling all our wishes: prosperity, employment and stability at all times for everybody. We frown upon cost-consciousness and financing constraints while complaining about high taxes, waste and a lack of long-term strategy. Of course, this does not work.

This book looks at one of the key tools of government, public expenditure. It asks how public spending has evolved over time and how it can serve both citizens and society to master the present and the future. The basic argument is this: in order to continue the success story and maintain the trust of our citizens in a fast-changing world, we need to spend public money wisely. Governments should focus on their core tasks, be lean, efficient and financially sustainable, reform where needed and prevent undue risk. This requires sound rules and institutions for both government and the economy!

I.2 The Role of Government in the Market Economy: The Classical View

What is the role and what are the core tasks of governments in the market economy? Classical economists and economic philosophers ever since Adam Smith (1937) have seen the main role of governments as setting the rules of the game for market economies (Hayek 1960; Buchanan and Tullock, 1962; Buchanan, 1975; Brennan and Buchanan, 1985). The rules of the game need to define safe property rights and a framework for their exchange in markets. Hence, there is a need for a well-functioning public administration with a secure code of law and regulation. We will refer to this as the 'rule of law'.

In the eighteenth century, Adam Smith realised that governments should prevent an obstruction of markets and competition. A strong antitrust system and open international trade rules can achieve this goal. Externalities are another reason to intervene in markets (Pigou, 1920, 1928; Coase, 1960). This includes, for example, environmental protection, safe medicine and consumer protection.

In recent years, the potential for externalities in financial markets has received increasing attention. Information problems and the sheer size of losses have fostered the recognition that both rules and regulation need to improve incentives in the financial system. In fact, many rules and regulations now have the objective of preventing damage that would be costly to citizens and government.

Beyond this rule-setting role of government, there are also good reasons for the provision of other public goods and services. Security is an obvious case in point: (almost) every country needs a defence force. There is also a strong reason for a domestic security force – the police – to protect internal security, complemented by a system of justice. The public administration and the justice system enforce property rights and contracts, and rules and regulations so that markets can work.

Beyond security and law enforcement, there are further core public goods. The most prominent one today is probably education. Since the nineteenth century, public education has become a widespread achievement in the world, starting at the primary level but now also including secondary and tertiary education. Without public education, people and societies would not invest enough in knowledge formation, and this would reduce the potential for society-wide progress, opportunity and prosperity.

Governments today also have an important role in enhancing social inclusion. Government provision of social safety nets, including health, poverty alleviation and elderly care, is not only socially desirable but has a strong public goods component. Health services should (inter alia) prevent diseases from becoming epidemics. Poverty reduction measures prevent people from becoming criminals out of desperation. Basic safety nets for the elderly reduce the need for costly self-insurance, in the face of ever more people becoming eighty, ninety or even a hundred years old. Many economists now refer to the 'social market economy' model when emphasising the need for well-targeted safety nets that complement markets.

Another 'popular' public good is infrastructure, such as roads, water and sewage systems or energy networks. Private provision of such infrastructure is often impossible, or at least difficult, because construction requires collective action and it is hard to charge for consumption. Private provision has become much easier with the spread of tolls or network charges, but there is still a considerable need for public engagement.

One should also add sound and sustainable public finances as a public good and a core task of government. Avoiding undue fiscal risk is part of this task. Sound public finances raise people's confidence that public services will still be available and of high quality in the future. Sound public finances also allow governments to run deficits in downturns without undermining confidence via the so-called automatic stabilisers. Over-indebted governments may need to undertake one-off cuts, especially in bad times. Over-indebtedness often results in instability and inflation via default or 'printing money' to finance the debt. All this is detrimental to both people's and countries' well-being.

An analogy to the game of football can illustrate the importance of 'good' rules of the game and their interplay with high-quality public goods and services. Football is a great game because it has rules that make it exciting, reward good skill and leave enough uncertainty for the occasional surprise result. But it would be far less successful and exciting if there were no clubs providing training opportunities and cities building infrastructure, especially in less privileged areas.

The benefits to society from 'good performance' on the core tasks of government are many and various and provide everybody with an opportunity to participate in economic and social life. In former times, being born to a poor family meant that you had no such opportunity, if you survived childhood at all. Today, everybody in a well-functioning industrialised market economy has the opportunity to access clean water and go to school. In the past, living in a poor quarter meant little access to the justice system and primitive, if any, roads. The much greater inclusiveness of modern market economies is often forgotten in today's debate.

A market process based on the rule of law with a lean, efficient and sustainable government is also the basis of individual freedom. Money in private hands gives freedom of choice to individuals, but rules prevent my choice impinging on the freedom of others (Hank, 2012). Governments that ensure the rule of law secure individual freedom.

Governments also promote freedom through doing well on core public goods and services. The case of security is obvious: no security, no freedom. However, good education and good roads also enhance individual freedom through the opportunities they create. If we know more, if we can access a broader market, we have more choice and we can live up to our potential more fully. One can therefore call this an important part of freedom.

Collier (2018) also emphasises the 'sense of belonging' – a culture of fairness and loyalty that a community of mutual obligations and rules creates. Rules based on values and morality then help communities and societies to live through long periods of adverse circumstances. One could see this as another social dimension of the rules- and market-based society whose value was already stressed by Adam Smith.

Trust in governments doing 'the right thing' is a prerequisite and a consequence of a well-functioning market economy. People will not want to follow the rules set by an untrustworthy government. With trust, society and the market economy function in an orderly fashion with limited friction. An order of high and growing complexity emerges without anybody specific in control of all the elements (Simpson, 2013). This is quite miraculous, but also a bit scary. In this order, freedom, opportunities and trust condition and reinforce each other. The outcomes – prosperity with growth, jobs and investment – are the 'symptom' of this order's success.

I.3 The Role of Government in the Market Economy: The Keynesian View

We can also see and define the tasks of government from the perspective of the intended outcome rather than process. Building on Keynes (1936), Richard Musgrave (1959) and many since have detected a threefold role for government. Public goods and regulation should improve the resource allocation of the economy, and economic growth would be a good way to measure this.

Public spending should also aim at actively stabilising the economy against undue fluctuations. Debt in downturns and surpluses in upswings would smooth demand and leave room to deal with unforeseen circumstances. Finally, the role of the state is to alleviate poverty and equalise incomes (and wealth) via redistribution. This would also be economically beneficial as, to simplify a little, the rich tend to save too much and the poor invest too little.

The process-oriented view of Adam Smith and other classical economists and the outcome-oriented view of Musgrave are rather different. But they overlap in many ways: a good, incorrupt public administration means a more efficient use of resources and more income potential for the poor. This, in turn, boosts growth and income equality. Good public education works in the same direction. It is equally important to measure and control outputs and outcomes so as to make governments both accountable and performance-oriented.

Balance is important, however. Too much focus on outputs may lead to a neglect of process. Outcomes are seemingly easier to measure than process and, hence, have a 'comparative advantage' for monitoring. But it is process more than outcomes that governments can influence. An exclusive focus on outcomes supports a view that economic results can be 'fine-tuned' like a machine and that government is responsible for them. This, however, is more than government can deliver (James, 2009).

I.4 Trust in Government

One can argue endlessly from different conceptual perspectives about the role of government. However, in a democracy, our citizens decide whether they support our market-based economic system, its direction and its governance. To do so, they need to have trust in government and what it is doing. The last decade has shown that this trust cannot be taken for granted.

What builds trust in government? There are good arguments and evidence that governments attaining core tasks and the rule of law are trusted more because that is what people want. For that, public spending is needed – but it is doing well on these tasks, not more spending, that builds trust (König and Schuknecht, 2019).

The link from the role of government to trust in government and the market economy is indirect (Figure I.2). If governments perform well on their core tasks, we are likely to witness better functioning markets, greater freedom and opportunities and more growth and prosperity. This boosts people's satisfaction and trust in the ability of government to deliver on their expectations. A virtuous circle arises when more trust means more compliance with rules, people paying taxes and investment boosting growth.

If governments do not deliver, we are likely to see poor performance of the economy, parts of society without opportunities and a general sense of frustration with the economic and political system. A sense of loss of control, of lawlessness and insecurity and of 'the rich having it all' starts to spread when corruption rises, public education deteriorates, the environment degrades or people's personal security depends on the income level of their neighbourhood.

Worse still, the poor performance of the market economy may induce governments to blame the market instead of themselves. This risks discrediting the economic system and may create a spiral of new intervention, worsening performance and further undermining of trust.

A simple analysis can illustrate these claims. Eurobarometer regularly conducts a survey of trust in government for most EU member countries.

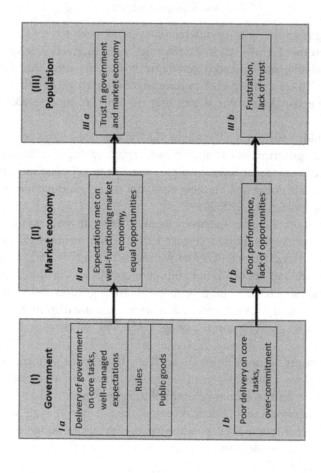

Figure I.2 Link from government performance to trust.

The survey results are compared, with measures of government spending as inputs and measures of outcomes on government core tasks.

There are many indicators from various sources, and we focus on a few which seem most suitable. The 'rule of law' indicator by the Fraser Institute is a proxy for good rules of the game in society. It compiles data on judicial independence, impartial courts, protection of property rights and contract enforcement, amongst others.

Total government spending or spending on public administration serves as a proxy for how much governments spend on providing the 'rule of law'. Similarly, public education spending measures inputs and the OECD PISA score measures outcomes in education. We can also see how trust relates to infrastructure spending and a World Bank infrastructure quality indicator. Social spending and the income share of the poorest 40% of households measure inputs and outcomes as regards safety nets and income distribution. Public debt serves as an indicator of the soundness of public finances.

Table I.1 provides the results for twenty-one European countries for the period 2005–2015. The numbers reflect the degree of correlation between spending and performance indicators on the one hand and trust on the other. An indicator near zero implies no correlation; the higher an indicator, the more one can speak of a relevant positive correlation, and a value of 0.3 is a good borderline. Correlations are important and illustrative but we should not overinterpret them; they do not necessarily imply causality.

The results are telling: there is very little correlation between trust in government and public expenditure. Even social expenditure does not correlate with more trust in government. The only expenditure component where the correlation is reasonably strong is education. We will see in Part II that there is very little correlation between spending and performance and some countries do very well with little public money.

By contrast, government performance matters a lot. The correlation coefficient is highest for 'rule of law' – the proxy for 'good' rules of the game. High-quality infrastructure also shows a relatively strong correlation with trust. The picture is modestly positive regarding education/PISA and income distribution.

Sound and sustainable public finances are also very relevant for trust. In fact, the correlation between trust and debt in the pre-enlargement EU is quite remarkable and the highest of all coefficients. Citizens are probably quite aware of the problems that over-indebtedness creates.

Table I.1 *Correlation between trust in government, public spending and performance on core tasks*

Role of government	Public spending	All EU Correlation with trust	Performance on core tasks	All EU Correlation with trust	Pre-enlargement EU Correlation with tust
Rules of the game	Total spending	0.03	Rule of law	0.69	0.69
			Regulation	0.33	0.38
			Globalisation	0.44	0.39
Infrastructure	Public investment	0.06	Infrastructure quality	0.42	0.48
Education	Spending on education	0.42	PISA	0.33	0.32
Social safety nets	Social spending	0.09	Income share 40% poorest households	0.32	0.54
Sound public finances			Public debt	−0.45	−0.73

Sources: OECD for all input variables and PISA; IMF WEO for debt; World Bank for the index for infrastructure, Fraser Institute for the indices on rule of law and regulation; WDI for income share of bottom 40%; KOF globalisation index. Trust from Eurobarometer, 2005–2015 vintages

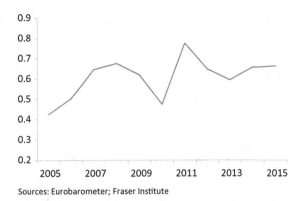

Sources: Eurobarometer; Fraser Institute

Figure I.3 Correlation between trust in own government and the rule of law.

Globalisation is often blamed for a loss of trust or the rise of populism (Potrakfke, 2018). The result here is the opposite: the correlation between open markets and trade integration on the one hand and trust on the other is strong and positive. Open, well-functioning international markets are a core function of government, trade boosts opportunities, prosperity and high-quality jobs.

The correlation between government performance on core tasks and trust in Europe has tended to grow over time. Figure I.3, for example, shows that the correlation coefficient for trust and the rule of law started out near 0.4 in 2005. Since then, it increased significantly and stood near a very high 0.65 in 2015. There was some bumpiness around the global financial crisis when all countries experienced a loss of trust.

The findings on trust and government performance are also encouraging from another angle. European adjustment programmes were much criticised for their effect on the economy and society. Many economists argued that higher spending rather than consolidation should have boosted growth. We will see later that the facts suggest differently. Crisis countries undertook expenditure reform and strengthened their rules of the game. The implementation of reform programmes went hand in hand not only with a resurgence of the economy but also with more trust by citizens in their government (Figure I.4). This confirms the role of sound policies and reforms to re-build trust.

All in all, governments are essential for our well-being and their role has rightly evolved over time. But for that we need 'good' (meaning effective and efficient), not necessarily 'big' government. If governments focus on their core tasks, well-functioning markets and high-quality government

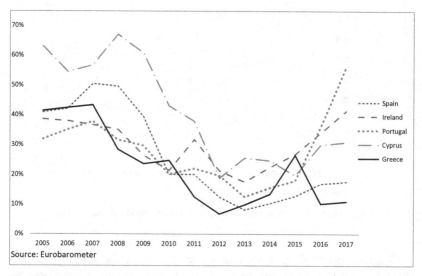

Source: Eurobarometer

Figure I.4 Trust in own government, European reform countries.

goods and services provide a high degree of freedom, opportunities, prosperity and trust.

I.5 Map of the Book

Twenty years ago, in our book *Public Spending in the 20th Century*, Vito Tanzi and myself demonstrated that governments have grown significantly since the late nineteenth century as they have taken on new tasks and extended the provision of existing ones (Tanzi and Schuknecht, 2000). At first, this focussed mainly on the core tasks discussed here. Over time, and certainly after the 1960s, many governments went far beyond that. Many have consequently become too big for their own (and their people's) good.

Part I (Chapters 1–3) looks again at the question of how the role of government has evolved over the past 150 years. It provides a historical and holistic perspective on the growth, composition and financing of government spending. It describes the rise of public spending until about 1960, the huge increase until the 1980s, the 'ups and downs' thereafter and the renewed growth of government since the turn of the millennium (Chapter 1). Public spending broadly followed the intellectual climate and fashions, but some countries' governments now spend more than half of their GDP while some others spend much less and have broken the trend of rising spending.

It is worth looking at the underlying composition and trends of public expenditure if we are to better understand its main drivers (Chapter 2). Most governments are spending an ever-growing share of resources on social objectives while other more productive spending such as investment sometimes gets short shrift.

In Chapter 3, we focus on the important question of how all this spending is financed: via revenue or via (visible and hidden) debt. We show that under-financing – or over-spending – has become chronic in many countries so that public debt and uncovered future liabilities are often at an all-time high.

Part II (Chapters 4–6) asks whether all this spending and debt is worthwhile. Most governments could be doing a good job with much less spending and, hence, much less financing difficulties, as we show in Chapter 4. There is evidence that small governments tend to perform better than big governments on many measures, though there are exceptions and differing objectives. Nevertheless, and much more so than twenty years ago, we need to compete with dynamic Asian economies that do well and have much smaller governments.

Many countries have undertaken significant fiscal reforms in three waves since the 1980s, and this is examined in Chapter 5. We will see that these efforts at containing spending, improving efficiency and regaining fiscal integrity have typically been very successful in economic and social terms. The findings also suggest some scepticism towards higher spending as a recipe for success.

Chapter 6 discusses how 'big' government should be. Putting together evidence on best practice as regards aggregate spending and core spending categories, we argue that the optimum size of government has remained broadly unchanged since 2000. Public spending of 30–35% or perhaps 40% of GDP is all that is needed. Vito Tanzi and I came to a similar conclusion twenty years ago. This is not surprising given that the core tasks have not changed much and population ageing is only just 'taking off' in many countries. But these figures are not dogmatic. Some emerging economies thrive with significantly less while some countries are doing well with a bigger government.

Part III (Chapters 7–9) discusses the key risks and challenges that governments will face in the future. These risks relate to the ever-expanding 'insurance role' of government (Chapter 7). Social spending, in particular, risks over-burdening governments, creating ever more debt and crowding out other core tasks. We call this the risk of 'social dominance' (Schuknecht and Zemanek, 2020).

The other main risk for government comes from the financial sphere. Given high debt and asset price levels, there are significant risks from fragile markets and rising financing costs. Financial developments also affect public finances via the real economy. Moreover, there are risks of financial sector turbulence turning into fiscal turbulence via bank, non-bank, central bank and international channels. Low public spending and low debt provide more buffers against fiscal financial risks. Chapters 8 and 9 discuss these challenges.

Part IV (Chapters 10–11) discusses the role of rules and institutions as possible remedies. Rules and institutions are at the heart of effective and well-managed governments that focus on their core tasks (Chapter 10). They ensure the sustainability of public finances and the stability of both economies and financial systems. They also guide expectations as to the limits of and constraints on government behaviour. This builds trust and prevents hubris and excess in what governments do. A brief Conclusion cum Epilogue (Chapter 11) concludes the book.

PART I

THE GROWTH OF GOVERNMENT

The Growth of Government Expenditure over the Past 150 Years

The fate of countries is determined to a huge extent by the amount of resources the state absorbs and how these resources are put to use.

Joseph A. Schumpeter

Government should be a referee, not an active player [in the economy].

Milton Friedman

Highlights

The role of government has evolved significantly over the past 150 years. In the late nineteenth century, only about 10% of GDP passed through the hands of government. This was consistent with the prevailing view that government should only be minimally involved in the economy (Figure 1.1).

By 1960, public spending had increased to 25–30% of GDP as governments focussed on delivering their core tasks: the rules of the game, public goods and services, basic safety nets. Private choice still predominated and safeguarded both economic and financial freedom.

The Keynesian 'revolution' from 1960 to about 1980 saw government grow to 50% and 60% of GDP in some countries and to over 40% on average. Over the next two decades, the classical 'counter-revolution' propagated smaller states. Many countries began fiscal reform and rules-based policy-making gained prominence. Spending growth came to a halt, and in some cases reversed.

The years since 2000 have seen a revival of Keynesian thinking. Countries engaged in expansionary policies before the global financial crisis and experienced new record highs in public expenditure and debt thereafter. Another wave of reforms brought spending down in some crisis countries in the 2010s. However, public spending ratios on average rose well above the level of 2000.

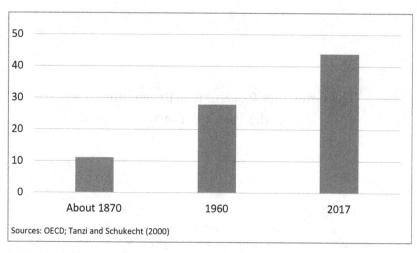

Figure 1.1 Public expenditure in advanced countries from a historical perspective, % of GDP.

1.1 The Emerging Role of Government

When economic philosophers like Hobbes, Locke and Smith started to write about what government should do in the economy in the seventeenth and eighteenth centuries, the role of the state was very different from what it is today. Governments had to pay for police and some administration, for an emperor or a king and occasionally for war. Governments did very little of what they do today, and often did it badly. There were few roads, few schools and little social welfare, except for that provided by churches or private benefactors. Poverty and misery prevailed.

Concrete information on what governments actually spent their money on and how much they spent is very limited until the mid-1800s. But we know they did not spend much in normal times and too much in times of war (when inflation often followed) or perhaps on palaces (that we can still admire). They also, with a few exceptions, played only a small role in development and growth. Progress until then had been due to private actors and not the state (Keynes, 1926).

This began to change gradually in many of today's advanced countries after about 1850. Technological progress and economic growth started to transform countries on a significant scale, with unprecedented progress in economic and social well-being. With the growth of the railways, an efficient land transportation system emerged. Public and private schooling began to flourish. At the end of the century, rudimentary social security emerged in a number of countries: Germany, under Bismarck, for example, invented the contribution-based social security system at that time.

What lay at the heart of this change was a new concept of the role of the market and the state that philosophers and classical economists such as Locke and Smith had propagated. The pursuit of private interests became a positive and the gains from trade and the division of labour gained their 'rightful' place as drivers of productivity and growth. Economists championed the beneficial role of the market in coordinating the free choices of consumers and producers. It was the time of 'classical' economics.

The role of government was small, but it evolved. Core functions of the government included first and foremost the development of basic rules and laws and public services. This included security and police, external defence, the outlines of public infrastructure, schooling and (later) basic social welfare. A functioning administration and judiciary ensured that people acted within the rule of law, which allowed markets to work with few limitations. Difficulties in developing effective systems of taxation may have constrained public spending as well (Tanzi, 2018c).

Adam Smith had already commented on the tendency in industry to form cartels. But this was not seen as something that governments should discourage, sometimes to the contrary. Nor did governments deal with the environment, or with energy networks or many other issues that have become important to us today. Still, the second half of the nineteenth century was a time of vibrant economies and significant progress, and all this happened with very limited public resources, especially by today's standards. By about 1870, data on government spending and on output had become available for a number of countries. Vito Tanzi and I found spending data for eleven countries, which are reproduced here (Table 1.1). The average public expenditure ratio was only 11% of GDP. Only every ninth Thaler, Forint, Pound or Lira went through the hands of government; almost 90% of spending was by the private sector.

We should read these early data with a bit of caution as the measurement of expenditure and output was not fully comprehensive and comparable at the time. Nevertheless, the figures are informative and suggest that differences across countries were quite large. In 1870, Sweden had the smallest government sector, at 5.7% of GDP, followed by the United States, at 7.3%. Japan, the Netherlands, the United Kingdom and Germany reported up to 10% of GDP. The largest government sectors featured in Australia and Switzerland. Austria, France and Italy had average-sized governments.

Table 1.1 *Total expenditure by general government*

% of GDP	About 1870	About 1913	About 1920	About 1937	1960	1980	2000	2017
Euro area								
Austria	10.5	17.0	14.7	20.6	35.7	50.0	51.0	49.1
Belgium[1]	..	13.8	22.1	21.8	30.3	54.9	49.1	52.2
Finland	..	..	..	..	..	40.0	48.0	53.7
France	12.6	17.0	27.6	29.0	34.6	46.3	51.4	56.5
Germany	10.0	14.8	25.0	34.1	32.9	46.9	44.7	43.9
Greece	..	..	..	..	..	..	46.4	48.0
Ireland[2]	..	..	18.8	25.5	28.0	48.9	30.9	26.1
Italy	13.7	17.1	30.1	31.1	30.1	40.6	46.6	48.9
Netherlands[1]	9.1	9.0	13.5	19.0	33.7	55.2	41.8	42.6
Portugal	..	..	..	..	..	32.3	42.6	45.9
Spain[1]	..	11.0	8.3	13.2	18.8	32.2	39.2	41.0
Other Europe								
Denmark	..	..	..	..	..	52.7	52.7	51.9
Sweden	5.7	10.4	10.9	16.5	31.0	60.1	53.4	49.1
Switzerland	16.5	14.0	17.0	24.1	17.2	32.8	33.8	34.7
UK	9.4	12.7	26.2	30.0	32.2	47.6	35.4	41.1
Other advanced economies								
Australia	18.3	16.5	19.3	14.8	22.2	33.6	36.4	36.4
Canada	..	..	16.7	25.0	28.6	41.6	41.4	41.1

Japan	8.8	8.3	14.8	25.4	17.5	32.0	38.0	39.2
South Korea	..	..	..	..	..	23.0	24.7	32.4
New Zealand	..	..	24.6	25.3	26.9	38.1	37.5	38.7
Singapore	..	..	..	..	..	..	19.6	..
US	7.3	7.5	12.1	19.7	27.0	34.9	33.7	37.8
Average[3]	11.1	13.0	18.9	23.4	27.9	43.2	42.7	43.9

Sources: OECD, Ameco, WEO, Tanzi and Schuknecht (2000). Year indicated or nearest year available
1. Central government until 1937.
2. When taking GNP instead of GDP for Ireland, the ratios for 2000 and 2017 are 35.5% and 32.9%, respectively.
3. Unweighted, excluding Singapore and South Korea.

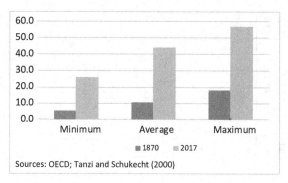

Figure 1.2 Public expenditure ranges, % of GDP, 1870 vs. 2017

All these figures are very small by today's standards (Figure 1.2). Public spending was hardly one quarter of the comparative ratio of today, where most countries report over 40% and some over 50% of GDP. The largest government then was smaller than Singapore, the advanced country with the smallest government today. The change in the country pattern is particularly surprising in three cases. Sweden, with the smallest government in 1870, has one of the largest today. The opposite holds for Australia and Switzerland.

In the following forty-odd years to 1914, the picture did not change greatly. Very small government in a vibrant economic environment continued to prevail. Despite the significant improvements in government services, public expenditure ratios increased little, from an average of 11% to 13% of GDP.

Some if not much of the increase on the eve of the First World War may have already been related to the growing hostilities in Europe and rising military spending. This is consistent with the fact that expenditure ratios in countries that were initially not involved in these hostilities (i.e. the United States, Australia and Japan, but also the Netherlands and Switzerland) changed little or even declined. Spending increases were strongest in Austria, France, Germany and Italy. At around 17% of GDP, Austria, France and Italy were the new record spenders.

1.2 First and Second World War

With the outbreak of the First World War in 1914, things changed dramatically. In fact, this was the first major, durable episode of a large increase in the size of government. The war economies that prevailed in most countries permitted governments to expand tax collection massively to finance the war effort (Peacock and Wiseman, 1961). When the war ended in 1918, some but definitely not all of the increase reversed. Average public spending in 1920 (or the nearest available year), was 6% of GDP higher than before the First World War: in other words, the ratio of government spending to GDP increased by almost half.

The main European adversaries of the First World War were also the countries with the largest public sector. Italy's public spending stood at 30% of GDP. France, Germany and the United Kingdom featured spending of 25% of GDP or more. Outside Europe, only New Zealand had a similarly large public sector.

By contrast, a number of governments still showed very small expenditure ratios near pre-1914 averages. The Netherlands, Sweden and the United States remained relatively close to the 10% of GDP ratio. Spain's figure was below 10%, but that only referred to central government.

In the 1920s, the role of government continued to evolve and became more active in providing core public goods and services. More countries introduced or expanded basic social security systems and developed public higher education. It was a turbulent time, with hyperinflation in countries such as Germany, Austria and Italy in the early 1920s and economic and financial booms in the second half of the 1920s in many countries.

The Great Depression of 1929–1939 placed a huge burden on social security and government budgets. Countries that could (when the markets gave them credit!), introduced public spending and infrastructure programmes such as the New Deal in the United States. As a result, public expenditure ratios had on average increased further by the late 1930s, when preparations for another war had also started to boost spending in countries such as Germany.

By 1937, public expenditure had increased to an average of 23.4% of GDP, almost twice the ratio of just twenty-five years earlier! The same four large European countries that had already featured record spending in 1920 – France, Germany, Italy and the United Kingdom – reported public expenditure near or above 30% of GDP.

On the eve of the Second World War in 1939, many countries had spending ratios between about 20% and 25% of GDP. Only the Netherlands, Spain and Sweden in Europe, plus Australia and the United States outside it, still reported public spending below 20% of GDP. Incidentally, Singapore still manages to provide all core tasks of government with a similar spending ratio today. Still, between 1918 and 1939, the prevailing economic model had been that of market economies, with growing but limited government involvement.

1.3 Government in the Post-Second World War Period
until about 1960

The intellectual environment moved away from classical thinking after the Second World War, although proposals for different systems had already emerged much earlier. Marxist thinking of the nineteenth century and the Russian Revolution had transformed that country after 1918. This provided both a boost and testing ground for socialist or communist thinking. The American New Deal and economic regulation in the wake of the Great Depression had also been a departure from the 'limited state' model and many European countries had become more interventionist.

Still, there was a lively debate over what the 'right' economic model might be, with the Hayekian liberals on the market-friendly side of the spectrum. In Germany, and perhaps as a reaction to the controlled economy under the Nazis, the 'ordo-liberal' model of the social market economy provided a renewed boost to a rules-based market economy approach complemented by a social component. Other countries, such as France or the United Kingdom, maintained more state control after 1945.

In the newly evolving theory of public finance, views shifted away from government underpinning a well-functioning market process to government affecting economic outcomes. Building on the work of Keynes (1926, 1936) and the experience with the New Deal spending programmes, a growing number of economists advocated a more active role for the state in stabilising short-term economic fluctuations. Galbraith (1958) advocated more spending from education to research, pollution control and development aid.

Most prominently perhaps, Musgrave (1959) defined an allocative, stabilising and redistributive role for government. This also opened the doors to the evolution of the welfare state without too much regard for the need to finance it or the implications for property rights and incentives. This shows the power of economic narratives and ideas: to this day, most public finance economists would categorise the role of fiscal policies along the lines defined by Musgrave.

With growing faith in the state and its 'fine-tuning role' for the macroeconomy, there was also a gradual erosion of fiscal rules and the consensus that budgets needed to be balanced in peacetime. This process had already started in the Great Depression and accelerated after the Second World War in several countries including the United States, Germany and Switzerland (Moser, 1994). Fiscal rules in Italy were uncertain from the outset and eroded in the 1960s (Eusepi and Cerioni, 1989).

Nevertheless, until the end of the 1950s, the movement in favour of big, redistributive government and macroeconomic fine-tuning had not yet fully influenced practice in finance ministries and had only just started to translate into higher public expenditure figures. In 1960, public spending averaged 27.8% of GDP, not much higher than the level in 1937. The 'Peacock and Wiseman' effect after 1914 was thus not very prevalent after 1945. Governments had cut back their military sector and public debt in an environment of strong growth.

Modest average spending figures by today's standards went hand in hand with more homogeneity in spending levels. In 1937, the largest government sector was 1.5 times the average; in 1960, it was 1.3 times. The biggest government in 1960 was Austria, with an expenditure ratio of 35.7%. Most European governments were in the 30–35% range; the United States had an average-sized government in 1960 and so did New Zealand and Canada. Switzerland, Spain and Japan had the smallest government sectors, still below 20% of GDP.

It is worthwhile pausing for a minute before proceeding to look at the next 50 years. What was the situation in 1960 in the advanced economies of the 'West'? They were rapidly growing countries at the forefront in terms of all economic and social indicators, with the world's highest per capita GDP, good school systems, rapidly growing infrastructure, and internal and external security. There was a sense of law and order, with strong democratic participation and virtually universal basic social welfare.

Hence, if one could, one would have perhaps 'stopped history' here, the 30% or so of public spending was fully sufficient for the state to play its core role. We could have continued living happily ever after, or so it seems looking back. But the story of government expenditure took a different turn.

1.4 The Keynesian 'Revolution': 1960–1980

The two decades between 1960 and 1980 saw the greatest expansion in public expenditure in peacetime history, which affected almost all advanced economies of the time. It followed the adoption of the 'Keynesian paradigm' by a new generation of policymakers and administrators. The average size of government increased from 27.8% to 42% of GDP, an increase by one-half in relative terms, reflecting an increase in the expenditure ratio by 0.7 percentage point for each year of a twenty-year period.

This staggering increase coincided with a strong faith in the beneficial role of additional government programmes. New programmes, and the expansion of existing ones, focussed especially on social welfare, but spending also increased strongly on subsidies, housing, education and more. Moreover, the modest downturn of the late 1960s became the first episode when many countries used fiscal expansion for 'stabilisation' purposes. Countries again applied expansionary policies in the 1970s in the context of the 1973 and 1979 oil crises. Except that expansionary policies often did not stabilise: the oil crises were huge supply shocks. Spending increases exacerbated inflationary pressures and were often neither timely nor followed by surpluses in good times, as Keynes would have advised.

Hence already by 1980 expenditure ratios in a number of countries had grown to 50% of GDP, or even more. 'Big' government was especially prevalent in small European countries: Austria, the record holder of 1960, reported public spending of exactly 50% of GDP; Belgium's spending had increased from 30% to almost 55% of GDP, with Denmark only slightly 'behind'.

The most staggering increase, however, happened in Sweden. The size of the state virtually doubled, from 31% of GDP in 1960 to 60% in 1980. To be fair, these countries were small open economies that were particularly hard hit by the two oil crises when import costs rose and export markets contracted. Therefore, a shrinking GDP and related higher spending both had a stronger effect on raising expenditure ratios than in larger countries. Still, it was an amazing period, when administrators at times had to devise ways how more money could be spent – unthinkable by today's standards.

There was also a group of larger countries where public spending had risen strongly – about 15% of GDP – but not as far and fast as in the first group. In France, Germany, Italy, the United Kingdom and Canada, public spending was near or above the average, but stayed below the 50% threshold. One could call this the group of 'intermediate'-sized governments.

There was a third group, where public expenditure was still below 40% of GDP. This group of 'small' governments included the United States, Japan, Australia, New Zealand and Switzerland. However, even in these countries, the size of the state had grown very strongly. Even these countries were already reporting in 1980 much higher public expenditure ratios than most newly advanced and emerging economies in Asia are today.

Finally, four countries are worth referring to which were still quite backward. Portugal, Spain, Greece and South Korea featured small or even very small public sectors, also because their revenue collection potential had not yet developed as far as in the other countries (Tanzi, 2018c).

1.5 The 'Counter Revolution': 1980–2000

In the following two decades, until the turn of the millennium, two things happened. First, the change in the intellectual climate towards more market and less government gained prominence amongst both politicians and administrators. The works of sceptics about the beneficial role of government spending and proponents of a greater role for the market, such as Hayek (1960), Buchanan (1975) and Friedman and Friedman (1980), had a growing influence. Olson (1982) warned of the stifling effect of rent seeking special interests on economic dynamism. Most prominently, on the policy side, Ronald Reagan in the United States and Margaret Thatcher in the United Kingdom promised to curtail the role of government and reinvigorate the market economy.

But there was also a pragmatic reason for such government scepticism in many advanced countries. The Keynesian 'revolution' had not brought the benefits it had promised. In the 1970s, it was widely felt that governments had been destabilising their widely fluctuating economies with high deficits, growing debt and much inflation in its wake. Some governments had reached the limits of what was financeable by taxes and begun to feel their negative incentive effects. Economic growth had declined and unemployment had increased significantly in many countries: higher spending had brought more bureaucracy and little additional benefits.

The 'classical counter revolution' succeeded in slowing down the growth of government drastically, and some countries managed to reduce their spending ratios. Reforms of the state differed in their ambition and took place in two waves in the 1980s and 1990s (see Chapter 5). However, some countries did not curtail the growth of government. On average, therefore, the expenditure ratio in advanced countries changed little over the two decades: the small increase from 42% to 43.3% of GDP was due to rising interest payments for the public debt.

The 1980s and 1990s were also a period when rules-based fiscal policy-making underwent a strong revival. The United States introduced a number of institutional reforms and rules; European countries signed up to the Maastricht Treaty and later the Stability and Growth Pact (SGP), which required countries to have broadly balanced budgets and reasonably low debt (below 60% of GDP). In the convergence process towards the European Monetary Union (EMU), all countries succeeded in bringing their deficits below the required threshold of 3% of GDP.

The individual country experience of the 1980s and 1990s is also worth looking at. A number of small European countries with the strongest expenditure increases in the 1960s and 1970s reversed their trend. Belgium's expenditure ratio declined from almost 55% to 49% of GDP, the Netherlands' ratio fell even more dramatically from 55% to 42%; Sweden reported a decline from 60% to about 53%. Ireland, with a government sector near 50% of GDP in 1980, reported the most remarkable decline to little over 30% by 2000. By contrast, Portugal and Greece saw further major increases in their public expenditure ratios.

Developments in the large advanced economies diverged significantly. France, Italy and Spain reported significant further spending increases. The French public expenditure ratio increased to well above 50% of GDP in 2000, having been 46% in 1980. Italy stood at slightly above 40% in 1980 and 6 percentage points higher in 2000. A similar increase from a lower base allowed Spain to stay below 40% of GDP. The United Kingdom, and to a lesser extent also Germany, reported lower expenditure ratios in 2000 than in 1980. In the United Kingdom, this reflects the Thatcher reforms and the strong growth phase of the 1980s and 1990s.

In Germany, unification resulted in more of a rollercoaster ride. The 1980s first saw some expenditure retrenchment, before the ratio went up after unification, followed by another phase of savings in the late 1990s. Similarly, Canada's small overall expenditure increase over the two decades reflects a strongly expansionary phase in the 1980s followed by reform in the 1990s (Schuknecht and Tanzi, 2005; Hauptmeier, Heipertz and Schuknecht, 2007).

The experience of countries with 'small' governments is also interesting. A number of them, including Australia, South Korea, Switzerland and the United States, saw virtually no change in the size of government over the two decades. New Zealand's reforms in the 1980s, following the UK example, allowed a major expenditure reduction, while the opposite happened to Japan.

Ireland's expenditure ratio declined strongly over the two decades. However, Ireland's GDP number reflects significant multinational enterprise value added so that the GNP figures could be seen as more representative: the respective figure for 2000 public expenditure would be 35.5% of GNP instead of 30.9% of GDP.

When looking at the end of the millennium, it also worth discussing the emerging economies of Eastern Europe and Asia, which had started to become serious competitors. We have already commented on South Korea and Singapore with their small public sectors. Table 1.2 reports expenditure figures for selected Central and Eastern European (CEE) countries, Russia and China. In 2000, most emerging European countries reported public expenditure ratios from the lower 30%s to the lower 40%s, with Slovenia being the only exception. This shows their successful transition

Table 1.2 *Total expenditure in Eastern Europe and selected emerging economies*

% of GDP	2000	2017
Europe		
Czech Republic	41.0	38.9
Estonia	36.4	39.2
Latvia	33.0	33.5
Lithuania	34.8	29.7
Hungary	47.1	46.5
Poland	42.1	41.2
Slovakia	52.0	40.4
Asia		
Russia	..	34.8
China	..	32.3

Sources: OECD; IMF WEO

over the 1990s away from 'super-big' government and towards a market economy. It also shows the competitive potential of these countries via low spending and low taxes.

The opening up of China and Eastern Europe in the 1990s gave rise to a further debate. To some economists, globalisation required larger government, notably in smaller countries (Rodrik, 1998), while competition between states was seen as putting downward pressure on public spending (Sinn, 1997; Tanzi and Schuknecht, 1997a; Schulze and Ursprung, 1999). The empirical evidence is inconclusive, with globalisation not playing a significant role in any specific direction (Dreher, Sturm and Ursprung, 2008; Potrafke, 2009, 2018).

In sum, the 1980s and 1990s were a very turbulent period. Many countries stopped or even reversed the continuous growth of government of earlier decades. Reform of the state led to leaner government sectors. There were, however, exceptions, notably much of Southern Europe and Japan.

1.6 The New Millennium: A Revival of Faith in Fiscal Activism

While the growth of government halted in the 1980s and 1990s, the intellectual climate slowly turned again, and faith in government activism returned. A new generation of technical tools – computable dynamic stochastic general equilibrium models that permitted simulating the behaviour of simple economies – emerged and allowed a seemingly precise calculation of the impact of government expenditure policies.

Moreover, in the booming early 2000s, with falling interest rates and debt service payments, sound public finances became less pressing. As a result of expansionary expenditure policies and considerable deficits, several European countries including Germany, France, Italy, Portugal and Greece broke the European fiscal rules (the SGP).

Things really turned, however, with the global financial crisis (Tanzi, 2018b). The financial liberalisation of the 1990s and beyond, without adequate regulatory and supervisory underpinnings, had been a significant contributor to the crisis. Insufficiently prudent fiscal and monetary policies had compounded financial sector policy failure. But the blame in popular discourse fell almost fully on bankers, markets and, with it, the market economy model.

The stabilising impact of expansionary fiscal policies at the height of the crisis further stoked belief in the need for governments to tame markets. Some observers argued that too much debt and too loose policies had reignited the crisis in Europe in 2011 in the first place – but such analysis only had a modest impact (Hauptmeier, Sanchez-Fuentes and Schuknecht, 2014). A few observers questioned whether this renewed trust in fiscal activism versus rules and institutions could live up to the expectations it created (James, 2009)

A renewed debate on a much more activist role for government and government spending emerged. Mazzucato (2013) argued that an 'entrepreneurial state' needed to take on a more active role in promoting innovation, investment and industry. While the role of government in basic research is uncontested, it is surprising that a debate on industrial policy re-emerged despite the well-known knowledge and incentive problems for governments and the questionable record of countries like Japan and France that had applied industrial policies extensively before.

Some observers began to argue that under-funded governments were unable to maintain good public services while top earners did not contribute their fair share to this funding, despite historically high spending and revenue ratios of over 30%, 40% or even 50% of GDP. Concerns about more unequal income distribution grew and resulted in further calls for more spending. Few argued that ineffective governments unable to prioritise high public spending towards the attainment of core tasks had caused this calamity: in other words, few people argued that government failure, rather than market failure, was at fault.

When looking at the size of government over the last two decades, developments have been rather turbulent, with a further overall increase in public expenditure ratios. From 2000 to 2017, total public expenditure

Table 1.3 *Public primary expenditure (non-interest expenditure)*

% of GDP	1960	1980	2000	2017	Change 2000–2017
Euro area					
Austria	34.9	47.6	47.5	47.2	−0.2
Belgium	27.5	48.3	42.4	49.8	7.4
Finland	..	39.0	45.3	52.8	7.5
France	34.1	45.0	48.5	54.7	6.2
Germany	32.1	43.3	41.6	42.9	1.3
Greece	..	..	39.6	44.8	5.3
Ireland	24.5	42.6	28.9	24.1	−4.8
Italy	28.3	35.9	40.5	45.1	4.6
Netherlands	32.4	51.4	38.5	41.6	3.1
Portugal		29.7	39.6	42.0	2.4
Spain	18.3	31.5	36.0	38.5	2.4
Other Europe					
Denmark	..	48.9	49.0	50.8	1.9
Sweden	30.0	56.0	50.0	48.7	−1.3
Switzerland	16.9	32.3	32.0	34.2	2.1
UK	29.5	42.7	33.0	38.4	5.4
Other advanced economies					
Australia	19.7	29.8	34.2	34.9	0.7
Canada	27.4	36.1	34.4	38.3	3.9
Japan	17.1	29.6	34.9	37.2	2.4
South Korea	..	22.4	23.1	31.1	8.0
New Zealand	24.3	34.2	34.8	38.0	3.2
Singapore	..	..	19.6	..	..
US	25.1	30.4	29.9	34.3	4.4
Average[1]	26.4	39.7	39.0	41.9	2.9

Sources: OECD, Ameco, WEO, Tanzi and Schuknecht (2000)
1. Unweighted, excluding South Korea and Singapore.

increased from 42.7% to 43.9% of GDP. However, this was a period of strongly falling interest rates and interest payments on public debt decreased from 3.7% to 2% of GDP. Primary (non-interest) spending, therefore, went up much more than total spending – from 39% to 41.9%, or almost 3%, of GDP (see Table 1.3). Primary expenditure reflects more truly the expenditure choices that government makes.

Finland, France and Denmark had primary expenditure in excess of 50% of GDP in 2017 and several other European countries came close to this. By contrast, the primary spending figures for a number of countries with relatively 'small' governments remained below 35% of GDP. Belgium,

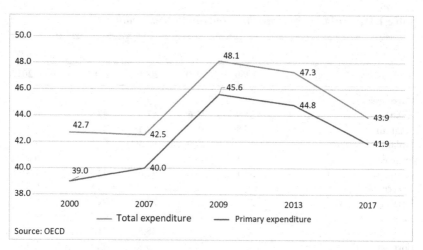

Figure 1.3 Total and primary expenditure dynamics in the new millennium, % of GDP.

Finland, France and South Korea reported the strongest increase in the new millennium by 6.2% to 8.0% of GDP. Ireland reported the lowest total and primary expenditure ratio in Europe, even when considering GNP instead of GDP in 2017.

Moreover, it is important to note that the overall increase in public expenditure since the turn of the century reflected at first a modest increase in the early 2000s, followed by a very strong rise during the global financial crisis and a gradual decline thereafter (Figure 1.3). This pattern was more pronounced in the countries that experienced financial and fiscal crisis. Portugal, Greece, Spain and Ireland showed strong increases in their expenditure ratios in 2007–2009/2010 and began to reform thereafter in the context of international programmes. The United Kingdom followed a similar pattern in the crisis and post-crisis period, though without IMF support.

France and Italy also reported increases in expenditure ratios between 2000 and 2017. France topped the league at 56.5% of GDP in 2017. In Germany, the expenditure ratio changed little over the whole period; however, in contrast to the fiscal 'boom and bust' of several of its European partners, it followed the opposite pattern: consolidation until the early 2010s (briefly interrupted by a crisis-related stimulus), and robust spending growth thereafter.

These diverging patterns show up very clearly in Figure 1.4, which looks at public primary spending. The European crisis countries reported expenditure growth well above trend growth after the start of the EMU. Even when assuming a generous real trend growth of 2% plus 2% inflation,

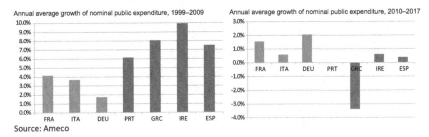

Source: Ameco

Figure 1.4 Public expenditure dynamics before and after the financial crisis.

expenditure growth should not have grown more than 4% per annum to keep the expenditure ratio stable. The actual figures for Ireland, Spain, Greece, Cyprus and Portugal were much higher, showing the significant expansionary policies in these countries between 1999 and 2009. In France and Italy, potential nominal growth was probably closer to 3% or 3.5%, so the expenditure dynamics were also too strong.

Figure 1.4 also illustrates the remarkable turnaround in expenditure dynamics as of 2010: very restrictive expenditure policies were part of the countries' reform programmes. Note the opposite dynamics in Germany, with restrictive pre-crisis policies and more expansionary policies in the late 2010s. This fact runs counter to the claims of unduly restrictive spending policies in Germany by some economists for the latter period. Towards the end of the 2010s, however, expenditure growth seemed to pick up more broadly again. In a number of countries, expenditure growth rose above sustainable rates (Fuest and Gros, 2019a; Thygesen et al., 2018).

The mainly non-European smaller governments also diverged considerably in their development of public expenditure. But most of them reported an increase. South Korea raised spending significantly, though from a much lower base. The United States also showed a much higher expenditure ratio despite the post crisis recovery. Singapore remained the country with the smallest expenditure ratio of all.

Expenditure on the Financial System

Finally, many countries over the past decade – and before – spent huge amounts of money on recapitalising their financial system when it got into trouble. The accounting of the costs of financial crises, however, is not straightforward. Some of the costs feature as capital transfers and, thereby, show up in government expenditure. In other instances, financial support

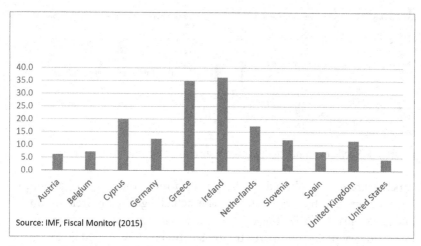

Figure 1.5 Fiscal costs of global financial crisis, % of GDP, gross impact by 2015.

affected only the debt via so-called financial transactions outside the budget. But as financial support is expenditure it should be added to the 'official' expenditure ratios reported above to get the full picture. Moreover, such transactions significantly raised public debt and, in some instances, brought countries to their knees.

The fiscal costs of the global financial crisis averaged over 7% of GDP (Figure 1.5). Fiscal costs reached 30% of GDP in Greece and Ireland. Governments recovered some of the losses so that net costs were typically lower, but these net calculations did not include an adequate reward for the risks that governments took on board when they supported their banks.

The occurrence of financial crisis costs should not have come as any surprise. There were precedents even amongst industrial countries, including the United States, Japan and the Nordic countries, during the late 1980s and 1990s. Nevertheless, the global reach and magnitude of costs amongst advanced countries was both unique and unexpected.

1.7 Conclusion

In the past 150 years, the spending role of government has grown hugely, in four major phases. The period of the classical consensus prevailed from the nineteenth century until about 1960 but, until 1914, this featured very limited government. An expansionary phase to cover what we today would call 'core tasks' lasted until about 1960.

Thereafter, the 'Keynesian revolution' saw governments venturing into many new activities and fiscal fine-tuning, bringing large increases in public expenditure, deficits and debt in its wake. New thinking on the limits of government and the instability of the 1970s gave rise to a period emphasising limited government, fiscal rectitude and government reform. This lasted until the late 1990s and saw government expenditure stabilise: it even fell in a number of reforming countries in the 1980s and 1990s.

The new millennium began a new period of Keynesian thinking. Expansionary fiscal policies predominated in the first decade. The global financial crisis and the subsequent criticism of the market model boosted faith in government to be able to fine-tune demand. This new phase has seen expenditure ratios, deficits and debt rise again. However, the crises in a number of European countries with unsustainable expenditure trends gave rise to another wave of expenditure reform in the 2010s.

Geographically, European governments have always tended to be bigger than their non-European counterparts, although this does not hold true for all of them. The Nordics and some Southern European countries started out with small public sectors and now have amongst the largest ones. The Anglo-Saxon countries tended to have smaller governments, but there were periods when this was not the case (e.g. Ireland and the United Kingdom around 1980). The current and former emerging economies of Asia mostly feature governments on the very small side. The overall variation is enormous and public expenditure ratios now range from about 20% to well over 50% of GDP.

Chapter 2 looks in more depth at the pattern of government spending across different categories before Chapter 3 turns to the financing of government. This will prepare us for the later discussion of 'value for money' from government spending, and of the risks and challenges for the future in Parts II and III.

The Composition of Expenditure

Europe needs to be competitive and we also need to be competitive if we wish to remain an interesting partner.

Angela Merkel

Politicians are the same all over. They promise to build a bridge even where there is no river.

Nikita Khrushchev

Highlights

The history of the composition of government spending is both complex and fascinating. Although government priorities have changed over the past 150 years, social spending has been the biggest 'winner' (Figure 2.1).

In the late nineteenth century, public spending focussed on public administration, investment, debt service and the military. In the following decades until about 1960, such growth focussed on developing public services and social safety nets, taking advantage of falling military spending after the two world wars. The following sixty years saw mostly further increases in social expenditure, especially on pensions, health and long-term care.

Public spending on 'goods and services' has always averaged nearly half of total expenditure. By contrast, social expenditure has grown from less than 10% a century ago to 55% in 2017. Education spending has been stable at about 10% of total spending in recent decades, after rising strongly in earlier years. The share of public investment has steadily fallen, from 20% in the late nineteenth century to only 7% in 2017.

2.1 Expenditure on Goods and Services or Public Consumption

Government spending grew four-fold from about 11% to 44% of GDP between 1870 and 2017. What have governments been spending their

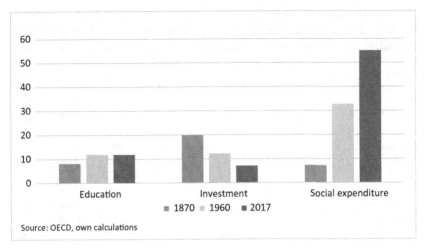

Figure 2.1 Rising share of social expenditure, % of total expenditure.

money on, how has this changed over time and what priorities does it reflect?

It is astonishing how simple the world of government spending was in the late nineteenth century. About half of total expenditure – 5% of GDP – was spent on public goods and services (Table 2.1). This expenditure is also often called 'real expenditure' or 'public consumption' (statistically, these concepts are very similar but not identical). With this money governments paid their employees, bought furniture or paper for the public administration and a few other things. The other half of government spending went into public investment and into servicing the public debt. Public spending on social welfare was virtually non-existent.

For the period up to 1914 and for some countries even 1937, data on public consumption and its components is quite scarce, as the missing values in Table 2.1 demonstrate. Public administration was an important, though by today's standards very small, category of expenditure. The civil service in the late nineteenth century was tiny, and only about 2.5% of total employment was in the public sector. Being a civil servant was truly an exception and, in many countries, a privilege. By 1914 public employment had increased somewhat to 3.7% of the workforce; public education absorbed more and more resources and contributed to the growing civil service.

A very significant share of public consumption went into the military, depending on the circumstances of war and peace. Tanzi and Schuknecht (2000), for example, report military spending of up to 6% of GDP around 1900. This share increased much further during the two world wars.

Table 2.1 *Government consumption*

% of GDP	About 1870	About 1937	1960	1980	2000	2017
Euro area						
Austria	..	..	13.2	18.3	19.2	19.5
Belgium	..	..	15.3	22.9	20.9	23.4
Finland	..	..	12.4	17.7	19.8	23.1
France	5.4	15.0	15.2	21.0	22.2	23.6
Germany	..	21.0	13.4	19.6	18.7	19.6
Greece	..	..	11.7	14.3	18.3	20.1
Ireland[1]	..	..	12.6	20.2	14.7	12.0
Italy	..	..	14.2	16.8	17.9	18.6
Netherlands	6.7	12.3	16.0	24.5	20.4	24.3
Portugal	..	..	9.0	13.4	19.0	17.6
Spain	4.9	10.7	8.8	13.9	16.7	18.5
Other Europe						
Denmark	..	..	13.4	27.1	23.9	25.0
Sweden	5.5	10.4	16.1	29.3	24.5	26.0
Switzerland	..	..	6.6	10.0	11.6	12.0
UK	..	11.7	17.2	21.7	16.4	18.3
Other advanced economies						
Australia	4.8	5.5	11.2	17.4	17.8	18.5
Canada	..	10.1	14.3	21.3	19.2	20.8
Japan	..	12.4	11.5	14.1	16.9	19.6
South Korea	..	..	..	12.1	11.3	15.3
New Zealand	..	..	12.2	19.6	17.0	18.0
Singapore	..	..	9.1	9.8	9.9	..
US	2.5	12.9	15.8	15.9	14.0	14.1
Average[2]	5.0	12.2	13.0	19.0	18.5	19.6

Sources: Ameco, WEO, Tanzi and Schuknecht (2000)
1. When taking GNP instead of GDP for Ireland, the ratios for 2000 and 2017 are 16.9% and 15.1%, respectively.
2. Unweighted, excluding South Korea and Singapore.

After 1918, there was a significant decline in military spending. In fact the losers of the First World War, Germany and Austria, reduced military spending in the early 1920s to below 1% of GDP, even less than countries spent after the end of the Cold War.

Government expenditure on goods and services recorded a major increase until 1937, when expenditure had more than doubled to over 12% of GDP (Table 2.1), but this was still roughly half of total government spending. The range across countries was huge: Australia spent only 5.5% of GDP, France spent 15% and Germany over 20% of GDP in this category. This reflects the huge spending increase on defence to over 5% of GDP in France and almost 10% of GDP in Germany as they prepared for war.

When we look at the post-war period around 1960, we find that spending on public consumption was 13% of GDP and had changed little on average, being still around half of total expenditure. Declining military spending paid for the development of stronger public administrations, more education and other public services. Public employment increased from an average of a little over 5% in 1937 (excluding military) to 12%.

Public consumption expenditure in the majority of countries remained in the 10–13% of GDP range just as before 1939. Japan, Spain and Switzerland reported the smallest figures (below 10%) while some European countries and the United States reported above 15% of GDP. After 1960, the 'Keynesian revolution' boosted public consumption. This was the time of strong faith in government programmes and countries significantly extended both public services and bureaucracies. Government consumption increased roughly by half, from an average of about 13% of GDP in 1960 to about 20% by 1980. European countries, including the Nordics, the Netherlands and Ireland, reported the strongest increases. Public employment also 'exploded': at the end of the period, every fifth worker in France, Sweden, Norway, the United Kingdom and Australia was in public service.

The decades until 2017 on average then saw a stagnation in public 'real' expenditure at around 20% of GDP and public employment crept up slightly further. But just to put the size of this spending category into perspective, its share of GDP was almost twice as big as that of total public spending 150 years earlier.

Country experiences again differed markedly. Ireland, Sweden and the United Kingdom reported significantly smaller public consumption in 2017 than in 1980. Southern European countries in particular showed the opposite trend. Switzerland, the United States, South Korea and Ireland reported quite small bureaucracies absorbing few resources. In Ireland, this also held for the less distorted ratio to GNP instead of GDP. Switzerland and Singapore remained near 10% of GDP throughout the period while, by contrast, several small and large European countries reported expenditure of about 20–25% of GDP.

It is also worthwhile looking at the components of public consumption in recent decades. Public expenditure on general public services, which includes public order, economic affairs and recreation and culture, declined significantly after 1980. Average expenditure fell from 17.3% of GDP in 1990 (when data first became available) to 13.6% in 2015.

Security has been surprisingly 'cheap'. The sub-component 'public order', which includes the police force and other security services, has only absorbed around 1.5% of GDP on average in the 2010s. Similarly, and despite popular perceptions, external security is also rather inexpensive: military spending in advanced economies ranges from 1% to a little over 3% of GDP and the NATO objective for 2025 is 2% of GDP. Total security related spending thus amounts to about 3.5% of GDP on average. This is less than one fifth of government consumption and less than one tenth of total public spending, and is less than security-related spending in both the nineteenth and twentieth centuries.

Public Education

The nineteenth century's most important policy innovation was probably the rise of public education. By 1900, public basic education was almost universal in today's advanced economies. Public expenditure was, however, low, averaging 0.6% in 1870 and rising to a little over 1% of GDP before the First World War (Table 2.2). France, Germany and Japan prioritised public education spending early on and thus reported the highest figures.

After the First World War, education expenditure started to take off and expand in more and more countries as the coverage and duration of public education increased and became a key instrument of economic development and social mobility. By 1937, education spending had almost doubled to over 2% of GDP before rising further to 3.2% in 1960. By that time, lower secondary education was virtually universal in the advanced economies.

There were, however, great differences across countries, as the education 'revolution' did not start everywhere at the same time and the private sector played a greater role in some countries than in others. Many countries reported public spending above 4% of GDP; Australia and Spain, however, reported only 1.3–1.4% of GDP in 1960.

The education revolution did not stop there, however, and continued in the 1960s as upper secondary and university education rapidly expanded. Public expenditure at first continued to increase. From 1960 to 1980, it grew from 3.2 to 4.9% of GDP on average. Several countries, including the Netherlands, Sweden, the United States and Canada, reported 6% of GDP or more, but Greece and Spain significantly lagged behind.

From 1980 to the mid-2010s, public expenditure ratios on education remained broadly constant, averaging slightly above 5% of GDP. Japan,

Table 2.2 *Public expenditure on education*

% of GDP	About 1870	About 1913	About 1937	1960	1980	2000	2015/16
Euro area							
Austria	..	..	2.5	2.9	3.8	5.2	4.9
Belgium	..	1.2	..	4.6	6.1	5.5	6.4
Finland	..	..	..	4.6	4.9	5.9	6.0
France	0.3	1.5	1.3	2.4	5	5.6	5.4
Germany	1.3	2.7	..	2.9	4.7	4.1	4.2
Greece	..	..	..	1.6	2.2	3.9	4.3
Ireland	..	..	3.3	3.2	6.6	4.3	3.3
Italy	..	0.6	1.6	3.6	4.3	4.4	3.9
Netherlands	..	..	1.5	4.9	7.6	4.7	5.3
Portugal	..	..	..	1.6	3.1	6.6	4.9
Spain	..	0.4	1.6	1.3	2.6	4.1	4.0
Other Europe							
Denmark	..	..	..	3.0	5.9	6.3	6.9
Sweden	..	..	..	5.1	9	6.5	6.6
Switzerland	..	..	..	3.1	6	5.2	5.6
UK	1.0	1.1	4.0	4.3	4.7	4.6	4.6
Other advanced economies							
Australia	..	..	0.7	1.4	4.5	5.0	5.3
Canada	..	..	..	4.6	6.9	7.3	7.2
Japan	1.0	1.6	2.1	4.1	3.7	4.2	3.4
South Korea	..	..	..	..	2.2	4.0	5.2
New Zealand	..	..	2.3	3.2	5.8	7.3	..
Singapore	..	..	..	..	..	..	..
US	..	..	..	4.0	6.6	6.1	6.1
Average[1]	0.9	1.3	2.1	3.3	5.2	5.3	5.2

Sources: OECD, Tanzi and Schuknecht (2000)
1. Unweighted, excluding South Korea and Singapore.

Ireland and Italy spent below 4% of GDP on public education, Belgium, Canada, the Nordics and the United States more than 6%. However, education is a good example where more spending does not necessarily mean better-educated people. We will return to this issue in Chapter 4.

In several countries, the private sector plays an important role in education provision and financing (OECD, 2018a). Private education expenditure ranges from less than 10% of total education spending in Norway, Luxembourg and Austria to 30–60% in a number of Anglo-Saxon countries. Private education is most important in New Zealand, the United Kingdom, Australia and the United States; in these countries, except the United States, public funding to private providers is also high.

Private provision is considerably more important for higher- than for lower-level education. Public financing of primary and secondary education ranges from 75 to 100% in OECD countries, but the figures for tertiary education are as low as 55% in the United Kingdom and 40% in the United States.

Private financing is also very relevant in professional training and education. In Germany and the Netherlands, 40–50% of professional training as part of the academic/vocational education system is financed from private sources.

Public Spending on the Environment and Climate

In past decades, public spending on the environment and climate change emerged as a relevant new public expenditure category. An in-depth discussion could easily use up a whole chapter. We want to at least briefly touch on this theme which is increasingly moving to the core of government responsibility. Nevertheless, governments tend to address environmental objectives predominantly via regulation and taxes/charges so that the expenditure role of the state is quite limited.

Environmental spending includes various types of spending that do not just belong to public consumption (such as for the environmental administration) but also to other categories. Spending on sewage infrastructure and treatment is part of public investment. Subsidies or tax credits are also important in some countries. Special financing facilities and guarantees (without immediate costs to the budget) matter in many countries.

Advanced countries spent almost 0.7% of GDP on average on the environment in 2000. This share increased marginally to 0.74% in 2017. Japan, the Netherlands and Greece reported spending over 1% of GDP in 2017. However, data for important countries, such as the United States and Canada, was missing.

2.2 Public Investment

The late nineteenth century was the time when many of the beautiful public buildings and infrastructure that still please the eye today were constructed. In fact, with education having such a high standing, many schools and universities in Germany, France and many other countries

Table 2.3 *Public expenditure on investment*

% of GDP	About 1870	About 1913	About 1937	1960	1980	2000	2017
Euro area							
Austria	..	..	..	4.2	4.3	2.7	3.0
Belgium	..	..	..	2.2	4.7	2.4	2.2
Finland	..	..	..	5.4	4.3	3.5	3.9
France	0.5	0.8	6.3	3.4	4.1	3.9	3.4
Germany	..	..	..	3.4	6.8	2.3	2.2
Greece	..	..	..	3.7	3.2	5.1	4.6
Ireland	..	..	..	2.8	5.6	3.5	1.9
Italy	..	..	..	3.7	3.0	2.9	2.0
Netherlands	..	2.1	4.5	4.3	3.8	3.8	3.5
Portugal	..	..	..	..	4.2	4.6	1.8
Spain	..	0.3	1.4	2.6	1.8	3.7	2.0
Other Europe							
Denmark	..	..	..	..	3.1	2.8	3.4
Sweden	..	..	..	3.2	3.3	3.9	4.5
Switzerland	..	..	..	3.7	5.6	3.0	3.6
UK	0.7	2.1	4.1	3.3	2.6	1.7	2.6
Other advanced economies							
Australia	6.9	8.9	7.0	3.9	3.4	3.0	3.5
Canada	1.5	3.8	3.8	4.0	3.0	2.9	3.9
Japan	1.3	3.7	3.3	3.9	6.1	5.5	3.7
South Korea	..	..	..	..	7.2	5.5	4.5
New Zealand	..	..	..	1.1	2.5	3.1	..
Singapore	..	..	..	..	..	..	..
US	2.2	2.7	5.1	2.9	4.3	3.6	3.2
Average[1]	2.2	3.1	4.4	3.4	4.0	3.4	3.1

Sources: Ameco, IMF WEO, Tanzi and Schuknecht (2000)
1. Unweighted, excluding South Korea and Singapore.

were often monuments and architectural statements rather than simply functional buildings, as is mostly the case today.

Public investment was thus an important expenditure category, averaging 2–3% of GDP in the pre-1914 period, not much different from today (Table 2.3). Australia, the United States and Canada, still 'frontier countries' at the time, reported the biggest numbers, but in many countries the figures probably underestimate infrastructure investment as the private sector financed much of the new rail infrastructure.

In the following decades, public expenditure on investment held broadly steady before increasing again. Figures for 1920 and 1937 showed around 3.5% of GDP, rising to 4.5% in 1960 and 1980. Above-average figures in Asia and in some European countries in certain periods reflected catching-up or reconstruction needs: Germany and Japan in the post-war period, South Korea and Singapore after 1960 and later Ireland and Greece.

After 1980, investment spending started to come down to an average of 3.5% of GDP by 2000 and about 3% by 2017. This does not only reflect fiscal difficulties in a number of countries; it also points to the fact that much of the 'hard' infrastructure in industrial countries had at some point been completed. Much infrastructure provision, such as in telecoms, energy, rail and road, also moved to the private sector and thus became part of private investment.

This reflects the fact that the 'public good' character of infrastructure has declined and the potential for user charges increased significantly. Modern procurement and budgeting techniques also allow more private financing and provision, for example, via public–private partnerships (PPPs). For new types of infrastructure such as high-speed internet services, the private sector seems to play a predominant role while the public sector sets incentives. As a result, public investment figures are difficult to compare across countries and are no longer fully representative when assessing infrastructure spending.

Some international organisations argue for expanding public investment. Based on simulations, they argue that multipliers for public investment tend to be particularly high (e.g. OECD, 2016 *Economic Outlook*). Others contest this claim (see e.g. Cogan et al., 2010). Ilzetzki, Mendoza and Végh (2010) found a growth multiplier of only 0.4 in the short run before a stronger long-term effect set in.

There is nonetheless significant evidence that public investment – efficiently provided – is good for economic growth and people's well-being (Fournier, 2016). Upkeep and modernisation of infrastructure, in particular, has become an important challenge in many advanced countries, given stiff competition for public funds.

Some economists doubt that innovation and development should be mainly left to the private sector. Mazzucato (2013), for example, argues that state funded investment in technology and innovation is more important for development than is often presumed. Perhaps this is more an argument for government support for basic research (that the private sector can then turn into marketable products) than for public investment. The disadvantages of government in running projects and enterprises need to be weighed against the public good content of the investment.

2.3 Interest Expenditure on Public Debt

Historically, governments have often spent a significant share of their resources on servicing the public debt. In fact, debt service was the third most important spending category in the late nineteenth century, on which governments spent on average over 2% of GDP (Table 2.4). Spending was higher when a war effort had raised the public debt.

After 1918, the situation changed significantly. A number of countries had so much debt that its monetisation resulted in hyperinflation. After 1923, Germany, for example, had no interest payments – though at the high

Table 2.4 *Public expenditure on interest*

% of GDP	About 1870	About 1920	About 1937	1970	1980	2000	2017
Euro area							
Austria	..	1.0	1.5	0.8	2.4	3.6	1.8
Belgium	..	6.6	3.4	2.8	6.6	6.7	2.5
Finland	..	..	..	0.9	1.0	2.7	1.0
France	5.2	4.5	5.4	0.5	1.2	2.9	1.8
Germany	0.3		0.9	0.8	3.6	3.1	1.1
Greece	..	..	..	0.7	1.7	6.9	3.2
Ireland	..	0.5	2.3	3.5	6.3	1.9	2.0
Italy	4.5	4.4	4.7	1.8	4.7	6.1	3.8
Netherlands	2.4		4.8	1.3	3.8	3.3	1.0
Portugal	..	..	..	..	2.6	3.0	3.9
Spain	3.3	2.3	3.9	0.5	0.7	3.2	2.6
Other Europe							
Denmark	..	..	..	..	3.8	3.7	1.1
Sweden	..	1.0	0.9	1.0	4.1	3.3	0.4
Switzerland	..	..	1.1	0.3	0.5	1.7	0.5
UK	1.7	5.7	5.3	2.7	4.9	2.4	2.7
Other advanced economies							
Australia	3.6	5.4	5.8	2.5	3.8	2.2	1.5
Canada	..	4.8	5.8	1.2	5.5	7.0	2.8
Japan	..	1.1	..	0.4	2.4	3.1	2.0
South Korea	..	..	..	..	0.6	1.6	1.3
New Zealand	..	..	6.3	2.6	3.9	2.7	0.7
Singapore	..	..	..	..	..	..	..
US	1.4	1.3	1.0	1.9	4.6	3.8	3.6
Average[1]	2.8	3.2	3.5	1.5	3.4	3.7	2.0

Sources: Ameco, WEO, Tanzi and Schuknecht (2000)
1. Unweighted, excluding South Korea and Singapore.

price of an impoverished middle class and elderly population. Other major war participants continued to honour their debt and, consequently, had high interest payments of 4% to over 6% of GDP – one fifth to one quarter of total expenditure, a huge burden.

After 1945, further dramatic changes happened. Once again Germany and a few other countries escaped an unsustainable debt burden through inflation. In several other countries, 'financial repression' forced low interest rates on the holders of public debt which, with strong growth, permitted a rapid decline in the debt service burden.

The period of declining debt service ended after 1970. By then, debt service payments had come down to an average of 1.4% of GDP, less than half of the ratio during the inter-war period and also much less than in the late nineteenth century. Only a few countries, including Ireland, the United Kingdom, Belgium and New Zealand, had much higher interest payments.

The 1970s, with two oil crises and rising inflation and deficits, saw interest payments increase rapidly. By 1980, spending on debt service had more than doubled to over 3% of GDP. Belgium, Canada, Ireland, Italy, Sweden, the United Kingdom and the United States reported above 4% of GDP and, with high deficits, high interest rates and rising debt continuing in the 1980s, expenditure on debt service increased further.

Debt service payments peaked at an average above 5% of GDP in 1990. During the European downturn and currency crisis of the early 1990s, Italian public interest payments rose to over 11% of GDP, one quarter of its total expenditure. Belgium reported almost 10% and Sweden almost 7% of GDP. Governments with high debt had to start paying major risk premia as liquidity and even solvency concerns began to emerge.

Some countries had already begun government consolidation and reform in the 1980s (see Chapter 5). But only after further reforms in the 1990s and falling inflation and real interest rates did interest payments also begin to come down. In 2000, interest payments of 3.5% of GDP were almost back to the level of 1980. 'Only' Belgium, Greece and Italy still had debt service payments above 6% of GDP and the lowest debt countries often reported less than 2%.

By 2017, and with record low interest rates feeding through, debt service payments as a share of GDP had almost halved to 1.9% of GDP, compared to the beginning of the millennium. This followed the favourable effect of declining interest rates that more than compensated for the impact of a much higher debt ratio (see Chapter 3). Net interest payments of government were below 1% of GDP in many countries, and even negative in South

Korea. Greece, Italy, Portugal and the United States had the biggest interest obligations, at 3–4% of GDP.

2.4 Social Safety Nets

Transfers and Subsidies

So far, we have said nothing about the most important expenditure categories of today: transfers and subsidies, and social expenditure. From a historical perspective, they did not matter much until well into the twentieth century. Transfers (e.g. for pensions) and subsidies refer to the so-called economic classification of expenditure. Most transfers and some subsidies serve the achievement of social objectives; other subsidies support, for example, certain industries. Transfers and subsidies also provide an incomplete picture of social benefits because they do not include transfers in kind such as health benefits, which count as public consumption. Getting a good statistical picture of the social role of the state is, therefore, not easy. Transfers and subsidies are still a good start because the data goes back much further than that for social expenditure.

Data for the late nineteenth century is very thin, but we have reason to believe that spending on transfers and subsidies did not exceed 1% of GDP on average and this may even include some non-social spending (Table 2.5). The United Kingdom had a level of social spending twice as high as this, but it was still only 2.2% of GDP.

This is not surprising. Germany only invented compulsory public social security in the 1880s. At the start, this covered a small share of the population with very limited health and pension benefits. A few other countries introduced compulsory health and pension regimes just before the First World War, and the United Kingdom and Ireland saw the first compulsory unemployment insurance in 1911 (Tanzi and Schuknecht, 2000).

Transfers and subsidies increased significantly in the first four decades of the twentieth century as welfare systems started to develop in many countries. By 1937, spending averaged 5.7% of GDP in the countries for which data is available. It already exceeded 7% of GDP in France and Germany and 10% of GDP in the United Kingdom. But even here, programmes were limited and coverage was below 50% of the work force; unemployment insurance sometimes covered very few people. By contrast, expenditure figures for Canada, Japan and the United States were still in the 1–2% range, and public social welfare was very limited.

Table 2.5 *Transfers and subsidies*

% of GDP	About 1870	About 1937	1960	1980	2000	2017
Euro area						
Austria	..	..	..	16.3	22.9	21.6
Belgium	0.2	..	12.7	16.9	17.5	19.8
Finland	..	..	..	13.8	18.4	21.7
France	1.1	7.2	11.4	17.0	20.3	24.5
Germany	0.5	7.0	13.5	15.8	21.0	19.1
Greece	..	..	..	..	15.6	21.2
Ireland	..	..	..	..	9.6	9.4
Italy	..	..	..	12.3	18.5	23.1
Netherlands	0.3	..	11.5	18.3	12.9	12.7
Portugal	..	..	..	6.6	13.9	21.3
Spain	..	2.5	1.0	12.9	14.7	17.1
Other Europe						
Denmark	..	..	..	15.7	20.0	19.7
Sweden	0.7	..	9.3	..	18.8	15.6
Switzerland	..	..	6.8	..	13.6	13.9
UK	2.2	10.3	9.2	11.8	14.2	15.6
Other advanced economies						
Australia	..	..	4.3	7.8	11.7	10.2
Canada	..	..	..	7.9	9.6	10.8
Japan	1.1	1.4	5.5	..	10.2	14.8
South Korea	..	..	..	1.7	5.3	10.9
New Zealand	0.2	..	..	..	13.0	12.8
Singapore	..	..	..	..	..	..
US	..	..	4.7	10.0	10.5	14.9
Average[1]	0.8	5.7	8.2	13.1	15.3	17.0

Sources: OECD, Ameco, Tanzi and Schuknecht (2000). As of 2000 transfers only
1. Unweighted, excluding South Korea and Singapore.

Rapid growth and declining military spending after 1945 allowed social security systems to be extended further. By 1960, the state provided basic social safety nets with widespread if not universal coverage in almost all countries. Spending on transfers and subsidies had increased to an average of 8.2% of GDP. Europe and notably Belgium, Germany and the Netherlands featured the highest spending ratios, but in most countries the core social tasks of government as defined by classical and Keynesian economists had probably been achieved or were within reach.

What happened next in the area of transfers and social expenditure, however, was not a slowdown or halt in expenditure growth: the growth of government continued and even accelerated. By 1980, transfers and subsidies had grown to 13% of GDP. A number of countries reported public transfers and subsidies above 15% of GDP, but a few countries were still reporting below 10%.

Over time, the data series greatly improved, and by 2000 data for all countries were available: transfers (excluding subsidies) reached 15.3% of GDP on average. Given that subsidies (of ca. 1–2% of GDP on average) were excluded, this increase masks a stronger increase of transfers. A further increase to 17% had occurred by 2017. European countries featured the highest expenditure ratios, with France reaching almost one quarter of GDP and Italy running a close second.

These figures, however, underestimate the social role of government. As mentioned, they do not include transfers in kind, which can reach another 10–15% of GDP. Total transfers in some countries were, therefore, well above 30% of GDP in the 2010s. Increases in cash and in-kind transfers were also much higher than those for cash transfers only, exceeding 4% of GDP in many cases for the 2000–2017 period. But these figures include capital transfers and other non-social transfers so that the picture is not very accurate and comparable across countries. Fortunately, the OECD had earlier developed a well-defined database of social expenditure.

Social Expenditure

Social expenditure as defined by the OECD includes the socially related transfers and subsidies and certain other government expenditure for social purposes. The main categories are pensions, health, long-term care, family, child and unemployment benefits. Education is mostly not included (except below primary education). Due to its productive role it is (rightly) part of public 'goods and service' expenditure. The first figures were available for 1960 and broad coverage started about 1980.

Patterns over time and across countries significantly mirror those for subsidies and transfers, as there are significant overlaps but also important nuances. In 1960, social expenditure averaged 9% of GDP (Table 2.6). Germany and Austria had the highest social spending, at 15% of GDP; Greece, Japan and Switzerland the smallest, at 3–4%. Surprisingly from today's perspective, social spending in Anglo-Saxon countries was not far from the average.

By 1980, the picture had changed dramatically and more strongly than the figures for subsidies and transfers. Average expenditure had nearly doubled as a share of GDP to 16.6%. Social spending consumed every sixth instead of every eleventh Dollar, Franc, Pound or Mark twenty years

Table 2.6 *Social expenditure*

% of GDP	1960	1980	1999	2007	2016
Euro area					
Austria	15.0	22.0	25.8	25.1	27.8
Belgium	11.4	23.1	24.6	24.9	29.0
Finland	8.2	17.7	23.8	22.9	30.8
France	12.0	20.2	28.6	28.0	31.5
Germany	15.4	21.8	25.5	24.1	25.3
Greece	3.3	9.9	18.0	20.6	27.0
Ireland[1]	7.1	15.7	13.7	15.8	16.1
Italy	10.7	17.4	22.8	24.7	28.9
Netherlands	9.6	23.3	19.1	19.9	22.0
Portugal	..	9.5	17.2	21.8	24.1
Spain	..	15.0	19.8	20.8	24.6
Other Europe					
Denmark	..	20.3	24.5	25.0	28.7
Sweden	12.6	24.8	28.0	25.5	27.1
Switzerland	4.2	12.8	17.0	16.8	19.7
UK	9.7	15.6	17.7	19.5	21.5
Other advanced economies					
Australia	5.9	10.3	17.3	15.9	19.1
Canada	8.1	13.3	16.0	16.2	17.2
Japan	3.5	10.2	16.0	18.5	23.1
South Korea	..	..	5.8	7.1	10.4
New Zealand	11.4	16.7	18.7	18.1	19.7
Singapore	..	..	..	..	..
US	7.0	12.8	14.2	15.9	19.3
Average[2]	9.1	16.6	20.4	21.0	24.1

Source: OECD, Social Expenditure
1. When taking GNP instead of GDP for Ireland, the ratios for 2000 and 2017 are 15.8% and 19.6%, respectively.
2. Unweighted, excluding South Korea and Singapore.

earlier. The continental European countries of Austria, Denmark, Sweden, Belgium, the Netherlands, Germany and France formed the group of large welfare states with spending of over 20% of GDP. Switzerland's spending was much lower, but it had still more than tripled to 12.8%, just about the ratio reported by Canada and the United States. Australia, Greece, Portugal and Japan showed the lowest share of social spending.

Subsequently, expenditure dynamics slowed somewhat, but the upward trend continued unabated. Two decades later, public social expenditure had increased another 4 percentage points of GDP to 20.4% on average.

France and Sweden were the champions of social spending, with 28% of GDP or more. Italy began with a low ratio of 10% in 1960 but it had doubled by 1980, followed by a further increase to almost 25% of GDP in 1999. Greece and Portugal also showed a remarkable catch-up. Non-Europeans all featured social expenditure well below 20% of GDP – though also significantly higher than two decades earlier.

The 1980s and 1990s, however, marked an important change across countries. A number of reform countries, including Canada, New Zealand, Germany, the Nordics and Spain, halted the upward trend in social spending. The Netherlands and Ireland were the first countries to bring down the social expenditure ratio over the two decades.

The following period until 2017 saw another increase in social expenditure by about 4 percentage points of GDP. The increase was slightly above average in Europe where Belgium, Finland, France, Italy and Denmark came close to or exceeded the 30% of GDP mark. In Europe, only Ireland was below the 20% threshold in 2016 (both on a GDP and the less distorted GNP basis). Japan reported the strongest population ageing, and its high social expenditure dynamics were only matched by much of Southern Europe.

We should not forget, however, that this period witnessed a 'boom and bust' cycle, with the worst, global financial and economic crisis since the Great Depression of the 1930s. It therefore deserves more discussion. Remarkably, social expenditure ratios continued to increase in the 'boom' phase between 1999 and 2007 and notably in the later crisis countries of Europe. This is consistent with the finding of strong expenditure dynamics during the boom described in Chapter 1, but it runs counter to the (Keynesian) logic that such spending should be scaled back in good times.

Social expenditure ratios jumped upwards in the global financial crisis as the adverse effect from falling growth and employment compounded the persistence of earlier expenditure dynamics. In the subsequent recovery, social expenditure ratios stayed broadly stable until 2016 as the crisis countries in particular reined in their expenditure growth.

The past two decades also brought to the fore a trend towards more social expenditure programmes, and increasing complexity may undermine the achievement of targets and have unintended consequences. Complexity also invites rent seeking and lobbying over the design of benefits (Tanzi 2018a).

When looking at social versus other expenditure, we find another interesting story. Social expenditure is now about five times as large as education spending. In the past forty years, the rise in social expenditure

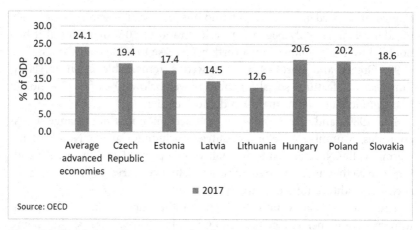

Figure 2.2 Social expenditure in central and eastern Europe, 2017.

has been faster than that of total and primary expenditure. The main 'victims' seem to have been public investment and some core administration expenditure. We will return to this in more depth in Chapter 7.

Finally, a word on emerging markets and other 'competitor' country groups. Social expenditure in the former socialist economies of Eastern Europe were typically much lower than in the West in 2017 (Figure 2.2). None of them showed social spending significantly above 20% of GDP, and two of the Baltics were well below the lowest ratio for non-Asian advanced economies: these countries had truly turned away from their socialist past. East Asian countries all reported much smaller welfare states, though with a strong upward dynamic.

2.5 Pensions, Health and Long-Term Care

Pensions

The strong growth of social expenditure in recent decades mainly reflects the dynamism of pension and health expenditure. Recall that social security was only introduced for the first time in the 1880s in Germany and only began to spread in the interwar period before expanding more fully after 1945. Public expenditure on pensions was initially very low. Around 1920, it was little more than 1% of GDP on average and above 2% in only a few European countries (Table 2.7). By 1960, pension spending averaged 4.5% of GDP, and still only 1–2.5% in several advanced countries such as Japan,

Table 2.7 *Public pension expenditure*

% of GDP	About 1920	1960	1980	2000	2013/latest
Euro area					
Austria	2.4	9.6	10.4	12.0	13.4
Belgium	0.3	4.3	8.7	8.7	10.2
Finland	..	..	5.4	7.4	11.1
France	1.6	6.0	9.2	11.4	13.8
Germany	2.1	9.7	10.4	10.8	10.1
Greece	..	..	5.2	10.4	17.4
Ireland	..	2.5	5.0	2.9	4.9
Italy	2.1	5.5	8.6	13.5	16.3
Netherlands	..	4.0	6.0	4.7	5.4
Portugal	..	..	3.7	7.8	14.0
Spain	0.9	..	6.1	8.4	11.4
Other Europe					
Denmark	..	..	5.7	6.3	8.0
Sweden	0.5	4.4	6.7	6.9	7.7
Switzerland	..	2.3	5.5	6.0	6.4
UK	2.2	4.0	5.3	5.1	6.1
Other advanced economies					
Australia	..	3.3	3.6	4.7	4.3
Canada	..	2.8	3.1	4.2	4.6
Japan	0.3	1.3	3.9	7.3	10.2
South Korea	..	..	..	1.3	2.6
New Zealand	..	4.3	7.0	4.9	5.1
Singapore	..	..	..	..	..
US	0.7	4.1	6.0	5.6	6.9
Average[1]	1.3	4.5	6.3	7.4	9.4

Sources: OECD, Tanzi and Schuknecht (2000). Old age and survivors pensions
1. Unweighted, excluding South Korea and Singapore.

Switzerland or Ireland. Only Germany and Austria were spending almost 10% of GDP on pensions in 1960.

The increase in pension spending accelerated after 1960. By 1980, the average had risen to 6.3%, and Belgium, France and Italy had joined Germany and Austria with spending near 10% of GDP. Thereafter, average spending rose further at a rate of 0.5% to 1% of GDP per decade, and Europe remained well above average in terms of level and dynamics.

In pensions, the main drivers of expenditure were population ageing, replacement rates and retirement ages. Initially, as of 1960, rising entitlements and shorter working lives contributed to rising pension expenditure. More recently, population ageing has been the main driver as the 'baby boomers'

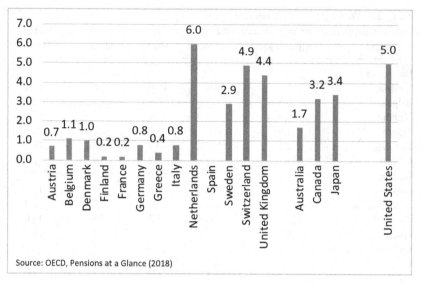

Source: OECD, Pensions at a Glance (2018)

Figure 2.3 Private pension benefits, % of GDP, 2015.

born in the late 1940s and thereafter started to reach retirement. This effect is often stronger than the countervailing effort to contain spending by raising the statutory and effective retirement age, and by lowering entitlements.

The total average of pension spending reached 9.4% of GDP in the early 2010s with a range from 2.6% in South Korea to 17.4% in Greece. Germany, Ireland, New Zealand and the Netherlands, however, managed to halt the upward dynamics. Southern Europe, by contrast, experienced a virtual explosion of pension expenditure before the global financial crisis triggered reforms.

Most advanced countries also feature private pension plans to complement the public pension system, and they play a particularly strong role in some Anglo-Saxon countries, Japan, the Netherlands and Switzerland (Figure 2.3). In these countries, private pension benefits amount to 3–6% of GDP and, thus, hugely complement public pensions. In other countries, private pensions play less of a role, or systems are still in the development phase, but they are not negligible either.

Health

Expenditure patterns in public health were similar to those for public pensions. Historical data confirm very low public health expenditure

Table 2.8 *Public health expenditure*

% of GDP	About 1910	About 1930	1960	1980	2000	2014/latest
Euro area						
Austria	..	0.2	3.1	4.7	5.9	6.5
Belgium	0.2	0.1	2.1	5.1	5.9	8.0
Finland	..	..	2.1	4.6	4.0	5.8
France	0.3	0.3	2.5	5.4	7.5	8.6
Germany	0.5	0.7	3.2	6.3	7.4	7.9
Greece	..	..	..	3.1	4.5	6.1
Ireland	..	0.6	3.0	6.1	4.2	5.5
Italy	..	..	..	5.3	5.5	6.8
Netherlands	..	..	1.3	4.8	4.7	7.9
Portugal	..	..	..	3.0	5.9	6.1
Spain	..	..	0.9	4.0	4.9	6.4
Other Europe						
Denmark	..	..	..	5.1	5.1	6.7
Sweden	0.3	0.9	3.4	7.2	5.7	6.6
Switzerland	..	0.3	2.0	3.3	4.6	6.6
UK	0.3	0.6	3.3	4.4	5.3	7.1
Other advanced economies						
Australia	0.4	0.6	2.4	3.7	5.2	6.4
Canada	..	..	2.3	4.8	5.7	7.1
Japan	0.1	0.1	1.8	4.4	5.8	7.8
South Korea	..	..	..	..	2.0	3.9
New Zealand	0.7	1.1	3.5	5.1	5.8	7.5
Singapore	..	..	..	..	..	..
US	0.3	0.3	1.3	3.5	5.6	8.0
Average[1]	0.3	0.5	2.4	4.7	5.5	7.0

Sources: OECD; Tanzi and Schuknecht (2000)
1. Unweighted, excluding South Korea and Singapore.

until the Second World War: few countries came even close to 1% of GDP
(Table 2.8).

The picture changed after 1945. Health and health insurance systems
expanded and so did expenditure, averaging 2.5% of GDP in 1960. Only
the United States stood at half that level, while several European countries
reported above 3%. Still, total spending on health was only half of that
on pensions and Europeans did not feature higher averages than other
countries.

By 1980, public health expenditure ratios had doubled to nearly 5% of
GDP. Germany, Ireland and Sweden posted the largest figures, the United
States was still near the bottom, at 3.5%. Upward dynamics continued

thereafter, though a little slower than for pensions. They were particularly steep for Japan, the United Kingdom and the United States. These countries were well below average in 1980 but moved well above the average in the 2010s.

Public expenditure in the mid-2010s averaged 7% of GDP, 1.5% of GDP higher than only fifteen years previously. Just as with pensions, the pace of spending growth has increased compared to earlier decades. But, unlike pensions, expenditure ratios are remarkably similar across the advanced economies, ranging mostly between 6% and 8% of GDP. Only South Korea and Singapore remain outliers at the lower end.

Again, there are significant differences as regards the role of the public and private sector (Figure 2.4). In most countries, public health provision covers 70–90% of health expenditure, but there are a few exceptions. In Australia, Portugal, Switzerland and Greece, private financing is 30–40% of total health expenditure, in South Korea and the United States this share is even 40–50%. A number of countries have mainly government (tax-financed) schemes, some have mainly contribution-based public insurance and a few feature mixed systems. The latter typically have the highest total health spending (see also Dauns, Ebert and Schuknecht, 2015; OECD, 2017c).

Long-Term Care

Since the 1980s and 1990s, another social expenditure category has come into significant prominence: long-term care. This was virtually no public responsibility a few decades ago; it was mostly the job of families. Also, many people died before diseases like Alzheimer's required intensive long-term attention.

Long-term care expenditure has grown rapidly from a very low level (Table 2.9). In 2016, it was particularly high in Sweden, Finland and the Netherlands, exceeding 3% or even 4% of GDP. In a number of countries, figures still ranged around or below 1% of GDP so that the average came out below 2%, but the trend remains clearly upward.

Other Social Expenditure

A number of further social expenditure categories add up to a significant total, unemployment benefits being the most prominent. Unemployment benefits were a rather negligible category in the 1960s. However, the value of having such a 'safety net' was high from a social perspective, buffering

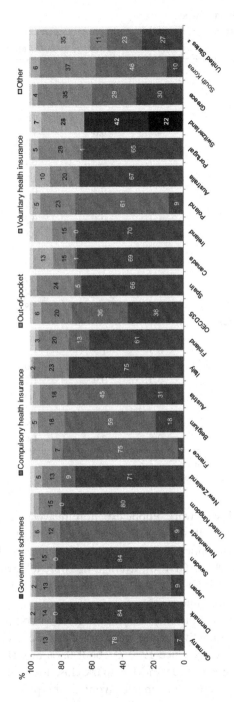

Source: OECD Health Statistics (2017)

1. France does not include out-of-pocket payments for inpatient LTC thus resulting in an underestimation of the out-of-pocket share.

2. Spending by private health insurance companies in the United States is reported under voluntary health insurance.

Figure 2.4 Health expenditure system financing, 2015.

Table 2.9 *Long-term care expenditure*

% of GDP	1980	2000	2015/latest
Euro area			
Austria	0.9	1.2	1.5
Belgium	..	0.7	2.2
Finland	..	1.1	1.9
France	0.2	0.8	1.7
Germany	0.4	1.4	1.8
Greece	..	..	0.1
Ireland	..	0.9	1.6
Italy	..	0.3	0.9
Netherlands	1.3	0.8	2.7
Portugal	..	0.1	0.2
Spain	..	0.1	0.8
Other Europe			
Denmark	..	1.9	2.6
Sweden	..	0.6	2.9
Switzerland	..	1.9	2.4
UK	..	2.0	1.8
Other advanced economies			
Australia	0.0	0.0	0.2
Canada	0.9	1.3	1.5
Japan	..	0.6	2.0
South Korea	0.0	0.0	1.3
New Zealand	..	..	1.3
Singapore	..	..	..
US	0.7	0.8	0.9
Average[1]	0.6	0.9	1.6

Sources: OECD, EU Commission
1. Unweighted, excluding South Korea and Singapore.

financial hardship due to loss of work. Public expenditure averaged mostly around 1% of GDP over time. It was significantly higher during the 1980s and 1990s and during economic downturns in some countries. Public spending was again near 1% of GDP on average in 2017, following the success of labour market reform in many countries and the favourable economic environment of the time.

All countries – but to significantly varying degrees – complement unemployment benefits with active labour market policies. Spending has been relatively stable on average since 1980 at about 0.5% of GDP, with the United States spending very little and Denmark close to 2% of GDP. 'Activation-related' expenditure found much favour in the policy debate because such policies facilitated people's re-entry into the labour market, despite some concern about 'capture', where the activation industry does not produce the skills that the economy needs.

Other work and family-related benefits include disability, maternity, family and child benefits, to name only some of the most important ones. Expenditure on families is perhaps the most important sub-component of these; this increased slowly after 1980, reaching on average slightly above 2% of GDP in the mid-2010s. Spending varies hugely between less than 1% of GDP in the United States and almost 4% of GDP in Finland, Sweden and the United Kingdom.

2.6 Conclusion

The composition and dynamics of total expenditure over the past 150 years shows some fascinating patterns. Especially after 1960, we see a clear orientation towards an increasing share for social expenditure. By contrast, some other components linked to core tasks, such as investment, are on the decline.

Public expenditure focussed on producing goods and services, investment and interest payments up to the First World War, and there was hardly any social role for government. Expenditure on goods and services increased in the following decades, building public administrations and providing core public goods and services. Public investment also increased, building modern infrastructure networks. Since 1980, public spending on goods and services has been broadly stable with some significant country variation, and public investment even began to decline.

By 1960, social safety nets were in place in all countries, albeit to varying degrees. However, the growth of social spending accelerated thereafter and the spending ratio almost trippled from 9% of GDP in 1960 to nearly 25% of GDP on average in 2016. After 1980, social expenditure continued to increase at a rate of roughly 2% per decade, increasing faster than total spending and thus 'mechanically' replacing other public spending categories.

Public pensions, health and long-term care are the most important components of social expenditure. Together, they account for about 20% of GDP on average for advanced countries and pensions are almost half of that. Other important components include unemployment and family benefits. European countries tend to feature the largest welfare states, with social spending ratios up to almost 33% of GDP.

We will return to many of these issues in Parts II and III. The financing of expenditure via taxes, deficits and debt are analysed next, in Chapter 3.

3

Financing Government

For a Minister it is very tempting to use debt to play the 'big man during his office' without raising taxes unduly. ... The practice of incurring debt is, therefore, almost without exception, to be expected from any government.

David Hume

What can be added to the happiness of 'man' who is in health, out of debt, and has a clear conscience.

Adam Smith

Highlights

Government expenditure needs to be financed. The two ways to do so are via taxes or via deficits and debt. For the first ninety of the past 150 years, public expenditure broadly grew in line with revenue, except during wars and times of crises. This changed fundamentally in the 1960s and early 1970s as the 'Keynesian revolution' took hold.

Over the past fifty years, revenue rose strongly, but public spending often increased even faster. Chronic deficits stoked a high and growing stock of public debt in much of the advanced world. Public debt in the largest countries is now similar to the level prevailing at the end of the Second World War (Figure 3.1).

Future governments will also face significant liabilities from increasing public expenditure related to population ageing, as well as fiscal risks from the financial sector. These liabilities and risks imply higher expenditure in the future that will need to be financed. At the same time, there are political and economic limits to both taxation and indebtedness.

3.1 Government Revenue

Understanding the past (and future) of public spending requires understanding how, and how well, it is financed. The history of taxes and government

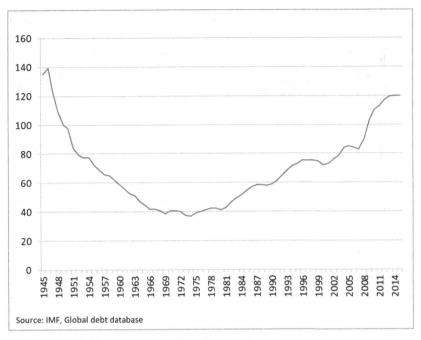

Figure 3.1 Public debt ratio, % of GDP, G7 countries.

revenue broadly mirrors that of public expenditure. But governments have the option to break that link by incurring deficits and public debt, at least for some time and up to a point.

When looking back at the period from 1870 to after 1960, it is interesting to note that peacetime public revenue and expenditure ratios were very similar. This, however, is hard to show in the figures because country data on the revenue side are not as readily available and sometimes not as comprehensive as on the expenditure side. Revenue ratios and averages, therefore, tend to be lower than the expenditure figures reported in Chapter 1, but the available data still has some interesting stories to tell.

Public revenue in 1870 on average stood at 9.3% of GDP and this ratio changed little until 1913 (Table 3.1). France, Italy and Australia managed to collect near or above 15% of GDP, but in general limited revenue collection probably also contributed to low public expenditure ratios in that period (Tanzi, 2018b). Figures for revenue in 1870–1937 in Canada, Germany, the Netherlands, Spain, Sweden and Switzerland only refer to central government. This, as mentioned, makes revenue and expenditure figures for these years difficult to compare.

Table 3.1 *Total government revenue*

% of GDP	About 1870	About 1913	About 1920	About 1937	1960	1980	2000	2017
Euro area								
Austria	..	..	9.0	15.7	37.9	49.6	48.6	48.4
Belgium	11.6	..	17.0	..	30.3	46.8	49.0	51.2
Finland	..	..	..	..	..	43.7	54.9	53.2
France	15.3	13.7	17.9	20.5	37.3	45.8	50.1	53.9
Germany	1.4	3.2	8.6	15.9	36.0	46.1	45.6	45.2
Greece	..	..	..	..	..	24.4	42.4	48.8
Ireland	9.6	11.8	23.2	26.3	27.5	35.9	35.7	25.7
Italy	12.5	14.7	24.2	31.1	24.8	34.5	44.2	46.6
Netherlands	..	6.4	11.8	11.9	33.9	52.0	43.6	43.7
Portugal	..	..	..	..	..	27.8	39.4	42.9
Spain	9.4	10.3	5.8	11.9	18.7	30.0	38.1	37.9
Other Europe								
Denmark	..	..	..	..	..	51.3	54.6	52.9
Sweden	9.5	6.7	7.2	8.5	32.5	56.1	56.6	50.3
Switzerland	..	2.5	3.8	6.0	23.3	32.8	34.2	34.7
UK	8.7	11.2	20.1	22.6	29.9	42.3	36.8	39.1
Other advanced economies								
Australia	17.8	16.7	19.4	14.9	24.4	30.3	35.1	35.0
Canada	4.1	5.5	16.6	22.6	26.0	37.9	44.0	40.0
Japan	9.5	..	..	..	18.8	27.6	31.3	35.4
South Korea	..	..	..	..	..	..	29.1	35.3
New Zealand	..	..	24.7	27.0	..	21.8	39.3	39.9
Singapore	..	..	..	..	..	..	..	..
US	7.4	7.0	12.4	19.7	27.0	31.3	34.5	32.9
Average[1]	9.7	9.1	14.8	18.2	28.6	39.3	42.9	42.9

Source: Ameco, WEO, Tanzi and Schuknecht (2000)
1. Unweighted, excluding South Korea and Singapore.

Public revenue jumped to almost 14% of GDP on average in 1920, due to tax increases during the First World War. Revenue increased further to almost 19% in 1937 as preparations for the Second World War required higher revenue in the late 1930s. The 'big' governments of the time were also the countries with the highest revenue ratios: Australia, France and Italy before 1914 and France, Italy, New Zealand, the United Kingdom and Canada before 1939.

As of 1960, data availability is much better, and revenue and expenditure patterns can be compared more directly. For the advanced countries, total general government revenue averaged 28.7% in that year, which was even slightly more than the total expenditure of 27.8%. Revenue collection was also relatively homogenous across countries: only Spain and Japan featured revenue ratios below 20% of GDP, while only France and Austria featured ratios above 35%. In fact, all countries with revenue ratios above 30% were European.

The following two decades saw an unprecedented increase in peacetime revenue – almost but not quite in tandem with expenditure. This period thus saw the beginning of the chronic decoupling of expenditure from revenue: in fact, while expenditure increased by over 15% of GDP, revenue had 'only' grown by a little over 10% of GDP on average. As a result, revenue stood at about 39.3% of GDP in 1980 compared to expenditure of 43.2% of GDP.

Still, the increase was impressive: it averaged 0.5% of GDP for each year of the two decades, despite the fact that two oil crises resulted in major recessions during the period. A main reason was the strong inflation in the 1970s, resulting in significant 'bracket creep' as rising nominal incomes catapulted people into higher tax brackets even when their real incomes were not rising. The 1960s and the 1970s were also the time when many countries introduced value-added taxes (VAT), which facilitated the collection of taxes on consumption.

Unsurprisingly, the biggest spenders also featured the highest revenue ratios. Belgium, the Nordics, the Netherlands, Germany and France collected 45% of GDP or more from their population. Australia, Japan, Greece and the United States were still below 30%. Already in 1980, a pattern of higher revenue European countries and lower revenue non-European countries had started to emerge, similar to the expenditure side.

With the end of the 'Keynesian revolution', growing inefficiencies in the tax system moved onto the radar. The 1980s and the 1990s saw a host of reforms on the revenue side. Countries moved away from very high top marginal tax rates, and base broadening and system streamlining was pursued in many countries. High interest payments and large deficits also forced many governments to seek more and more growth-friendly financing of their expenditure.

As a result, in the period between 1980 and 2000, public revenue increased in the advanced countries by 3.8 percentage points of GDP to 42.9% of GDP. The Nordic countries raised their revenue ratios to above 50% of GDP, and Austria, Belgium and France were near 50%. The two countries with the strongest further increases were Italy (+ 12% of GDP) and Greece (+ 18% of GDP). These two countries respectively raised revenue ratios by an impressive 0.6% and 0.9% of GDP on average each year over that period.

Divergence across countries, however, increased. In a few 'small government' countries such as the United States or Japan, revenue rose moderately above 30% of GDP. Government reform on the expenditure side in many countries permitted a reduction in the tax burden. The revenue ratios of the Netherlands and the United Kingdom fell significantly, by over 5% of GDP, while Austria and Germany also posted small declines from high initial levels.

In 2017, average public revenue was the same as in 2000, at 42.9% of GDP. However, this masks two significant developments. First, divergence continued. Southern European countries tended to show further increases in revenue ratios while those of most other countries either changed little or even declined slightly. Finland and France continued to collect well above 50% of GDP; Ireland, South Korea and the United States were around 30%.

Second, it appears that in many countries, the potential to raise revenue ratios further had reached the limit. Akgun, Bartolini and Cournède (2017) argue that many countries are yielding at or near the maximum possible revenue from personal income tax, corporate income tax and VAT. This is particularly true for the countries with large governments and weak institutions. Hence, in many countries, further revenue increases are hardly possible beyond the levels reached in the mid-2010s. This limits their ability to tax-finance future expenditure increases.

For personal income tax, the authors argue that an effective rate close to 50% might already be above the revenue maximising tax rate. An employee with as little as 167% of average income faces taxation beyond that rate in many countries. Figure 3.2 illustrates the same argument for VAT, showing estimations for the maximum potential revenue that countries can collect relative to the 2015/16 actuals. It shows that revenue maximising VAT rates are not much higher than 20% and mostly somewhat below it. In many countries, actual VAT rates are already near or above the

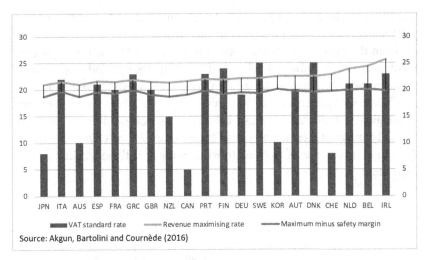

Source: Akgun, Bartolini and Cournède (2016)

Figure 3.2 VAT standard rate vs. revenue maximising rate.

estimated maximum revenue, especially when allowing for a safety margin for measurement errors.

It is worth spending a little time on revenue composition. The pre-First World War period saw a strong dependence of government revenue on indirect taxes including customs duties (Tanzi and Schuknecht, 2000). Direct taxes averaged little over 2% of GDP, or about 20% of total revenue, and the strong reliance on indirect taxes continued until 1939.

By 1960, the pattern had changed significantly, as countries expanded income taxation and, in many cases, introduced contribution-based social security systems. Indirect taxes contributed about 40% to revenue, income taxes 33%, and social security 25%. The contribution of social security contributions, and thus the burden on labour, continued to rise thereafter and, as mentioned, VAT became a more and more important revenue component.

3.2 Deficits

When governments cannot collect enough revenue to finance their expenditure, they incur deficits. These, in turn, raise the public debt. In this regard, the period from 1870 until after the Second World War was rather turbulent as the two World Wars resulted in huge deficits. In peacetime, the unwritten rule was broadly to avoid deficits, and this practice prevailed until the 1960s as classical economic thinking continued to dominate amongst policymakers and, after 1945, growth was strong.

Given the deficiencies in the data, however, a reliable picture of government balances is only available as of 1960. In that period, government finances were on average broadly in balance. The year 1960 showed a small average surplus of 0.4% (Table 3.2). This is a figure virtually unimaginable today and has not been seen for several decades. In 1960, the only major deficit country was Belgium, at 7% of GDP. Austria, at 2.6% in that year, seems 'nothing to write home about' today, but it looked high then.

Table 3.2 *General government surplus/deficit*

% of GDP	1960	1980	2000	2017
Euro area				
Austria	−2.6	−2.6	−2.4	−0.7
Belgium	−7.3	−9.5	−0.1	−1.0
Finland	4.2	3.7	6.9	−0.6
France	0.8	−0.4	−1.3	−2.6
Germany	3.0	−2.9	0.9	1.3
Greece	0.3	−2.6	−4.1	0.8
Ireland	−1.5	−11	4.9	−0.3
Italy	−1.0	−7.1	−2.4	−2.3
Netherlands	1.3	−3.8	1.9	1.1
Portugal	2.7	−7.5	−3.2	−3.0
Spain	..	..	−1.1	−3.1
Other Europe				
Denmark	5.9	−2.4	1.9	1.0
Sweden	..	−5.4	3.2	1.3
Switzerland	..	..	0.4	0.4
UK	−1.2	−2.9	1.4	−1.9
Other advanced economies				
Australia	0.3	−3.3	−1.2	−1.4
Canada	..	−2.9	2.6	−1.1
Japan	1.1	−4.8	−7.4	−3.8
South Korea	..	−1.1	4.4	2.8
New Zealand	..	..	1.7	1.2
Singapore	..	..	..	..
US	−0.2	−3.6	0.8	−4.9
Average[1]	0.4	−4.1	0.2	−1.0

Source: OECD, AMECO
1. Unweighted, excluding South Korea and Singapore.

The 1970s were the first extended period of significant and chronic deficits in many countries outside wars. By 1980, when the second oil crisis had its full fiscal impact, deficits averaged almost 4% of GDP. Belgium and Ireland reported (near) double-digit deficits, and Italy's deficit reached almost 6% of GDP. Finland was the only country with a significant surplus, while France had a near balanced budget.

Rising expenditure, high deficits and rising debt led to two major reform 'waves' by government in the 1980s and 1990s (see also Chapter 5). A number of countries brought down expenditure ratios, thus allowing reductions in deficit and debt. The commitment to enter the EMU in 1999 also induced countries to cut their spending and deficits. This and a good economic climate resulted in the near disappearance of average deficits by 2000. It may also have helped that all the EMU entrant countries had to report deficits below 3% of GDP in 1999, and they succeeded. Only Greece reported a deficit of 4% in that year and increasing figures thereafter.

The global economic boom period continued until 2007, with a short 'soft patch' in the early 2000s after the bursting of the dotcom bubble. However, governments did not use the good times to achieve or maintain sound public finances. A number of countries showed significant deficits when the global financial crisis struck. These included the later European crisis countries Portugal and Greece, but also France, Italy, the United Kingdom and the United States. In these countries, fiscal deficits skyrocketed during the crisis and reached double-digit levels in 2010. Expenditure ratios had grown hugely and revenue had shrunk as the economy contracted and 'old' expenditure habits proved hard to break.

A few European countries experienced a growing concern in the financial markets over their financial health, especially after Greece's major misreporting of public deficits became public in 2009. Greece and Portugal had to go to the International Monetary Fund (IMF) for a bailout. Newly created European support facilities also bolstered Ireland, Spain and Cyprus, which sought international help after experiencing rising deficits and financial sector difficulties.

In the following period, consolidation efforts in a number of countries plus low interest rates and a strengthening economic recovery produced a significant reduction in average deficits from 7% of GDP in 2010 to about 1% in 2017. The United States and Japan maintained the highest deficits of near 4% and 5% of GDP, respectively. France, Portugal and Spain had ratios near 3%.

The evaluation of deficit dynamics in the 2010s is complex. In a number of countries like Germany, the economic recovery had prevailed for eight or nine years by 2017, while in some Southern European ones it only began in 2014. It is thus less surprising that Spain and Italy had not advanced as far as Germany with deficit reduction by 2017. At the same time, the United States and France could have used the long recovery period better to bring down their deficits.

The assessment of the 'true' fiscal position of a country also proved much more difficult than expected. Measures of the structural fiscal balance (which excludes influences from the business cycle) and their changes turned out to be less reliable than hoped. There was quite some uncertainty over the level of spare capacity in advanced economies (the output gap), and how much special factors had affected fiscal balances.

3.3 Public Debt

Public debt is a very old phenomenon. Since virtually the first existence of money and the state, governments have borrowed money to finance wars and, rather less often, beautiful buildings. Government debt has thus never been absent in the past 150 years. In 1870, public debt averaged about 60% of GDP in today's advanced countries (Table 3.3); Australia and Spain reported well above 100% and France and Italy were high debt countries as well.

It seems perhaps surprising that governments could sustain high debt ratios when revenue was only around 10% of GDP. The absence of major wars plus sustained economic growth and broadly balanced budgets contributed to significant debt reduction until 1914: expenditure obligations were low and the potential for revenue increases quite large, as the First World War demonstrated. Nonetheless, there were government bankruptcies in the late nineteenth century, in Greece for example.

The First World War resulted in huge deficits and debt increases. However, not all countries honoured their obligations and maintained stability. Germany defaulted on its debt through inflation. Italy, France and the United Kingdom suffered a major debt burden, which the Great Depression did not lighten. While many people have criticised the lack of fiscal expansion in the Great Depression, they often forget that governments' market access was very limited at that time.

The Second World War was another watershed. Germany defaulted again via inflation before introducing a sound currency, the Deutsche Mark, in 1948. A number of other countries, such as Japan, were also hit hard by inflation or hyperinflation. On average, the G7 debt averaged over 120% of GDP after 1945.

The subsequent period until the 1960s featured mostly balanced budgets and strong growth and, in some cases, financial repression kept debt service

Table 3.3 *General government debt*

% of GDP	About 1870	About 1913	About 1920	About 1937	About 1945	1960	1980	2000	2017
Euro area									
Austria	69.6	63.3	24.1	35.6	35.2	17.7	35.5	66.1	78.4
Belgium	32.1	43.5	128.5	67.8	131.2	69.4	74.2	108.8	103.1
Finland	..	10.9	14.1	9.7	58.6	5.1	11.2	42.5	61.4
France	95.6	66.3	169.6	..	44.3	28.5	21.0	58.6	97.0
Germany	25.4	38.5	4.2	19.3	17.8	18.4	30.3	58.9	64.1
Greece	73.8	64.7	80.4	73.0	23.6	11.6	22.7	104.9	178.6
Ireland	..	..	14.9	31.3	27.1	44.9	66.9	36.1	68.0
Italy	91.6	77.2	159.7	72.1	72.4	31.4	54.0	105.1	131.8
Netherlands	87.0	64.1	62.0	120.9	223.0	66.7	43.7	51.7	56.7
Portugal	62.6	49.2	45.0	29.4	24.6	16.4	29.1	50.3	125.7
Spain	161.7	76.7	37.9	61.5	22.4	20.5	16.0	58.0	98.3
Other Europe									
Denmark	24.2	15.6	12.5	17.9	10.6	20.1	39.2	52.4	36.4
Sweden	12.7	15.3	12.1	20.1	41.6	25.4	37.4	50.8	40.6
Switzerland	..	2.7	28.9	30.5	78.9	16.2	43.9	54.5	42.5
UK	77.4	27.9	137.8	158.7	234.7	117.9	48.1	37.0	87.7
Other advanced economies									
Australia	120.1	120.1	61.2	74.3	89.7	31.5	21.3	41.1	64.6
Canada	29.0	20.7	58.4	87.9	155.5	66.1	45.6	105.4	109.1
Japan	34.0	53.6	25.6	57.0	56.0	8.0	50.1	139.0	235.9

(continued)

Table 3.3 (*continued*)

% of GDP	About 1870	About 1913	About 1920	About 1937	About 1945	1960	1980	2000	2017
South Korea	..	..	..	..	..	13.7	17.0	17.6	37.9
New Zealand	45.8	112.0	132.7	148.0	147.2	68.0	52.3	35.8	30.0
Singapore	..	..	..	..	..	15.7	72.3	87.4	104.7
US	29.9	3.2	27.9	39.6	116.0	54.3	41.2	53.1	107.8
Average[1]	63.1	48.7	61.9	60.8	80.5	36.9	39.2	65.5	90.9

Sources: OECD, IMF, Historic Public Debt Database, AMECO
1. Unweighted, excluding South Korea and Singapore.

costs low. Public debt ratios declined significantly to an average of 36.9% for the advanced countries and less than 50% of GDP for the G7. This was a remarkable achievement.

The United Kingdom reduced its debt from 235% of GDP, Canada from 155%, the Netherlands from 223%, New Zealand from 147% and the United States from 116%, all to less than half the post-1945 ratio. Finland, Germany, Japan, Greece (!) and South Korea reported very little debt in 1960. This period of low spending, no deficits and low debt seems like a fiscal paradise in retrospect!

After a further decline until about 1970, public debt started creeping up. In the 1970s, high inflation and low interest rates on the outstanding stock of debt helped 'finance' part of it at the expense of the holders of 'old', low- interest debt, and the figure therefore remained below 40% on average in 1980. But by then the interest environment had turned and the composition had changed from low- to high-interest debt. High inflation translating into higher nominal and real interest rates meant much higher debt service costs.

In the next twenty years, therefore, public debt increased exponentially, in two waves: first, in the high-interest rate low-growth phase of the early 1980s and then again in the recession of the early 1990s. In the upswing phases, average debt did not decline much if at all and deficits persisted. By 2000, average debt was near 70% and G7 debt near 80% of GDP. Canada, Japan, Italy, Belgium and Greece had debt ratios at or above 100% of GDP, numbers last seen during and after the Second World War.

A number of countries had reformed the role of the state and successfully brought down spending, deficits and debt (see Chapter 5). A few countries, therefore, only reported debt ratios around or below 40% of GDP at the turn of the millennium. These included the United Kingdom, Ireland and Finland in Europe and Australia, South Korea and New Zealand outside it. The Nordic countries had also started to accumulate significant assets in both sovereign wealth and pension funds.

After the turn of the millennium, there was initially little change in the debt ratio, despite the boom years until 2007, primarily due to expansionary fiscal policies in many countries. If countries had pursued neutral fiscal policies, the level of debt would have fallen much more (Hauptmeier, Sanchez-Fuentes and Schuknecht, 2011). This would have created larger fiscal buffers, especially in Italy, Portugal, Greece and Cyprus, who later experienced fiscal crises.

The next explosion of public debt followed during the global financial crisis of 2007. Average public debt in 2017 stood at 94% and at near 120% of GDP for the G7, almost back to the level of 1945. Belgium, Italy, Greece, Canada, Japan (236%!) and the United States were above 100%. France, Spain and the United Kingdom were in the near 90–100% range. Germany – much rebuked by international organisations for excessively restrictive policies – still reported debt above pre-crisis levels and above the legal debt ceiling of 60% of GDP in Europe. Very few countries showed debt below 60% of GDP.

With these figures, it seems astounding that there was no sense of urgency about public debt reduction in the advanced countries in the late 2010s. An obvious reason for this nonchalance was the development of short- and long-term interest rates after the 1980s and especially after the global financial crisis. In the early 1980s, interest rates were very high (Figure 3.3a). With declining inflation, nominal and real rates fell. In the course of the 1990s, inflation went down to the (by-then widely accepted) 'ideal' inflation level of 2%. Interest rates came down to similar levels, particularly after the euro and the European Central Bank (ECB) had instilled expectations of monetary stability. With the global financial crisis, interest rates came down further to near zero or even into negative territory.

With the Greek crisis of 2009, markets started to differentiate sovereign risks, and financing costs for a number of European governments increased significantly. This only reversed with the introduction of adjustment programmes in crisis countries and with the ECB's promise to do 'whatever it takes' to keep the Eurozone together. Real rates were negative

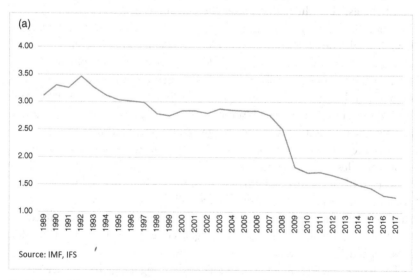

Figure 3.3a Advanced economies, annual real economic growth rate, 1989–2017.

(b)

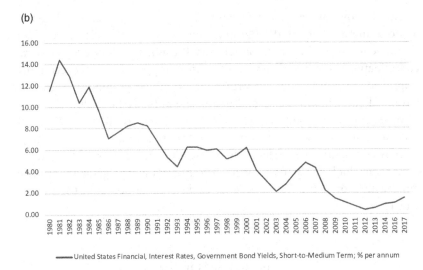

────── United States Financial, Interest Rates, Government Bond Yields, Short-to-Medium Term; % per annum

Source: IMF, IFS

Figure 3.3b Interest rate on US government bonds, 1980–2017.

at all horizons in much of Europe and Japan and only became positive again at the long horizon in the United States in 2017.

These interest rate developments would have been an unambiguous 'good' for public finances if it were not for three factors. First, growth has come down in the Western world in recent decades and even more so when looking at per capita growth. Average growth was above 3% per annum in the 1980s and below 2% in the second decade of the 2000s (Figure 3.3b). It may come down further for a number of reasons, including population ageing and low interest rates that undermine the efficient allocation of capital and the process of creative destruction espoused by Joseph Schumpeter (Borio et al., 2015; Gordon, 2016; White, 2017).

Second, interest rates may not stay this low. Real interest rates are likely to be lower today than a few decades ago because higher savers such as China have entered the world economy and high savings cohorts (people in their forties and fifties) are particularly strong. This is likely to change as people 'everywhere' age and as China changes its economic model. Inflation could also return, so that the price at which people are willing to lend money to governments may rise as well, especially those with high debt. Debt levels that are easy to finance at near zero rates today might then become much scarier.

Third, a low-interest rate environment takes away the sense of urgency to do something about deficits and debt, and there is also less of an incentive to undertake structural reforms. It is not a coincidence that fiscal consolidation in most advanced countries stopped when the economy improved in 2014–2015. Reforms also declined significantly in the advanced countries in the second half of the 2010s (OECD, 2019c).

Well-known economists such as Stiglitz (2018) or Blanchard (2019) even suggest that low interest rates permit more debt and more spending, thereby adding to the temptation to be fiscally profligate. Fiscal moderates, by contrast, look like 'party poopers' who prevent all the 'good' that can be done with more debt. We will come back to these points in Chapters 9 and 11.

3.4 Financing Needs in the Future

Future public expenditure and fiscal stability depend on both future trends and risks. Upcoming challenges relate especially to the growing insurance role of the state (Schuknecht, 2013): insurance against ageing-related risks and financial sector difficulties are likely to have a significant effect on future expenditure (see also Chapters 7–9).

Population ageing will be the greatest societal change of the coming decades. The good thing is that it is quite foreseeable, the bad thing is that its magnitude is huge and democracies are not very good at building fiscal buffers against it. A key indicator is the old-age dependency ratio, which measures the ratio of the population older than 65 (who tend not to work and need assistance) to those between 15 and 64 (who are to a significant extent likely to work). Future developments of this indicator are staggering (Table 3.4). In 2015, the old-age dependency ratio roughly ranged from below 20 in South Korea to above 40 in Japan. In other words, one elderly to five potential workers in South Korea and a little over two in Japan. The actual numbers are in fact less favourable because not everybody is working: in Germany, there were only about two workers per pensioner, even though the dependency ratio is one in three.

By 2050, we expect the dependency ratios to have risen much further. The United States will feature a ratio similar to that of Italy today, all others will fare worse. In South Korea, Italy and Japan, there will be two people above the age of 65 for every three below. Germany will not see much better figures, with little more than one worker for each pensioner if nothing changes.

Table 3.4 *Old-age dependency ratio*

(Ratio of 65+/15–64 olds per 100 population)		
	2015	2050
US	22.3	36.9
Germany	32.2	58.6
France	30.6	46.3
Italy	35.1	67.6
China	13.0	46.7
Japan	43.3	70.9
South Korea	18.0	65.8

Source: UN *World Population Prospects* (2015)

What does this mean for the development of public expenditure in general, and pensions, health and long-term care in particular? We will look at some key insights here before a more in-depth discussion in Chapter 7. The biggest increases in social expenditure are expected for countries where systems are still in the development phase. In South Korea or China, additional expenditure will easily amount to 10% of GDP if current retirement ages and benefit dynamics stay unchanged (Figure 3.4).

For most of the advanced economies, additional expenditure obligations will potentially be much smaller, but still significant. Projections for Japan, the United States, Italy and Germany point to additional spending of about 4% or 5% of GDP. France seems to be 'luckier', as projections only point to higher spending of 1% of GDP.

Additional expenditure of 3–4% of GDP at first sight does not seem too scary. But when this is put in perspective it is rather a lot, being more than total public investment. Total expenditure on education averages around 5% of GDP. If this additional spending comes on top of existing expend-iture, it will drive the average spending ratio in the advanced countries to near 50% of GDP, and much higher in some countries.

If such an increase had to be financed via taxes it would require major increases in social security contributions, consumption and/or income taxes. Four per cent of GDP represents about one third of average revenue in each of these categories, and we have argued earlier that a number of countries are already at the limit of taxation. In other countries, such a tax increase would have important adverse implications for incentives and growth and it would be politically very difficult, if not impossible, to implement.

Countries with small public sectors of around 30% of GDP would seem to be able to raise revenue more easily than countries with 'big'

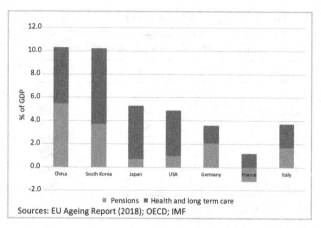

Figure 3.4 Projected increase in ageing-related spending, 2015–2050.

government sectors, but the magnitudes projected here would also be a huge challenge for these countries. Debt financing of such magnitude is also not an option, given the record debt ratios already prevailing in many advanced countries.

Moreover, this is only one set of projections. These are 'baseline' scenarios that tend to be optimistic; there are fiscally much less optimistic scenarios. To give just a flavour of the difficulties: The expenditure projections depend on reforms being maintained and not reversed – a major challenge given that the constituency of retirees will grow strongly. As Figure 3.4 shows, most expenditure increases will fall on health-related spending. In the past, both technical progress and higher incomes have driven expenditure dynamics well in excess of GDP growth and predicting these dynamics for the future is rather difficult.

Figure 3.4 also fails to show another major challenge: spending related to long-term care. This may well increase on average by another 1–2% of GDP, and we do not know whether the future old will need more or less care and where medical progress will alleviate the problem.

3.5 Financial Sector Liabilities

The financial sector has become a fiscal burden on various occasions in the past and it could well become so again in the future. During a financial crisis in particular, the stabilisation of the banking system often requires government support, while the recessionary effects of a crisis reduce tax revenues and raise spending obligations.

Table 3.5 *Financial crisis support before 2007*

Country	Crisis dates	Total gross fiscal cost (% of GDP)	Total net fiscal cost (% of GDP)	Recovery ratio (% of gross fiscal cost)
Average all	1970–2007	14.8	13.0	17.8
EU countries	1970–2007	6.6	5.5	23.9
Finland	1991–1994	12.8	11.1	13.4
Norway	1991–1993	2.7	0.6	77.8
Sweden	1991–1994	3.6	0.2	94.4
Argentina	2001–2005	9.6	9.6	0.0
Brazil	1994–1996	13.2	10.2	22.7
Chile	1981–1987	42.9	16.8	60.8
Indonesia	1997–2002	56.8	52.3	7.9
Japan	1997–2002	14.0	13.9	0.6
South Korea	1997–2002	31.2	23.2	25.6
Mexico	1994–1997	19.3	18.0	6.7
Malaysia	1997–2002	16.4	5.1	68.9
Russia	1998–2000	6.0	6.0	0.0
Thailand	1997–2002	43.8	34.8	20.5
Turkey	2000–2003	32.0	30.7	4.1
Uruguay	2002–2005	20.0	10.8	45.8

Sources: Laeven and Valencia (2008) and EU Commission

The fiscal costs of a financial crisis have often been huge in the past. Table 3.5 shows that fiscal cost can be in the double-digit range of GDP, even when taking into account the recovery of some losses after the crisis is over: Finland and Brazil, for example, showed net fiscal costs of around 10% of GDP. The Asian financial crisis on 1997–1999 featured the highest costs of recent decades, reaching about 50% of GDP in Indonesia and about 30% in Turkey and Thailand. However, such figures should perhaps be taken with a grain of salt, as measurement is notoriously difficult.

The global financial crisis that started in 2007/2008 was also very costly, but it was perhaps even more unexpected that it affected industrial countries so strongly when earlier crises had mostly hit emerging or developing economies. Fiscal costs from banking problems exceeded 10% of GDP in a number of countries, including Greece, Cyprus, Ireland, Slovenia and Germany. Gross losses exceeded US$ 2 trillion (IMF, *Fiscal Monitor*, April 2015).

The US (and German) banks made most of their losses in the US subprime crisis. Ireland and Southern European countries experienced mainly home-grown crises related to weak banks, expansionary public finances, loose monetary policies and weak financial regulation. Another important feature was the high levels of private sector debt in many countries coupled with high asset prices and in particular real estate prices and securitisation often hiding the very low quality of such debt. For fear of instability and unpopularity, governments allowed the migration of private debt and losses to the public balance sheets. Risks and liabilities may well arise in the future through banks and other channels, despite public commitments to the contrary. We will look into this challenge in more depth in Chapters 8 and 9.

3.6 Conclusion

Governments managed to finance the growing role of government quite well in peacetime until the 1960s, and rising revenue financed rising expenditure. The main exception was the two World Wars, when many countries accumulated huge debt. This debt was, however, brought down again in the periods following 1918 and 1945.

This pattern changed with the 'Keynesian revolution'. Government revenue continued to rise but not quite as fast as expenditure. By the 1970s, deficits had become endemic and public debt ratios ratcheted up in most countries with every recession, and sometimes even during upswings.

The 1980s and 1990s were turbulent, with a further increase in revenue and debt in most countries. At the same time, expenditure restraint and reform allowed many countries to halt the upward dynamic of spending ratios and contain unsustainable deficits and debt. With the boom of the late 1990s and early 2000s, however, Keynesian thinking came back. Buoyant expenditure dynamics and the costs of the banking crisis resulted in another major increase in both deficits and debt.

Moreover, we know that population ageing will bring about major increases in public expenditure that require financing in the coming decades, and fiscal costs from any renewed financial crisis cannot be excluded. These challenges will be subject to much deeper discussion in Part III. Chapters 4–6 in Part II will focus on government performance and efficiency, or 'value for money'.

PART II

VALUE FOR MONEY

4

Government Performance and Efficiency

Little else is requisite to carry a state to the highest degree of opulence from the lowest barbarism but peace, easy taxes, and a tolerable administration of justice.
Adam Smith

When there is no middle class, and the poor greatly exceed in number, troubles arise, and the state soon comes to an end.
Aristotle

Highlights

Governments should provide value for money from public spending. They do so when they perform well on core tasks and ensure efficiency by spending wisely. Core tasks on which we measure performance and efficiency include the quality of public administration, education, health and infrastructure, as well as economic stability, prosperity and income distribution.

The picture on performance and efficiency is very mixed across countries. The three 'small' governments of Switzerland, Australia and Ireland perform best overall, with a 50% higher score than the worst performers. Efficiency differences are even greater (Figure 4.1).

'Small' governments as a group tend do best as regards public administration, the economy and overall. 'Medium'-sized governments perform least well on the whole but show a wide divergence: some of them are very efficient in providing education, health and infrastructure. 'Big' government countries show more equal income distribution but at the 'price' of higher taxes and unemployment. Needless to say, this analysis is illustrative and perhaps needs to be taken with a grain of salt.

4.1 Value for Money from Public Spending

In most of the advanced countries, more than 30% or 40% of GDP goes through the hands of government and, in some countries, this share is

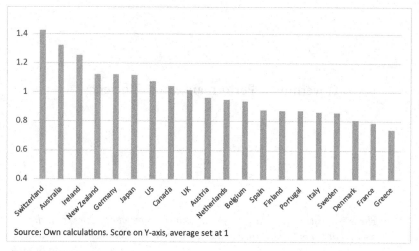

Figure 4.1 Government efficiency scores, 2017.

more than 50% of GDP. But are governments performing well when they spend so much money? Do 'big' governments perform better than 'small' ones? Is public spending efficient so that citizens get value for money?

These are difficult questions to answer. Some countries do not seem to be providing core public goods and services very well. For some others, the question is whether 'good performance' requires so much spending. What is clear, however, is that the minimal states of the late nineteenth century, with limited public services and virtually no social security, are not a desirable alternative. It certainly feels much better living today in a rich country with good schools, roads, hospitals and social programmes.

Country indicators on the attainment of the core tasks of government measure performance. Comparing performance to the relevant public spending provides a measure of 'efficiency'. The analysis focusses on the same advanced countries as in Part I. Measuring government performance and efficiency, however, is complicated and a number of caveats as regards our analysis are necessary:

- In some countries, the private sector plays a significant role in providing certain public goods and services. However, it is impossible to disentangle the contribution of private and public spending to infrastructure quality or education outcomes, for example.
- The quality of public goods and services often reflects the cumulative impact of public spending over a long period. Road networks emerged over decades and indicators of infrastructure quality reflect

this cumulative impact. High or low public spending in one particular year thus says little about efficiency.

- Technical progress makes a big difference. Life expectancy today is much higher than fifty years ago even where there is little public health because many lifesaving drugs have now become very cheap. Measures of 'good' public sector performance may thus change over time.

- Public expenditure in one area can affect outcomes in another. Life expectancy has increased because water and sanitation has improved. Investment in infrastructure thus affects performance in health. High-quality education for all enhances opportunities and equalises income distribution.

- Moreover, other variables than public expenditure can influence government performance and efficiency. These can include the age structure of a population, labour regulations or the positive growth effects of favourable terms of trade. Tax and revenue systems can influence expenditure policies and efficiency (Afonso, Tovar Jalles and Venancio, 2019).

- The federal dimension may also affect performance and efficiency, although the direction of impact is not self-evident. Decentralised spending may better reflect citizens' preferences and better local accountability. Centralised decision-making may take advantage of economies of scale and centralised procurement (Alesina, Angeloni and Schuknecht, 2005).

Two Approaches to Government Performance

As discussed in the Introduction, there are two approaches to what governments should do. The classical economic approach stresses functioning markets and equal opportunity in these markets. Governments perform well when they set sound rules of the game and implement them via a strong state administration. Public goods and services, such as schools, health and infrastructure allow all citizens to participate irrespective of origin or wealth. We call these respective indicators 'opportunity indicators'.

The second approach, following Keynes and Musgrave, focusses on certain outcomes of government activity. The state's role is to strengthen the allocation of resources in the economy to increase aggregate prosperity. Government spending should prevent undue fluctuations of economic activity, and the related hardship from unemployment and poverty. Government should also redistribute income via public spending. More equal income distribution would not only be socially desirable but also economically beneficial as the rich tend to save too much and the poor invest too little (to simplify a little). The relevant 'Musgravian indicators', therefore, refer to economic outcomes (Musgrave, 1959).

Of course, the roles of creating a level playing field to support markets and of 'optimising' economic outcomes are complementary and interdependent. A good education system is the main determinant of economic growth across countries and over time (Woessmann, 2016). A more effective government administration supports the functioning of markets and benefits in particular the poor (Fournier and Johansson, 2016). When analysing 'value for money' from government spending, it makes sense to look at both approaches. Governments should do well in both roles, and at reasonably low expense.

4.2 Performance Measurement and Indicators

Measurement

The two concepts of opportunity and economic outcome are a good starting point for the assessment of value for money from an international perspective, and both sets of indicators are relevant for government accountability to their citizens. We look at the performance of the advanced country governments at two points in time, the turn of the millennium and the most recent years.

We identify measures of performance and expenditure across countries for administration, education, health and infrastructure (opportunity) and income distribution, economic stability and economic performance (economic outcomes). These seven sub-indicators aggregate to an overall performance and efficiency measure. Indicators of performance and efficiency follow the methodology of Tanzi and Schuknecht (1997a, 1997b) and Afonso, Schuknecht and Tanzi (2005), and Figure 4.2 maps the relevant tasks and indicators.

We do not include fiscal sustainability and public debt as a separate indicator, even though it seems particularly relevant for trust in government (see the Introduction). However, changing the methodology compared to earlier studies seems too far-reaching. Moreover, we do not include incidators of environmental spending and performance as this is mostly influenced by regulation and taxes/charges (see also Chapter 2).

Four country groups help structure the discussion and derive patterns across groups. First, there is the overall, unweighted average across

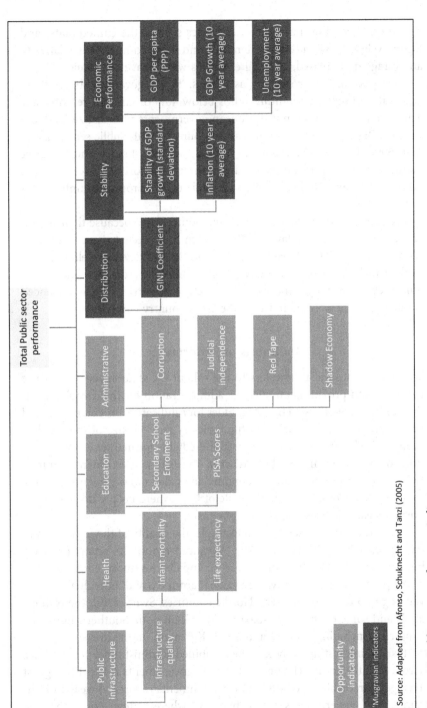

Total Public sector performance

Public Infrastructure	Health	Education	Administrative	Distribution	Stability	Economic Performance		

Infrastructure quality

Infant mortality

Life expectancy

Secondary School Enrolment

PISA Scores

Corruption

Judicial independence

Red Tape

Shadow Economy

GINI Coefficient

Stability of GDP growth (standard deviation)

Inflation (10 year average)

GDP per capita (PPP)

GDP Growth (10 year average)

Unemployment (10 year average)

Opportunity indicators

'Musgravian' indicators

Source: Adapted from Afonso, Schuknecht and Tanzi (2005)

Figure 4.2 Public sector performance indicator.

countries. Given the sheer size of countries such as the United States and Japan, weighting would skew the results and make comparisons relative to an average quite biased, as small countries would have little weight.

The three further groups are as follows. 'Small' governments are those that feature public expenditure ratios below 40% of GDP in recent years. This group includes six non-European governments plus Switzerland and Ireland. 'Big' governments comprise the countries with public sectors larger than 50% of GDP. These include Austria, Belgium, France and the three Nordics. The other 'medium'-sized governments report public expenditure between 40% and 50% of GDP and include eight European countries plus Canada.

The grouping excludes Singapore and South Korea because their figures are skewed by factors related to their much more recent rise to advanced economy status. They have had much less time to develop welfare states, so their inclusion would strongly bias the comparison on some indicators. Still, they are amongst the main 'competitor countries' of the advanced countries, so they are included in the cross-country comparison.

Indicators of Performance

The first set of indicators refers to the role of the state in setting rules of the game and providing an effective administration for their implementation, or 'the rule of law'. The set includes four indicators for corruption, red tape/bureaucracy, the quality of the judiciary and the size of the 'shadow economy'. The first three are essential ingredients for market economies to function well: the higher the indicator, the better government administrations perform. The 'shadow economy' indicator shows how much of the economy takes place outside the 'rule of law', where people do not follow normal legal practices and do not pay taxes.

Two indicators will serve as an example: the quality of the judiciary and corruption (Figures 4.3a and 4.3b). Advanced economies report relatively high values for the two indicators (compared to most emerging and developing countries): the average value is around 8 and individual country values go up to almost 10. The Nordic countries, Switzerland, the Netherlands and some of the Anglo-Saxons do well on both. Southern European countries (including France) and South Korea are on the low side.

It is also interesting to look at the combined administrative performance across country groups (Figure 4.4). 'Small' governments report the highest average score, while 'medium'-sized governments report the weakest indicators. 'Big' governments are in between, whereas they scored the best

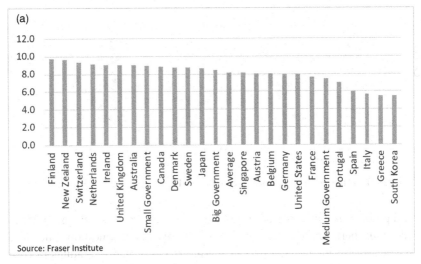

Figure 4.3a Quality of judiciary index, 2017.

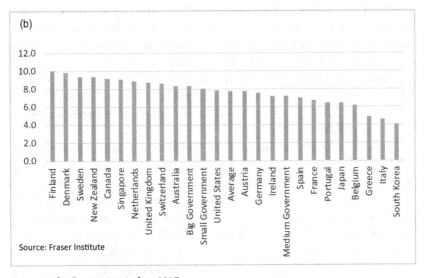

Figure 4.3b Corruption index, 2017.

marks on average twenty years ago. Overall, the development of administrative performance has been mixed over the past two decades, with corruption going up and red tape down.

The next indicator refers to performance in education. The indicator of choice is the OECD PISA score, which combines the scores for maths, reading

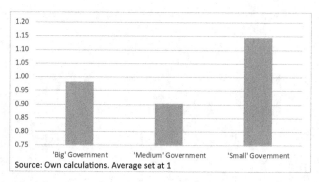

Figure 4.4 Administrative performance score, 2017.

and problem-solving skills of ca. 15-year-olds. This provides a snapshot of the education performance at the end of lower secondary education. But PISA scores are also highly indicative of the future performance of adults in core skills and in the ability to adapt to new learning challenges.

PISA scores are very good predictors of the future growth performance of a country (Hanushek and Woessmann, 2015). Years of schooling, another possible indicator, by contrast, has little impact. But education does much more than increase the cognitive skills that enhance productivity and growth. Education is the great equaliser of opportunity across rich and poor, and is at the basis of research and innovation. Schleicher (2018), Hanushek, Piopiunik and Wiederhold (2019) and Schleicher and Schuknecht (2019) discuss some of the factors that underpin successful education policies.

Education performance as measured by PISA in the advanced economies is high and averages over 500 points (Figure 4.5). Japan, South Korea, Singapore, Finland and Canada are the best performers. A few other Asian economies from Vietnam to Hong Kong that are not part of this study do similarly well or even better. Greece and Italy are the only countries with scores below 490. Portugal made the biggest jump in the past twenty years, from 456 to 497. Austria and New Zealand fell significantly, by over 20 points. The overall average has decreased somewhat during the past twenty years (see also OECD, 2018a). If the past is a guide to the future, Asian economic prosperity will continue to catch up rapidly. At some point, Asian countries may surpass the 'West' due to very strong education systems.

The measurement of public sector performance in health is particularly problematic, for two reasons. First, there are significant differences concerning the role of the private sector across countries. In the United States, private health spending amounts to almost half of total health expenditure;

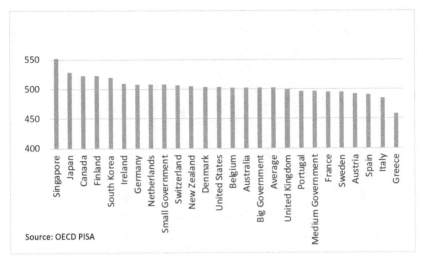

Figure 4.5 Education/PISA index, 2017.

in some countries, it is close to zero. Second, health has many dimensions that are often hard to quantify. We, therefore, stick to two indicators that, ultimately, matter most: the chances of surviving the infant phase and overall life expectancy.

However, even infant mortality may not be fully comparable across countries. In some countries, still-births are accounted for differently than in others. In the United States, doctors appear to attempt to save infants with a lower probability of survival than in other countries, and this biases upward the figure for infant mortality. International comparisons thus always have to be treated with caution.

Infant mortality rates are extremely low by historical and international standards in the advanced countries. Only 3.3 children of every 1,000 die in their infancy, a decline of 30% compared to almost 5 around the turn of the millennium. The comparable figure in some developing countries is over 100. This figure is still low from a historic perspective. Some estimates suggest a child death rate of about 500 in Europe only two centuries ago, as about half of all children died before reaching adulthood.

This decline is a truly remarkable achievement. Still there are significant differences between the 1.9 reported by Japan and Finland and the 4.7 in the United States. On average, 'big' governments are the best performers on this indicator.

Life expectancy differs relatively little across countries. The average has increased from 78.3 to 81.6 years since 2000. In 2017, the United States

Value for Money

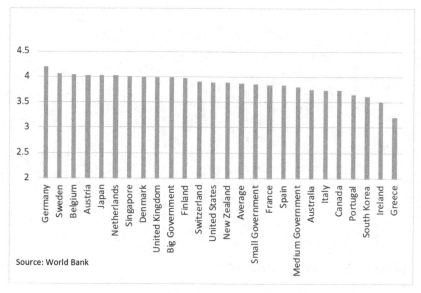

Source: World Bank

Figure 4.6 Infrastructure quality index, 2017.

ranked lowest, with a figure of 78.6 years; the 83.9 years in Japan are testimony to their renowned longevity. A number of countries comes close to Japan's record: France, Italy, Sweden, Australia, Canada, Switzerland and Singapore all feature above 82 years.

The measurement of infrastructure quality is difficult. The legacy of past policies casts a long shadow into the future (Figure 4.6). The most well-known indicator is perhaps that of the World Bank and includes logistics and transport-related elements in particular. It has been available for a few decades and Germany comes out at the top, followed by a group of rather similarly ranked countries. Greece and Ireland report the worst scores. The overall average has increased slightly in the past decade.

The World Bank indicator, however, is of limited coverage. Moreover, a top-scoring Germany seems to run counter to the claim of some observers that the country's infrastructure is crumbling. That these claims are exaggerated (to say the least) is confirmed when looking at alternative indicators: the Hertie Composite index on Infrastructure Quality and Governance shows similar results. The two indicators are very highly correlated, with a correlation coefficient of 0.81. The countries at the top (Germany, France, Switzerland, the Netherlands) and bottom (Greece, Italy) of the Hertie indicator feature similar rankings to those of the World Bank score. The Hertie indicator is more comprehensive, but it is only available for one year (2016) and there are a number of important countries missing. Therefore, we use it only for checking the robustness of our results.

Turning to the Musgravian 'economic outcome' indicators, and income distribution in particular, this is affected by both government expenditure and tax policies (Tanzi, 1998). There are three main types of indicators measuring income distribution: the income share of the poorest quintile or the poorest two quintiles, the poverty ratio in absolute or relative terms and the Gini coefficient.

The Gini coefficient is perhaps the most well-known indicator of income distribution, though not the most easily understood. It describes the income distribution across society, with a value of zero reflecting total equality. It is readily available and quite comparable across countries and, therefore, seemed a good choice. A value of 100 would signal that all income is in the hands of one person. A smaller value thus signals more equality.

The most common and comparable indicator is the Gini coefficient for net or disposable income, which already reflects the impact of government redistribution via taxes and spending. The net indicator is, therefore, always lower than the Gini for gross (or market) income and the difference can be quite significant (see Johansson, 2016). The average Gini coefficient is around 31 for all countries, ranging from 26 to 39 (Figure 4.7).

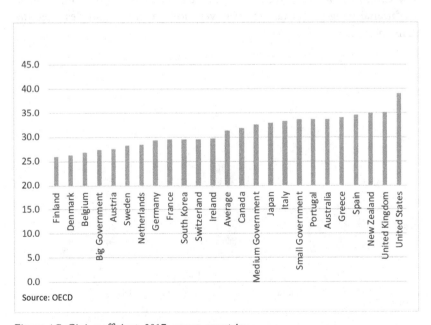

Source: OECD

Figure 4.7 Gini coefficient, 2017, across countries.

Two developments are worth noting when looking across countries and country groups. First, 'big' governments show more equal income distribution (lower Ginis) than 'small' governments. But the United States exerts a strong influence on the latter group's figure. South Korea, Switzerland and Ireland are 'small' government countries with a below-average Gini, which means above-average equality of income distribution. Ireland and France have a similar Gini indicator, even though France reports twice the size of government.

Second, the average Gini index has hardly changed compared to ten years ago, which is the longest period with comparable OECD data for all countries (Figure 4.8). Only four countries report a change in the Gini by more than 2 points: the Netherlands and the United Kingdom to the more equal side and Sweden and Spain to the more unequal side. The most 'equal' country (Denmark) and the least 'equal' one (the United States) both report more inequality today. However, the claim of growing income divergence in the West seems to have lost relevance for the past decade.

Turning to economic stability, it is advisable to look at ten-year periods for growth and inflation. There have been important changes since the first studies on government performance emerged fifteen years ago. Average real economic growth has declined in recent decades and the average for a few countries was negative for the decade 2008–2017. Inflation, another traditional gauge of instability, was very low in most countries over the same period.

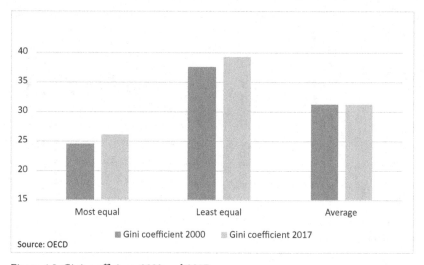

Figure 4.8 Gini coefficient, 2000 and 2017.

We have therefore chosen the standard deviation of growth for the past decade and the 1990s as an indicator for output stability, capping the lower volatility at 1. Calculations also exclude the exceptional growth of 26% for Ireland in 2015, which was due to special factors. We took average inflation as the price stability indicator.

The stability of economic growth decreased somewhat compared to the 1990s because the figures for the past decade reflect the impact of the global financial crisis. Unsurprisingly the former crisis countries, Greece, Ireland, Portugal and Spain, experienced the greatest volatility in the 2010s. Output volatility was somewhat lower in the countries with 'small' governments than in the other two ('big' and 'medium' government) groups. Inflation was low everywhere, so there was not much instability to report. Japan and Ireland featured positive average inflation but not much above zero. Australia reported the highest average (at 2.4%) for the decade.

Finally, three variables reflect economic performance: average real growth, average unemployment and per capita income. The indicators reflect the average for the 1990s and for 2008–2017. Average growth was significantly higher in the 1990s at 2.7%, compared to 1.0% in the later decade. Unemployment rates were higher than in the 1990s, even though a few countries including Germany improved their labour market performance significantly (Figure 4.9).

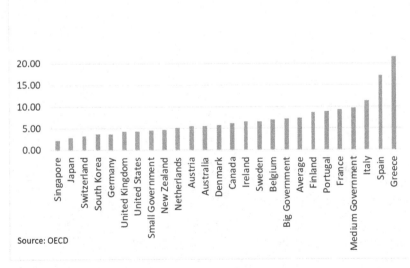

Source: OECD

Figure 4.9 Unemployment rate average, 2008–2017.

The former crisis countries Italy, Greece, Portugal and Spain, reported negative average growth and unemployment much above average (though rates had come down rapidly as of 2014). Only Australia, New Zealand and Ireland showed average growth rates above 2% up to 2017. This reflects the strong growth rebound in Ireland after the crisis and the greater dependency on raw materials that cushioned the impact of the crisis in New Zealand and Australia.

Growth declined almost everywhere in the 2008–2017 period compared to the 1990s. However, 'small' government countries clearly fared better than 'medium'-sized and 'large' government economies in both periods (Figure 4.10). This also implies that per capita GDP diverged between these groups by about 10% over twenty years, or 0.5% per year. This is not negligible.

If we set per capita GDP in 'small' government countries as 100, relative incomes declined from 90% to below 80% in 'medium'-sized government countries. Countries with 'big' governments reported a decline in relative income from near 100 to 90% (Figure 4.11). The richest countries in 2017 included Ireland, Switzerland, the United States and Singapore.

Of course, one could look at many more performance indicators. However, our selected ones seem to be fairly intuitive, comprehensive (relative to core tasks), robust and comparable across countries and over time. The aim is not an exhaustive discussion but a good intuition of where governments stand.

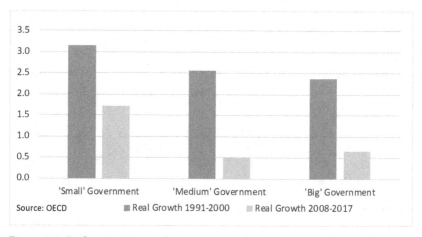

Figure 4.10 Real economic growth, average annual % change.

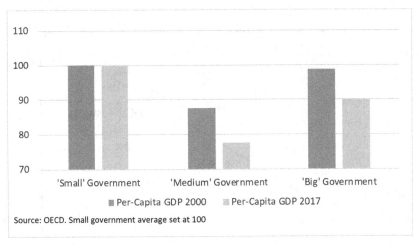

Source: OECD. Small government average set at 100

Figure 4.11 Development of per capita GDP.

4.3 Aggregate Performance and Performance over Time: A Synthesis

How did advanced economies perform overall in 2017, and how did this change over time? To facilitate comparison and aggregation across indicators, we set the average for each indicator at 1. The value of each country is then compared with the average: we call this 'normalisation'. For example, if the average growth rate is 2% and a country reports 2.5%, its value is set at 2.5/2 = 1.25. When a bigger value means a worse outcome, the value is inversed. If the average unemployment rate is 5% and a country features 7.5%, its value is set at 1/(7.5/5) = 0.67.

The results of the normalisation process for administrative performance are shown in Figure 4.12. Countries above the 45-degree line improved their performance after the start of the millennium, countries below it showed less favourable results compared to two decades earlier. Japan, Germany and Portugal reported significant increases in their performance score. The opposite holds for Austria, Finland, Denmark and Sweden. Switzerland remained the best performer, and Greece replaced Italy at the bottom of the scale.

Aggregation of the indicators follows the mapping presented earlier in Figure 4.2. Each of the computed administrative indicators counts one fourth towards administration performance. The normalised PISA score is the education performance indicator. The normalised health indicators contribute 50% each to health performance, and so on. All indicators are aggregated

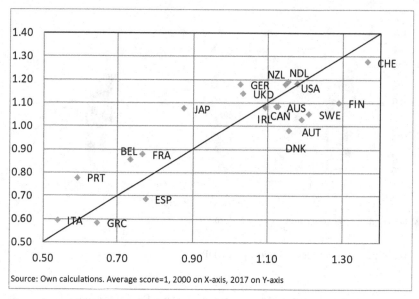

Figure 4.12 Administrative performance, 2000 and 2017.

Table 4.1 *Government performance by country group, 2017*

Performance	'Big' government	'Medium' government	'Small' government
Administration	0.98	0.90	1.15
Education	1.00	0.99	1.01
Health	1.06	0.97	0.97
Infrastructure	1.03	0.98	1.00
Distribution	1.13	0.95	0.93
Stability	0.98	0.92	1.10
Economy	0.85	0.75	1.43
Total government	1.01	0.92	1.08

Source: Own calculations. Average score set at 1

to an overall performance indicator with the weight of 1/7th each. The results do not change much with different weights, unless extreme values are chosen.

Table 4.1 reports the aggregated performance results by government size. The group of 'big' governments performed about average for the overall aggregate score 'total government'. This is reflected in a score of 1.01. 'Big' governments performed better than average on income distribution and health and much worse on the economy. The Nordics tended to be the better-performing countries in this group. 'Medium'-sized governments

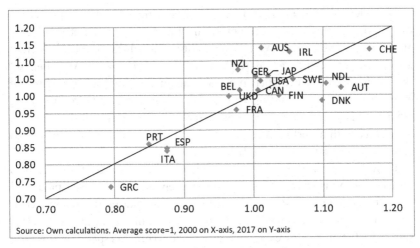

Figure 4.13 Aggregate government performance, 2000 and 2017.

showed below-average performance across the board but are a very diverse group. 'Small' governments had the highest aggregate score and featured the strongest public administration and economic stability and growth.

Country features and trends on government performance are also quite interesting (Figure 4.13). Switzerland, Ireland and Australia almost had the same top score in 2017. This was 10–15% above the average of '1' and 50% better than that of the worst performers (Table 4.1). There was a strong upper mid-field near to well above average, including Austria, Germany, the Netherlands, Sweden, New Zealand and a few others. While the aggregate performance of Australia and New Zealand score had improved, Denmark and Austria show a worsening between 2000 and 2017. The group of weaker performers included the four Southern European countries, despite much reform.

4.4 Efficiency Indicators and Measurement

The discussion on efficiency can proceed much faster than that of performance. Chapters 1 and 2 of this book have already discussed in depth the development of expenditure categories, and these form the basis for our efficiency assessment. We relate our government performance data to a set of government expenditure measures. As already mentioned, however, the findings are more illustrative than 'definite', given all the factors that we do not take into account.

We calculate efficiency measures by following the same approach as for performance. Expenditure per country and category is set relative to an average value of 1. If average expenditure on education is 5% of GDP and a country spends 4% it receives a value of 4/5 = 0.8. We then set the normalised performance measures against normalised measures of expenditure. Lower spending with equal performance thus implies more efficiency. Higher performance with equal spending is also more efficient. A country with a performance score of 1 and an expenditure score of 0.8 receives an efficiency score of 1/0.8 = 1.25.

Turning to indicators, we have to identify the relevant expenditure to measure administrative efficiency. Adequately staffed and well-paid civil servants and courts contribute to strong administrations at moderate cost. Over-staffed bureaucracies are likely to cost a lot of money and are a clear sign of inefficiency. However, what exactly governments spend on this core task of government we do not know, but government real expenditure, which pays for the civil service and related non-wage expenditure, seems a reasonable proxy.

Matching education performance and expenditure seems a bit easier. Education expenditure include teacher salaries, school buildings, etc. Similarly, public health spending includes running and capital expenses and seems a good proxy. There are also good reasons to match public infrastructure quality with public investment. However, for these three categories the caveat already mentioned holds, that the contribution of private spending to performance cannot be deduced. Therefore, the performance of government and the efficiency of public spending tends to be over-estimated to varying degrees across countries (see also Chapter 2).

Fiscal policies affect income distribution via tax and expenditure policies and regulation. Any spending proxy is, therefore, an imperfect way to measure government inputs towards distributional performance. High spending requires high (and often progressive) taxation, however, so that a spending measure may also capture some of the redistributive effect of the tax system. We choose social expenditure as an input measure because it captures most closely those categories that affect the income of the most vulnerable.

As regards the stabilisation and resource allocation role of government, total government expenditure seems the best proxy. Total spending reflects broadly this role of government via automatic stabilisers. Total spending is again also a crude proxy for the intervention of government in the total economy via all channels, including the incentive effect of higher or lower taxes.

As mentioned before, public sector performance is not determined by the expenditure of one year alone; it typically reflects the impact of spending over a long time. Therefore, the average expenditure ratio of the 1990s and the 2008–2017 decade can serve as measures of government expenditure inputs.

4.5 Government Efficiency

The discussion in Section 4.3 showed that 'small' governments tended to perform better on average and in the aggregate. Given the lower spending ratios of 'small' governments, we can expect this pattern to be accentuated when looking at efficiency. Nevertheless, the efficiency analysis reveals some interesting patterns, and some of the results are quite unexpected.

There is, however, no surprise as regards administrative efficiency. The picture from the performance discussion is reinforced, and 'small' governments came out ahead even more strongly for 2017 (Table 4.2). Germany, Switzerland, New Zealand and the United States were very efficient as they spent below average on an administration that performed above average.

Government efficiency and its change over time and across countries can be illustrated in a similar manner as performance. Figure 4.14 displays the results for administrative efficiency in 2000 versus 2017. Overall, the distribution of countries differs significantly, ranging from near 0.5 to over 2 (for Switzerland). This suggests that the Swiss administration was about four times as efficient as the Greek one. It also shows relative improvements or declines across countries. However, given all our caveats, these figures should be taken with a grain of salt.

The efficiency picture is particularly interesting for education, health and infrastructure (see Table 4.2). 'Medium'-sized governments showed

Table 4.2 *Government efficiency by country group, 2017*

Efficiency	'Big' government	'Medium' government	'Small' government
Administration	0.81	0.85	1.35
Education	0.88	1.07	1.03
Health	1.00	1.02	0.97
Infrastructure	1.01	1.03	0.98
Distribution	0.92	0.97	1.09
Stability	0.81	0.88	1.29
Economy	0.68	0.71	1.62
Total government	0.87	0.94	1.19

Source: Own calculations. Average score set at 1

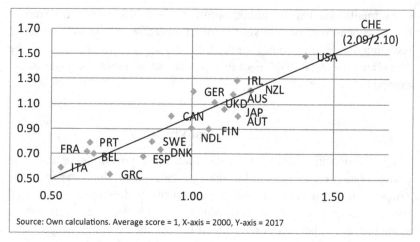

Figure 4.14 Administrative efficiency, 2000 and 2017.

the highest efficiency scores on average by a small margin, despite the fact that they did not show the strongest average performance. However, performance was reasonably good and spending low, so that this translated into high efficiency. Japan reported the highest scores on education and health. Finland, Spain, Australia and South Korea were also strong on health efficiency, Germany and Belgium on infrastructure.

As regards income distribution, 'big' governments showed lower Gini scores and, thus, a more equal distributional performance. However, social spending was much higher (28% of GDP versus less than 20% of GDP by 'small' governments). As a result, a 10% better performance turned into 15% less efficiency when taking expenditure inputs into account. This suggests a declining marginal product from more social spending as regards income distribution. Canada reports the highest score and the biggest improvement over time. Switzerland and Ireland are close behind. These three countries show average or high equality and low spending, while France and Italy show the opposite pattern.

As regards economic stability and prosperity, 'small' governments showed by far the greatest efficiency. Australia, Switzerland, New Zealand and the United States reported the highest indicators. Southern Europeans and Finland did poorly, with low growth and much turmoil over the past decade.

Finally, the picture for overall efficiency is worth looking at. The efficiency of 'small' governments was considerably higher than that of the other groups. The average for this group changed little compared to the 1990s

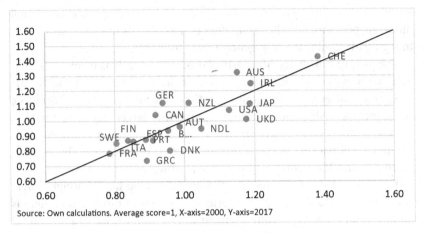

Source: Own calculations. Average score=1, X-axis=2000, Y-axis=2017

Figure 4.15 Aggregate government efficiency, 2000 and 2017.

while that for 'big' governments declined slightly. Switzerland, Ireland and Australia came out on top, with a score that was about twice as high as the worst performers (Figure 4.15). Germany, New Zealand and Japan also showed above-average scores. Australia, Canada, Germany and New Zealand improved their score the most compared to the 1990s, while the United Kingdom, Denmark and Greece fell back somewhat.

4.6 Conclusion

This chapter has discussed the performance and efficiency of the advanced country governments in fulfilling their core tasks. A government performs well when it provides a strong institutional framework with equal opportunity for its citizens via a well-functioning administration, a good education and health system and high infrastructure quality. A well-performing government also contributes to a reasonably equal income distribution, a stable economy and high growth and income.

Governments are efficient when they achieve their objectives at low cost; inefficient spending requires higher taxes and hurts both growth and opportunities. The 'value for money' question is, therefore, important.

Findings on government performance and efficiency suggest that 'small' governments tend to perform best and be most efficient overall: Switzerland, Australia and Ireland stand out. 'Medium'-sized governments do least well as a group, although they are very diverse and tend to be slightly more efficient than the other groups on health, education and infrastructure. 'Big' governments spend a lot of money on an overall moderate performance; the group does best as regards income distribution, though with significant divergence across countries.

The picture can change if a particular objective, such as income redistribution, receives a very large weight. This could be the case for the Nordic countries. However, an important question remains: is a (somewhat) more equal income distribution worth a significantly larger public sector with correspondingly higher taxes and more unemployment? Or is lower spending and a still reasonably equal income distribution the preferable option? Countries and their citizens may arrive at different conclusions.

The demand side indicators may give guidance on how to weigh different objectives and there are a few proxies. As regards distribution, there is no indication of a very strong preference for or shift towards more social spending and social objectives. Surveys show that over 60% agree to fair societies showing only small differences in standards of living. By contrast, almost 40% of the citizens of ten European countries see social benefits as putting too much strain on the economy. Both figures changed little between 2008 and 2016 (Table 4.3).

When trust in government is relevant for weighting the difference indicators, rule of law indicators receive the greatest and a growing emphasis (see Chapter 1). Putting all this together, the sectoral and

Table 4.3 *Survey results on social expenditure and equality*

	I agree with the statement that social benefits and services place too great a strain on the economy			I agree with the statement that for fair society, differences in standard of living should be small		
	2008	2016	Change	2008	2016	Change
Belgium	38%	37%	−1%	63%	67%	4%
Finland	20%	33%	13%	66%	68%	2%
France	53%	53%	0%	61%	61%	0%
Germany	38%	29%	−9%	56%	61%	5%
Ireland	58%	49%	−9%	62%	64%	3%
Netherlands	25%	23%	−2%	45%	52%	8%
Portugal	41%	57%	16%	84%	81%	−2%
Spain	37%	38%	1%	80%	76%	−4%
Sweden	26%	24%	−2%	56%	59%	3%
Switzerland	34%	35%	1%	65%	61%	−3%
UK	51%	53%	2%	50%	54%	4%
Average	38%	39%	1%	62%	64%	2%

Source: European Social Survey Round 4 and Round 8

aggregate indicators developed here may not be a bad choice, although results are illustrative and should perhaps be taken with a grain of salt.

Many countries experienced significant challenges with rising spending and its financing in recent decades. Many of them chose to reform public expenditure and did so with significant success. Chapter 5 looks at the experience of all these countries in more depth.

5

Reforming Public Expenditure

Wer zu spät kommt, den bestraft das Leben (Those who are late will be punished by life itself).

Mikhail Gorbachev

I sit on a man's back, choking him and making him carry me, and yet assure myself and others that I ... wish to lighten his load by all possible means – except by getting off his back.

Leo Tolstoy

Highlights

Public expenditure reforms over past decades have reinvigorated states and economies in many countries. A first group of countries already started to reform their public expenditure in the early to mid-1980s, as the negative side effects of high spending, taxes and deficits grew. A second group of reformers followed in the early to mid-1990s.

These countries reduced public expenditure significantly as part of comprehensive reform agendas (Figure 5.1). Reforms focussed on consumption-related expenditure and the welfare state, and improved economic structures and institutional frameworks. This strengthened public finances, growth and employment. Only a few countries did not reform, and their public expenditure continued to rise strongly.

In the 2010s, a third group of countries in Europe started to reform in the context of the global financial crisis. These countries also curtailed expenditure significantly and undertook institutional reform to the benefit of fiscal sustainability, growth and employment.

5.1 The Logic of Reforming Public Expenditure

Public expenditure should serve the attainment of government objectives in an effective and efficient manner. Governments require sound financing

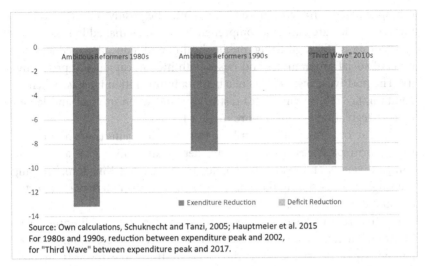

Figure 5.1 Expenditure reforms and expenditure and deficit reduction, % of GDP.

to permit long-term planning and avoid concerns about the sustainability of fiscal policies and public debt. When these conditions are not fulfilled, governments risk losing the confidence of their citizens and they should consider expenditure reforms.

There are two main ways for governments to undertake expenditure reforms. First, they can reduce their commitments and, thereby, expenditure. This could include, for example, the sale or closure of loss-making state-owned enterprises (SOEs), the termination of 'white elephants' in public investment and the abolition or shrinkage of ineffective social programmes. Governments can cease to provide low-priority services in public administration and save the relevant wage and non-wage costs.

Governments can also become more efficient in pursuing given tasks, for example, by lowering the costs of a programme and improving its targeting and effectiveness. Means-testing is a good way to improve the efficiency of social safety nets.

Second, governments can realise significant improvements in performance and efficiency from better public governance. Better accountability tends to make administrations more efficient; competitive procurement tends to lower the cost of both public services and infrastructure provision. Fiscal rules can harden government budget constraints and reduce the risks of liquidity and solvency concerns. We will return to these issues in Chapter 10.

Better policies and better governance are closely interrelated. Policy reform may become easier with improved governance if the latter, for example, makes problems more transparent. The positive effects of reform increase if they are part of a comprehensive package that addresses several shortcomings. Strengthening public health and education reduces the costs of social programmes and raises both human capital and productivity. The positive growth effects of a better administration increase when, in addition, tax reform eliminates distortions and when product and labour market regulation becomes more market-friendly.

Other reforms may also contribute to the positive effects of comprehensive reform packages. Exchange rate depreciation may give a boost to competitiveness and external demand. In the United Kingdom, entering the single market during the Thatcher reforms is likely to have supported economic performance.

Positive reform effects are greatest when they are so comprehensive that they change people's expectations about the future economic policy regime. Reforms that change the rules of the game towards market-friendliness of the economy, that enhance the attainment of core government objectives and that increase the efficiency of spending and taxes are most likely to have both major positive fiscal and growth effects. Tanzi and Schuknecht (1997b, 2000) provided case studies of such regime changes for the early 1980s, including in New Zealand, the United Kingdom and Chile, amongst others.

At the same time, there are formidable reasons to oppose reform and expect its failure. These include political deadlock due to a lack of reform-oriented government majorities and opposing special interests, given that such reform will have redistributional effects. The short-termism of policy-makers in the face of elections, and the lack of a comprehensive approach, are further reasons for the absence of reforms or their lack of success (Alesina, Favero and Giavazzi, 2019). Although reforms should ideally take place in good times, these political economy factors make reform more likely in crisis periods because there is more urgency (EEAG, 2019).

Despite these obstacles, the past forty years have been full of fiscal reform episodes. Some were more, some less, ambitious and many occurred during crisis or near crisis periods. Alesina et al. (2019) provide the most comprehensive empirical account. They find that expenditure reforms had positive confidence and expectation effects that mitigated adverse demand implications. This helped create a positive dynamic of less public (and more private) spending, less debt, often less taxes and more growth. Revenue-based adjustment, by contrast, had much higher output costs due to the absence of positive confidence and supply side effects.

The European crisis countries that reformed expenditure in the 2010s also experienced less output loss than the countries that focussed on tax increases. Moreover, many governments that conducted expenditure-based adjustment were re-elected, thus allaying fears that reform would be a political 'kiss of death'. And with reforms and success they regained the trust of their citizens (see Introduction).

Nevertheless, there was significant criticism of the European consolidation and reform process. Some observers argued against 'austerity' on the basis of presumed large negative growth effects (multipliers) (e.g. Blanchard and Leigh, 2014). Their claim, however, did not receive support in newer research by Górnicka et al. (2018) and the survey by Ramey (2019).

Alesina et al. (2019) synthesised and developed further the discussion of expenditure reform and non-Keynesian effects that had started already in the late 1980s. Giavazzi and Pagano (1990), Alesina (1995, 1996), Perotti (1998) and Alesina and Ardagna (2010, 2013) and the studies by Schuknecht and Tanzi (2005) and Hauptmeier et al. (2007) are some of the earlier literature.

We will review experiences with expenditure reform in the advanced countries since the early 1980s, using case studies instead of econometrics to analyse reforms and their impact; the results are very consistent with the findings of Alesina and others. The case studies focus on three reform episodes – the 1980s, the 1990s and the 2010s – and look at many of the performance and efficiency indicators examined in Chapter 4 before and after the reforms.

Methodology to Analyse Reform Experiences

Expenditure figures reveal when countries undertake expenditure reform, at which time, typically, expenditure ratios start coming off their peaks. We, therefore, take the year of the highest public expenditure ratio as our starting year. We then assess the impact of reforms by looking at expenditure developments since the peak. This approach is not perfect, as reforms may take time to take hold and there may be favourable economic developments rather than reform that drive down expenditure ratios. In practice, however, this approach seems reasonable because the starting point of reform is typically in periods of stress and not in the 'good times'.

In addition to expenditure variables, we look at indicators of financing and fiscal sustainability – notably revenue, deficits and debt. We also examine performance, including growth, employment, private spending and income distribution, after the start of reform. Finally, we check whether expenditure reforms are part of a broader, more comprehensive reform package.

The first set of case studies looks at reform experiences in the 1980s and 1990s, grouping countries by their ambition. This is based on the approach by Schuknecht and Tanzi (2005) and Hauptmeier et al. (2007). Countries that reduced primary expenditure by at least 5% of GDP were 'ambitious' reformers, countries with more modest expenditure reductions were 'timid' reformers and 'non-reformers' did not reduce primary expenditure at all.

The group of countries that started expenditure reform in the 1980s were the 'early' reformers and those that started in the 1990s were the 'late' reformers. This yields five groups: (1) ambitious and (2) timid early reformers, (3) ambitious and (4) timid late reformers and (5) non-reformers. Case studies look at the expenditure situation in the early 1980s, the peak of expenditure when the reform started, and the situation in the early 2000s. This provides a comprehensive picture of fiscal and economic developments for the twenty-year period.

Following the two waves in the 1980s and 1990s, a third wave of expenditure reform followed the global financial crisis in some European countries in the 2010s. As this group is small and only includes five countries, we do not differentiate further between them. But we will compare these countries' experiences with those of the three biggest euro area countries which showed little reform ambition in that period.

5.2 Expenditure Reform Experiences in the 1980s and 1990s

The 1980s and 1990s were a turbulent period for governments. The expansionary policies of the 1970s and the second oil crisis and, later, the recession of the early 1990s and the European Exchange Rate Mechanism (ERM) crisis went along with a significant increase in public expenditure in many advanced economies, coupled with large increases in fiscal deficits and public debt. Rising fiscal pressures and impending crises induced many countries to undertake reforms and reduce expenditure and deficits to sustainable levels. The fiscal figures for the 1980s and 1990s tell the story (Table 5.1).

Total Expenditure

Expenditure ratios had averaged 46.5% of GDP in 1982 (column 1). At their peak, when reforms started, these ratios had increased significantly further to average 51.6% of GDP (column 2): peaks were above 55% in

Table 5.1 *Total expenditure 1982, year of maximum spending ratio and 2002*

% of GDP

	1982 or nearest	Maximum public expenditure ratio	Year of maximum	Fiscal balance in that year	Public expenditure 2002 or nearest	Change maximum–2002
	(1)	(2)		(3)	(4)	(5)
Australia	38.1	40.2	1985	-6.9	35.6	-4.6
Austria	49.0	57.3	1995	-6.2	51.3	-5.9
Belgium	60.8	61.0	1983	-14.9	50.5	-10.5
Canada	46.5	52.8	1992	-9.2	41.4	-11.4
Denmark	57.8	60.7	1994	-3.6	55.8	-4.9
Finland	41.3	60.4	1993	-8.1	50.1	-10.3
France	49.8	55.5	1996	-3.4	53.6	-1.9
Germany	48.1	50.3	1996	-3.9	48.5	-1.8
Greece	35.4	51.0	1995	-5.1	46.8	-4.2
Ireland	49.8	49.8	1982	-14.5	33.5	-16.4
Italy	48.3	57.1	1993	-9.7	48.0	-9.1
Japan	32.9	40.0	1998	-10.2	39.8	-0.2
Luxembourg	49.5	49.5	1982		44.3	-5.2
Netherlands	58.6	58.7	1983	-5.2	47.5	-11.2
New Zealand	56.5	56.5	1985	-6.3	41.6	-14.9
Norway	45.6	54.1	1994	0.0	47.5	-6.6
Portugal	40.0	46.3	2001	-4.8	46.0	-0.3
Spain	35.9	47.6	1993	-7.3	39.9	-7.7
Sweden	64.3	68.0	1993	-10.9	58.3	-9.7

(*continued*)

Table 5.1 (*continued*)

% of GDP

	1982 or nearest	Maximum public expenditure ratio	Year of maximum	Fiscal balance in that year	Public expenditure 2002 or nearest	Change maximum–2002
Switzerland	32.8	35.7	1998	−1.2	34.3	−1.4
UK	44.8	45.4	1984	−3.2	41.1	−4.3
US	36.2	37.2	1992	−6.3	34.1	−3.1
Average	46.5	51.6		−6.7	45.0	−6.6
Euro area	47.2	53.7		−6.8	46.7	−7.0
Ambitious reformers, early	56.4	56.5		−4.6	43.3	−13.2
Ambitious reformers, late	47.1	56.7		−8.0	48.1	−8.6
Timid reformers, early	44.1	45.0		−5.7	40.3	−4.7
Timid reformers, late	45.5	49.4		−6.4	45.7	−3.7
Non-reformers	36.1	45.8		−7.5	44.2	−1.6

Source: Schuknecht and Tanzi (2005)

many countries. Moreover, fiscal deficits had grown strongly and averaged nearly 7% of GDP in the year of peak expenditure (column 4). High deficits thus required action to re-establish confidence in the sustainability of public finances, while high spending ratios suggested significant room for savings and efficiency gains.

By the year 2002, public expenditure ratios were on average slightly lower than in the early 1980s. The average decline across countries from earlier peaks was a strong 6.6% of GDP (columns 5 and 6). The 1980s and 1990s were, thus, a rather remarkable period, with a strong increase in public expenditure up to their peaks followed by a major decline.

Ten countries undertook ambitious reforms, with impressive expenditure adjustments. Ireland and New Zealand reported the strongest declines in total expenditure by around 15% of GDP or more. Canada, the Netherlands, Belgium and Finland featured reductions of over 10% of GDP, while Sweden, Spain, Norway and Austria showed falls of more than 5% of GDP in primary expenditure. Belgium, Ireland, Netherlands and New Zealand started their reforms early, while Austria, Canada, Finland, Norway, Spain and Sweden came later. This defines the two groups of ambitious reformers in Table 5.2.

Another ten countries also brought down public primary expenditure ratios but to a more limited, 'timid' extent (less than 5% of GDP primary expenditure reduction). Australia, Luxembourg and the United Kingdom started in the 1980s. Denmark, France, Germany, Italy, Switzerland and the United States form the group of (late) timid reformers of the 1990s.

Three countries – Greece, Japan and Portugal – did not reduce but rather increased public primary spending before the turn of the millennium: we call them 'non-reformers'.

Table 5.2 *Reform ambition and timing*

Categories	Countries
Ambitious and early reformers (early–mid-1980s)	Belgium, Ireland, Netherlands, New Zealand
Ambitious and late reformers (early–mid-1990s)	Austria, Canada, Finland, Norway, Spain, Sweden
'Timid' and early reformers	Australia, Luxembourg, UK
'Timid' and late reformers	Denmark, France, Germany, Italy, Switzerland, US
Non-reformers	Greece, Japan, Portugal

Expenditure Composition and Comprehensive Reforms

The composition of expenditure reform was quite remarkable and conducive to positive confidence effects. Table 5.3 provides the data across countries and expenditure categories. One third of the spending decline was due to falling interest payments. Interest rates came down in the 1980s and 1990s with falling inflation. Government reform helped this process through lower (re-) financing costs for falling deficits and more favourable debt dynamics.

Two thirds of the expenditure reduction fell on primary expenditure, especially transfers and subsidies, but also public consumption. This must have been politically difficult as it meant less social benefits and fewer civil servants.

The achievement of the ambitious reformers was impressive. Two thirds, or about 5% of GDP, of the primary expenditure cut affected transfers and subsidies. Canada, the Netherlands and New Zealand even reported a cut by 7–8% of GDP and the Nordic countries also introduced major social welfare reforms. Another quarter of the savings – 2% of GDP – affected public consumption, with Ireland and Canada being the most thrifty. Social welfare reforms are particularly important from a 'signalling' perspective, because they showed government resolve and improved incentives to both work and invest.

The decline in public investment and education was rather moderate for most of the countries. Still, the decline in public education amongst the ambitious reformers was 0.6% of GDP, or 10% of total education spending on average. Canada, Finland and the Netherlands stand out, with cuts of about 2% of GDP, but about half of the reformers left education spending little changed or increased it.

The increase in primary spending by non-reformers mostly went into public consumption. Public investment declined moderately and almost as much as in the reforming countries.

Finally, expenditure reform took place in the context of broader comprehensive reform packages in the ambitious reform countries. Hauptmeier et al. (2007) provide more details on eight of the ten countries, including Ireland, Sweden, Canada, Finland, Belgium, the Netherlands, Spain and the United Kingdom. Jonung, Tujula and Schuknecht (2009) discussed the experience of Finland and Sweden in the 1980s and 1990s. The European Economic Advisory Group (EEAG, 2019) looked at Denmark and Sweden and reached similar conclusions.

All eight reform countries except Belgium undertook complementary reforms of their fiscal institutions. This included the strengthening of the

Table 5.3 *Expenditure reform and its impact on expenditure composition*

% of GDP

	Change total expenditure	Thereof interest	Change primary spending	Transfers & subsidies[1]	Government consumption	Investment	Education
Australia	-4.6	-3.1	-1.5	1.5	-2.0	-1.0	-0.5
Austria	-5.9	-0.8	-5.1	-1.5	-1.8	-1.8	0.3
Belgium	-10.5	-3.0	-7.5	-4.0	-1.2	-2.3	-0.1
Canada	-11.4	1.5	-12.9	-7.0	-5.5	-0.5	-2.0
Denmark	-4.9	-3.7	-1.2	-1.5	0.4	0.0	0.6
Finland	-10.3	-2.3	-8.0	-5.4	-2.6	0.0	-1.8
France	-1.9	-0.8	-1.2	-0.7	-0.3	-0.2	-0.2
Germany	-1.8	-0.6	-1.2	0.1	-0.8	-0.5	-0.2
Greece	-4.2	-6.5	2.3	1.4	0.3	0.6	0.9
Ireland	-16.4	-6.8	-9.5	-3.1	-5.8	-0.7	-1.5
Italy	-9.1	-6.1	-3.0	-1.3	-1.0	-0.7	-0.4
Japan	-0.2	-0.4	0.2	-1.1	2.4	-1.1	0.1
Luxembourg	-5.2	-1.1	-4.0	-2.6	-1.5	0.0	
Netherlands	-11.2	-2.5	-8.7	-7.7	-1.0	0.0	-2.1
New Zealand	-14.9	-6.4	-8.5	-8.0	-0.6	0.1	1.9
Norway	-6.6	-1.2	-5.4	-5.0	-0.1	-0.4	-1.3
Portugal	-0.3	-0.2	-0.1	0.2	0.3	-0.6	0.0
Spain	-7.7	-2.2	-5.5	-3.7	-1.0	-0.8	0.0
Sweden	-9.7	-2.6	-7.0	-5.2	-1.3	-0.5	0.2

(continued)

113

Table 5.3 (*continued*)

% of GDP

	Change total expenditure	Thereof interest	Change primary spending	Transfers & subsidies[1]	Government consumption	Investment	Education
Switzerland	-1.4	-0.2	-1.2	-1.2	0.3	-0.3	0.0
UK	-4.3	-2.8	-1.4	1.2	-1.6	-1.1	-0.7
US	-3.1	-1.9	-1.1	0.2	-1.5	0.1	-0.4
Total average	-6.6	-2.4	-4.2	-2.5	-1.2	-0.5	-0.3
Ambitious reformers, early	-13.2	-4.7	-8.6	-5.7	-2.1	-0.7	-0.4
Ambitious reformers, late	-8.6	-1.3	-7.3	-4.6	-2.0	-0.7	-0.8
Timid reformers, early	-4.7	-2.4	-2.3	0.1	-1.7	-0.7	-0.6
Timid reformers, late	-3.7	-2.2	-1.5	-0.7	-0.5	-0.3	-0.1
Non-reformers	-1.6	-2.4	0.8	0.2	1.0	-0.4	0.3

Source: Schuknecht and Tanzi (2005)

1. Calculated as residual of primary spending minus investment and consumption.

Finance Minister's power to control budgets, an agreement on fiscal contracts to underpin reforms, multiannual fiscal frameworks for policy planning, expenditure rules and other institutional provisions that were still very innovative in the 1980s and 1990s. All countries except Canada featured other macroeconomic reforms. All countries improved labour market incentives and all except Belgium reformed taxes and privatised their SOEs.

5.3 Implications of Expenditure Reform

In order to evaluate the impact of reform, we look at a number of indicators from the 'value for money' analysis in Chapter 4. This includes indicators of fiscal, administrative and economic performance and income distribution. The results are favourable for reforming countries with very limited trade-offs regarding equality.

Deficit and Debt

The countries that undertook ambitious expenditure reforms experienced a remarkable improvement in their fiscal sustainability indicators (Table 5.4). The early ambitious reformers brought down their average deficit from 7% of GDP in the mid-1980s to 4% a few years later and to 1.5% of GDP by the mid-1990s. Ambitious late reformers saw their deficit go up until the early 1990s but this rapidly turned into a major surplus five years later. Expenditure reforms were so extensive that countries could afford major tax cuts as well. The decline in the revenue ratio was almost 6% of GDP for the early group and 2.5% for the ambitious late reformers.

The pattern for timid reformers was similar to that of the ambitious ones, though less pronounced. With smaller deficit cuts of about 3% of GDP, late reformers still had a deficit around the turn of the century and revenue ratios also fell much less. Non-reformers, by contrast, reported high deficits throughout the 1980s and 1990s.

These diverging experiences as regards deficits also affected public debt dynamics. In the mid-1980s, the early ambitious reformers had debts of 90% of GDP. This came down gradually in the 1990s to reach 60% around the turn of the millennium – a remarkable decline by 30% of GDP, and perhaps the strongest debt decline since the 1950s and 1960s.

The other reformers also succeeded in bringing down public debt. But since the late reformers only started in the mid-1990s, there was only a moderate decline in the few years until 2002. Hence, only the early reformers ended the 1990s with less public debt than in the mid-1980s. Chronic deficits by the

Table 5.4 *Deficit and debt performance*

% of GDP	First reform wave		Second reform wave		Change since reform
	1983–1987	1988–1992	1993–1997	1998–2002	
a. *Fiscal balances*					
Average, all countries	−3.8	−2.9	−3.3	0.2	
Euro area	−4.9	−3.9	−4.1	−0.5	
Ambitious reformers, early	−7.0	4.2	−1.5	0.6	7.6
Ambitious reformers, late	−1.5	−1.6	−3.6	2.5	6.1
Timid reformers, early	−1.1	−0.7	−1.9	1.8	2.9
Timid reformers, late	−4.5	−3.5	−3.7	−0.8	2.9
Non-reformers	−6.1	−4.9	−5.9	−4.8	
b. *Gross public debt, 5-year averages*					
Average, all countries	55.9	58.2	68.5	62.1	
Euro area	56.1	62.2	72.8	65.5	
Ambitious reformers, early	91.1	91.8	81.9	61.1	−30.0
Ambitious reformers, late	47.3	50.1	68.8	60.8	−8.0
Timid reformers, early	28.8	22.6	29.4	21.1	−7.6
Timid reformers, late	52.5	56.6	70.1	66.1	4.0
Non-reformers	60.4	68.3	86.0	99.4	

Source: Schuknecht and Tanzi (2005)

three non-reformers produced a strong increase in public debt from an average of 60% in the mid-1980s to nearly 100% by 2002.

Administration and Institutions

One might suspect that major expenditure reform would come at the expense of the quality of government institutions and services. This would be particularly detrimental if it affected the rule of law via a well-functioning administration. The evidence on this question is favourable for the ambitious reformers of the 1990s; for the earlier decade we do not have the relevant data. The change in the indicators of corruption, red tape and quality of judiciary for that period indicates that ambitious reformers experienced significant improvements in these indicators relative to the overall average (Table 5.5). Timid reformers, but much more so non-reformers, show a worsening of indicators relative to the average.

Economic and Distribution Performance

The reforming countries experienced a remarkable revival in their real economy. Trend growth increased strongly in the group of early reformers, both ambitious and timid (Figure 5.2). The rise in trend growth averaged 1.5%: a huge increase. For ambitious late reformers, Figure 5.2 also shows trend growth increasing by 0.5%, even though only little time had passed for the reforms to take hold.

Table 5.5 *Rule of law indicators, change relative to the average, 1990–2001*

	Corruption	Red Tape	Quality of judiciary
Ambitious late reformers	1.3	0.2	0.9
'Timid' late reformers	−0.4	−1.0	−0.2
Non-reformers	−0.5	−1.1	−1.9
Average all	0.2	−0.6	0.0

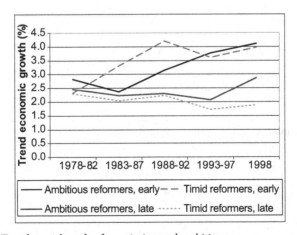

Figure 5.2 Trend growth and reform timing and ambition.

The countries that undertook ambitious expenditure reform saw their employment ratio rise markedly. The early group reported an increase in the employment ratio by 8 percentage points from 56% to 64.4% over the fifteen-year period. The increase for the early timid reformers was half as high. Late reformers also started to see the benefits of reform relatively quickly, with a 2–3% increase in the employment ratio over five years. Some people argue that employment is the most inclusive social policy, and from this perspective expenditure reform has also been a social success.

It is worthwhile spending a little additional time on income distribution. The picture for the Gini coefficient is mixed, but the shift towards more inequality is limited. The Gini coefficient in the 1980s and 1990s showed an increase in inequality from 28 to 29.4 for all the advanced countries (Table 5.6a). The increase was higher for the ambitious reformers, but income distribution remained more equal than the average. Inequality also increased somewhat for the other three groups of reforming countries. Non-reformers had the most unequal Gini amongst advanced economies and also reported an increase in inequality.

When discussing the income distribution effects of reform, one can also look at indicators of absolute poverty. From data on purchasing power

Table 5.6 *Income distribution and expenditure reform*

(a) Gini coefficient	Mid-1980s	2000	mid-1980s–2000
Average, all countries	28.0	29.4	1.3
Ambitious reformers, early	27.8	29.7	1.9
Ambitious reformers, late	23.6	26.3	2.7
Timid reformers, early	29.9	31.5	1.6
Timid reformers, late	28.3	29.2	0.9
Non-reformers	34.5	35.0	0.5

(b) Per capita GDP poorest quintile, 1995 prices, PPP US$		% change
Average, all countries	7,374	9,893	34.2
Ambitious reformers, early	7,273	10,400	43.0
Ambitious reformers, late	9,213	11,813	28.2
Timid reformers, early	6,936	9,036	30.3
Timid reformers, late	7,735	9,860	27.5
Non-reformers	4,299	5,819	35.4

Source: Schuknecht and Tanzi (2005)

parity (PPP)-based per capita GDP, the income share of the poorest quintile and economic growth rates, we can deduce the per capita GDP of the poorest quintile in an economy and its change over time (Table 5.6b).

Between the mid-1980s and 2000, the poorest quintile raised their income by 34%. However, there were significant differences across groups. For the early ambitious reformers, the per capita income of the poor had increased by 43%, 9 percentage points more than the average. The positive growth and employment effect on income of the poor seems to have dominated any worsening effect, for example from reductions in transfers.

In the other three reform groups, the income of the poorest quintile grew somewhat less than average. For the late reformers, this was perhaps also because the reforms did not have enough time to develop their full positive distributional effect via growing employment. The non-reforming countries showed average income dynamics despite their low starting income levels, so that the income gap to the average remained unchanged. The overall effects of reforms on inclusiveness were thus broadly positive. The benefit to the poor accrued through lower unemployment and rising incomes, while income distribution became somewhat less equal in many cases. However, income distribution in all reform groups remained much more equal than in the group of non-reformers.

5.4 The Third Reform 'Wave' of the 2010s in Europe

A third group of countries undertook expenditure reform in the 2010s following the global financial crisis. But again, the seeds of fiscal problems had been sown well before the crisis. Just as fifteen or twenty-five years earlier, many countries had experienced quite expansionary policies in the 'good times' of the late 1990s and 2000s. An explosion of expenditure, deficits and debt occurred with the financial crisis, before major reforms reversed fiscal and economic fortunes. Expenditure reform in the 2010s in fact had some quite common features with the experiences of the 1980s and 1990s.

Five European countries broadly followed this pattern: Greece, Ireland, Portugal, Spain and the United Kingdom. We call this the 'boom–bust' group. There were three other big, continental European countries following a different pattern of behaviour and experiences: France, Germany and Italy. Germany undertook early reforms and experienced a rapid rebound after the crisis. France got through the crisis relatively unscathed but there were no reforms until 2017. Italy undertook limited reforms in the context of a prolonged crisis. As in Section 5.3, we will discuss the individual country experiences, including fiscal, economic and social performance.

The Pre-reform Phase

The pre-crisis phase up to 2007 was one of strong growth and low infla-tion. Public revenue was strong as house prices boomed and filled govern-ment coffers through their effect on various tax bases in many countries (Eschenbach and Schuknecht, 2004). In this period, public expenditure grew strongly in a pro-cyclical manner in many industrialised countries (see also Figure 1.5). Most governments 'wasted' the opportunity of the 'good times' to put their fiscal house in order.

Seven of the eight countries followed this expansionary course. In these countries, expenditure ratios changed little or even increased between 1999 and the end of the boom in 2007 (Table 5.7). The strongest increase, despite high growth, is visible in the figures of the United Kingdom: +5.6% of GDP. This was a remarkable record for a 'boom' period. France, Greece, Portugal and Ireland also raised their expend-iture ratios. Strong expenditure growth stoked incomes and demand and, thereby, also the asset price boom, especially in Spain, Ireland and the United Kingdom.

Table 5.7 *Total expenditure, 1999–peak*

% of GDP	1999	Change 1999–2007	2007	Peak	Year	Change 2007–peak	deficit (Peak)
Boom–bust countries							
Greece[1]	46.2	0.9	47.1	55.4	2012	8.3	−6.5
Ireland	34.0	1.9	35.9	47.0	2009	11.1	−13.8
Portugal	42.6	1.9	44.5	51.8	2010	7.3	−11.2
Spain	40.9	−2.0	38.9	48.1	2012	9.2	−10.5
UK	35.3	5.6	40.9	48.9	2010	8.0	−9.5
Average (5)	39.8	1.7	41.4	50.2		8.8	−10.3
Big continental countries							
France	52.1	0.2	52.2	57.0	2013	4.8	−4.0
Germany	47.7	−4.9	42.8	47.6	2009	4.8	−3.2
Italy	47.4	−0.6	46.8	51.2	2009	4.4	−5.3
Average (3)	49.0	−1.8	47.3	51.9		4.6	−4.2

Source: Ameco, OECD
1. Greece excludes 2013, as data strongly affected by bank recapitalisation costs.

Two countries looked better at first sight, but this was due to special factors, not expenditure restraint. Spain showed a declining expenditure ratio, but that was due to growth very much above potential and a big windfall from falling interest payments on public debt. The primary expenditure ratio actually increased over this period. Similarly, Italy reported a small decrease in overall expenditure of –0.6% of GDP, which masks the fact that interest expenditure had decreased by 1.6% of GDP over the period so that primary, non-interest expenditure increased by 1% of GDP.

Finally, there was Germany. The 'post-unification blues' had forced the country to reform in the early 2000s: total expenditure was brought down by almost 5% of GDP between 1999 and 2007. Public expenditure hardly grew in nominal terms for almost a decade as social benefits were axed and nominal public wages and staffing declined.

Hence, when the global financial crisis started in 2007, the fiscal position of several countries was decidedly unsound. The fiscal balance of all countries except Spain and Germany had worsened compared to 1999. Deficits were near 3% of GDP in the United Kingdom, France and Portugal and well above that figure in Greece. Public debt had declined significantly in Spain and Ireland and modestly in Italy but much less than more neutral fiscal policies would have suggested (Hauptmeier et al., 2011). And when the crisis hit, debt was near or above 100% of GDP in Italy and Greece.

The Crisis Phase

Between 2007 and 2009, global financial markets and the economy deteriorated and then tanked after the Lehman Brothers default. Public revenue in many countries went down while expenditure dynamics continued on their pre-crisis path. Spending received a further boost from fiscal stimuli that most countries undertook. While stimuli in such an environment seemed reasonable, they were often of questionable effectiveness for stabilisation: poorly targeted, late and irreversible (Tanzi, 2018c). By the peak year, total expenditure ratios had increased on average by 8.8% of GDP in the most strongly hit boom–bust group, Greece, Ireland, Portugal, Spain and the United Kingdom. The equivalent figure for the other three countries was 4.6% of GDP (Table 5.7, column 6).

Fiscal balances fared even worse, deteriorating by about 10% of GDP on average in the five boom–bust countries. This is because public revenue declined and boom-related revenue from the real estate and financial sectors collapsed. Revenue, for example, fell by 3% of GDP in Ireland and by 6% of GDP in Spain. The big continentals, France, Germany and

Italy, showed a more 'normal' pattern of broadly stable revenue ratios in downturns, and these countries also did not experience a strong 'bust' in their housing sector (see also Chapter 8).

Expenditure ratios typically peaked in 2009 or somewhat thereafter, depending on the country-specific chronology of the crisis. In five countries, public expenditure ratios peaked well above 50% of GDP. France and Greece topped the league at above 55% of GDP; only Germany, Spain and the United Kingdom stayed slightly below 50%. As mentioned, in the boom–bust countries, public expenditure averaged 8.8% of GDP more than in 2007 and over 10% more than in 1999. Historically, these kinds of changes rarely occurred outside wartime.

Deficits had mostly peaked already in 2009, when average deficits in the boom–bust country group stood at 12% of GDP. Ireland reported a huge deficit of 32% of GDP in one year to cover the cost of recapitalising the banks and bailing out their creditors. For the three big continentals, deficits peaked at 4–8% before beginning to fall.

As a result, public debt sky-rocketed. In 2012, at the height of the euro fiscal crisis, Greece's debt stood at 160% of GDP, with Portugal and Ireland at 110%, Spain and the United Kingdom at 85%. By that time, Portugal, Ireland and Greece had fully fledged adjustment programmes and Spain had embarked on a financial sector programme. The United Kingdom decided to act before the markets tested it. In all countries, the reform programmes entailed major expenditure reform. For the three big continentals, the debt increase was 'only' about 20–30% of GDP by the time their expenditure peaked; however, for Italy, this was from a very high base.

Expenditure in the Reform Phase

The five boom–bust countries undertook major expenditure adjustment in the 2010s. Expenditure ratios came down by almost 10% of GDP between their peak and 2017. This was very similar to the decline experienced by the ambitious reform countries of the 1980s and 1990s (Table 5.8). Ireland topped the record of previous periods with a reduction of over 20% of GDP. But this fact relates also to some special features of the (relatively small) Irish economy and the shifting of activity to Ireland by some large multinationals. The total spending of Greece, Spain and the United Kingdom went down by over 7% of GDP. The 5.9% for Portugal reflects a 7% decline in primary spending partly 'eaten up' by rising debt service payments.

By 2017, total expenditure ratios had come down to 48% in Greece, to 46% in Portugal and to 41% in the United Kingdom and Spain. Nevertheless,

Table 5.8 *Total expenditure post-peak*

% of GDP	Peak	2017	Change peak–2017	Change 1999–2017
Boom–bust countries				
Greece[1]	55.4	48.0	−7.4	1.8
Ireland	47.0	26.1	−20.9	−7.9
Portugal	51.8	45.9	−5.9	3.3
Spain	48.1	41.0	−7.1	0.1
UK	48.9	41.0	−7.9	5.7
Average (5)	50.2	40.4	−9.8	0.6
Big continental countries				
France	57.0	56.5	−0.5	4.4
Germany	47.6	43.9	−3.7	−3.8
Italy	51.2	48.9	−2.3	1.5
Average (3)	51.9	49.8	−2.1	0.7

Source: Ameco, OECD
1. Greece excludes 2013, as data strongly affected by bank recapitalisation costs.

most of these figures were above the 1999 number; only Ireland, at 26%, was well below the 34% of 1999. The expenditure ratio of the United Kingdom was still 5% of GDP above the 1999 figure.

The figures for the three big continental countries were much less impressive. In Section 5.3, they would have been put in the category of 'timid' or 'non-reformer' countries. France's spending reduction of 0.5% of GDP between 2013 and 2017 was exclusively due to falling debt service costs. Public expenditure of 56.5% of GDP stood only slightly below an all-time high. Germany managed to bring down public expenditure almost back to the 2007 ratio; however, when interest payments are taken out, the reduction since 2009 was less. Italy brought total expenditure down by 2.3% of GDP between 2009 and 2017, but half of this was due to lower debt service costs.

Expenditure Composition and Comprehensive Reforms

The decomposition of expenditure reductions also yields quite interesting results. Most of the adjustment focussed on non-social primary expenditure (Table 5.9). This went down by almost 7% of GDP on average in the boom–bust countries and above 13% in Ireland. Government consumption accounted for almost 4% of GDP, with Greece much above and Ireland much below this figure. Public investment declined by almost 2% of GDP on average and by more than 3% in Spain. The strong fall in investment

Table 5.9 *Expenditure reform and the effect on expenditure composition*

Change peak–2017

% of GDP	Social expenditure	Non-social primary expenditure	Government consumption	Public investment	Public education	Total revenue
Boom-bust countries						
Greece	-1.0	-3.5	-1.8	2.1	0	2.9
Ireland	-6.1	-13.3	-8.0	-1.8	-0.7	-7.6
Portugal	-0.4	-7.7	-3.1	-3.5	-0.5	2.3
Spain	-1.5	-4.0	-1.2	-0.5	-0.6	0.3
UK	-2.3	-4.4	-2.6	-0.2	0.5	-0.1
Average (5)	-2.2	-6.6	-4.0	-0.8	-0.3	-0.5
Big continental countries						
France	0.1	-0.4	-0.5	-0.6	0	1.0
Germany	-1.4	-0.6	-0.1	-0.2	0.1	0.9
Italy	1.2	-2.3	-2.0	-1.4	-0.4	0.7
Average (3)	-0.1	-1.1	-0.9	-0.7	-0.1	0.8

Source: Ameco, OECD

124

spending gave much rise to criticism, although it was not clear that Spain and Portugal still suffered from infrastructure under-investment after years of expansion.

Social expenditure declined much less than in earlier adjustment episodes. Only Ireland reported a major decline in its expenditure ratio by 6% of GDP. For the other four, the decrease was only around 1% of GDP. In the 1980s and 1990s, transfers had often contributed 50% of total savings and investment had declined only modestly. Given the importance of bringing down less productive rather than productive spending, one can argue that the 'quality' of adjustment in the 2010s was often lower than in the 1980s and 1990s.

As regards education spending, the average decline was a modest 0.3% of GDP (similar to the 1980s and 1990s). There was no change in the ratio in Greece and an increase by 0.5% of GDP in the United Kingdom. The other three countries reported a decline near the average.

For the three big continentals, the adjustment composition does not show a strong focus on productive spending, with the partial exception of Germany. The ratio of social expenditure increased further in Italy and stagnated in France after the crisis. In Germany, it fell overall before increasing again after 2012 (despite the robust economy). At the same time, government consumption and public investment declined, though only marginally in Germany. Education spending declined in France and Italy and increased slightly in Germany.

Another difference between the 2010s on the one hand and the 1980s/ 1990s episodes on the other relates to public revenue. Reform programmes in the boom–bust countries did not feature major tax cuts because deficits were too large. In fact, revenue increased between the peak year of expenditure and 2017, except in Ireland. The increase was strongest in Greece (about 3% of GDP) and ranged between 0.5% and 2% of GDP for the others. The revenue ratio also increased in the three continental countries; in France it rose to an all-time high of 53.9% in 2017.

Finally, we should stress that the expenditure reform in the boom–bust countries was typically part of rather comprehensive reform packages (Hauptmeier et al., 2014). All countries featured reforms of the financial sector and labour markets, while Greece and Portugal undertook a privatisation programme.

All five countries strengthened their fiscal institutions by introducing fiscal councils (independent bodies to evaluate fiscal policy) and signing the so-called fiscal compact which enshrined EU fiscal rules in national law. Greece strengthened its public financial management. Portugal also strengthened its fiscal framework and improved its budgetary process. Ireland introduced a multiannual expenditure framework and performance budgeting. Spain improved its debt management and implemented local government expenditure rules. The United Kingdom delegated the production of its macroeconomic framework to an independent institution, the Office for Budget Responsibility (OBR).

5.5 Implications of the Third 'Wave' Expenditure Reforms

Deficit and Debt

Comprehensive reform in the five boom–bust countries, including major expenditure reform, enhanced the performance and credibility of these countries and their economies. Expenditure restraint brought down fiscal imbalances significantly. Deficit reduction after expenditure reforms began amounted to 7–8% of GDP in Greece, Portugal, Spain and the United Kingdom and 13.5% in Ireland (Figure 5.3). This was a huge correction of similar ambition as the earlier reform 'waves'.

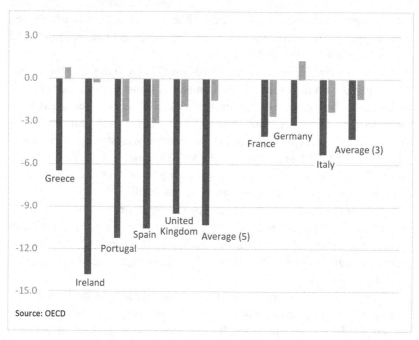

Source: OECD

Figure 5.3 Deficit reduction since expenditure peak, % of GDP.

Table 5.10 *Debt dynamics in 2009, year of debt peak, and 2017*

% of GDP	2009	Debt peak	Year	2017	Change Peak–2017
France	78.9	97.0	2017	97.0	0.0
Germany	72.6	81.0	2010	64.1	−16.9
Italy	112.5	132.6	2016	131.8	−0.8
Average	88.0	103.5		97.6	−5.9
Greece	126.7	181.3	2016	178.6	−2.7
Ireland	61.7	119.6	2012	68.0	−51.6
Portugal	83.6	130.6	2014	125.7	−4.9
Spain	52.7	100.4	2014	98.3	−2.1
UK	64.5	89.2	2016	87.7	−1.5
Average	77.8	124.2		111.7	−12.6

Source: OECD

The average deficits had fallen to 'only' 1.5% by 2017 in this group; however, Portugal and Spain still showed deficits around 3% of GDP despite four years of good growth. Amongst the three big continentals, Germany reported a surplus. The French deficit only came down below 3% in 2017 and the Italian deficit, at 2.3, was only marginally below the figures of earlier years.

This deficit pattern had important implications for debt dynamics (Table 5.10). By 2017, debt had been stabilised in all eight countries; however, it had only come down significantly in Ireland and Germany. In the other countries, the debt decline had not started in earnest despite a robust economic recovery. French and Spanish debt was stagnating at near 100% of GDP, the United Kingdom near 90%, Italy above 130% and Greece near 180% (though financed at very favourable terms). Portugal's debt came down significantly for the first time in 2017. Even Germany and Ireland still featured debt ratios above the 60% Maastricht convergence ceiling and above 2007 levels.

Administration and Institutions

It is also interesting to observe how the quality of the administration and institutions evolved. Results were mixed for both groups as regards the rule of law and administrative quality indicators (Table 5.11). We look at the change in the indicator values between 2000 and 2017 relative to the average of the advanced countries. Amongst the boom–bust countries,

Table 5.11 *Administration and rule of law, changes between 2000 and 2017*

	Corruption	Red tape	Quality of judiciary	Size of shadow economy	No. of indicators with above-average changes in performance
Boom–Bust					
Greece	0.1	−0.2	−2.0	−2.1	1
Ireland	0.5	−1.1	0.1	2.0	3
Portugal	0.2	0.8	3.0	1.8	4
Spain	−1.0	−1.3	0.3	−1.1	1
UK	−0.2	1.3	0.3	0.7	3
Big Continental					
France	0.6	0.8	0.4	0.4	4
Germany	0.8	1.7	−1.7	3.4	3
Italy	0.7	−0.4	0.9	−2.1	2

Source: Fraser Institute, Medina and Schneider (2018) for the shadow economy
A negative change is a worsening of corruption, red tape and judiciary and an increase in the shadow economy relative to the average of the advanced countries.

Portugal, Ireland and the United Kingdom showed a relative improvement on three or four indicators. For Greece and Spain, this only held for one indicator. The big continentals showed a slightly better picture: France performed better than average on all four indicators, Germany on three and Italy on two.

Economic and Distribution Performance

On economic performance, developments were quite positive in the boom–bust countries, which showed a remarkable economic rebound, except for Greece where the recovery lagged (Figure 5.4). Leaving aside booming Ireland, real economic growth averaged slightly below to well above 2% in Portugal, Spain and the United Kingdom in 2014–2017. This was more than in France, Italy and Germany. Consumption and investment also recovered strongly and dynamics in the four reform countries outside Greece were well above that of the three big continentals.

The most impressive achievement of the reforming boom–bust countries was probably the reduction in unemployment. In 2014–2017, unemployment in the big continentals came down by about 1% in France, Germany and Italy. The reforming boom–bust countries did much better,

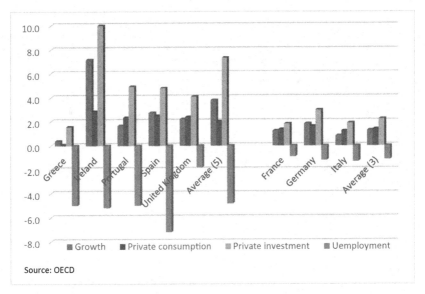

Figure 5.4 Economic dynamism: Annual real economic and consumption growth, change in unemployment rate, 2014–2017.

albeit mostly from higher levels. The decline in Greece Ireland and Portugal was about 5%, in Spain over 7% and in the United Kingdom almost 2%. This was a remarkable achievement for economic and social well-being, although there was some further way to go in all countries except Germany, Ireland and the United Kingdom.

Public infrastructure and income distribution are also worth looking at. Despite lower investment spending, the quality of public infrastructure improved in all countries except Ireland between 2007 and 2017 (Figure 5.5). This finding, however, should not be over-interpreted: spending affects infrastructure quality only over a long time horizon.

Income distribution changed little over the same period in both country groups. Recall that the average for all countries stayed constant at 31, and most countries reported very little or no change in their Gini indices. Only Italy saw a rising Gini coefficient from 31 to 33 while Portugal reported a decline (more equality) from 36 to 34 and the United Kingdom from 37 to 35. This is indicative of the fact that the reforming boom–bust countries had if anything a slightly more favourable development of income distribution than the big continentals and the average (Figure 5.6). Income distribution in the group of reformers improved by 0.5 point, while it worsened by 1 point in the three big continental European countries.

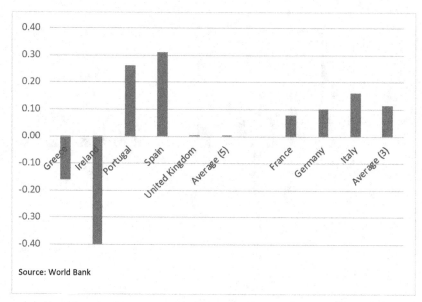

Source: World Bank

Figure 5.5 Change in infrastructure quality index, 2007–2017.

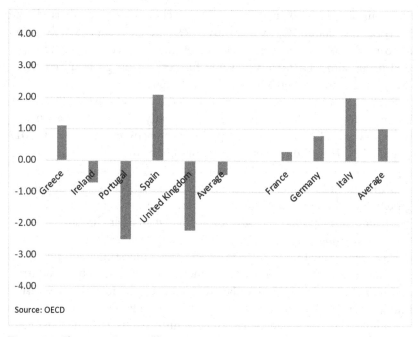

Source: OECD

Figure 5.6 Change in Gini coefficient, 2007–2017.

All in all, the boom–bust countries that undertook major expenditure reforms fared well in terms of fiscal, economic and social indicators. An exception is Greece, where perhaps too little time has passed to show success. The three big continentals showed a much less impressive record in the recovery period.

5.6 Conclusion

Many countries undertook important expenditure reforms in the 1980s and 1990s. These episodes resulted in major expenditure retrenchments so that the size of government on average amongst the advanced economies did not rise further between 1980 and the turn of the millennium. A third reform wave followed in the 2010s. These reform efforts by European countries in the 2010s were of similar ambition as the earlier waves. However, they still left the countries with somewhat higher spending ratios than around the turn of the century, in line with a general tendency towards higher spending.

The first two reform waves constituted important regime changes in several countries, and focussed strongly on curtailing the welfare state. Comprehensive reform strategies magnified positive effects for fiscal variables, growth and employment. The latest reform wave was also ambitious, comprehensive and successful, although the quality of adjustment was probably somewhat lower, with a smaller focus on less productive expenditure.

Some observers have argued that these reforms have come at the expense of public institutions, infrastructure and equality of income distribution. The analysis for the 1980s and 1990s points to modest 'costs' in this regard in a number of countries. However, the reforming countries experienced higher economic and employment growth and improvements in other indicators. The analysis for the 'third wave' of reforming boom–bust countries does not confirm this distributional trade-off, while having similar positive fiscal and economic effects to earlier reforms.

6

The 'Optimal' Size of Government

*The positive evils and dangers of the representative, as of every other form
of government, may be reduced to two heads: first, general ignorance
and incapacity . . ., secondly, the danger of its being under the influence of
interests not identical with the general welfare of the community.*

John Stuart Mill

*Freedom is never more than one generation away from extinction . . . It
must be fought for, protected, and handed on for them [our children] to
do the same.*

Ronald Reagan

Highlights

How 'big' should government be? How much lower can public spending be, if
countries still want to be amongst the better or even best performers? A pragmatic
'optimum' for the size of government, something that is realistic and reachable, is
normally not more than 30–35% or perhaps 40% of GDP (Figure 6.1). This is
the spending ratio of top-scoring countries, such as Switzerland and Australia,
and they do well on their core tasks. Ireland and Singapore do so with even
lower spending.

This implies a lot of room for expenditure savings in many countries, given a total
average of almost 44% and highest spending above 56% of GDP. 'Big spenders' with a
poor performance and an unequal income distribution can gain in particular from
cutting the size of the state.

There is also a group of countries with high spending and good performance, such
as the Nordics. For these, the picture for the optimal size of government is nuanced.
Experience nonetheless shows that comprehensive reform can make a big difference
to performance and efficiency everywhere.

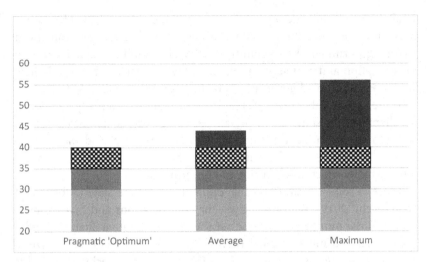

Figure 6.1 A pragmatic 'optimum' versus average and maximum size of government, % of GDP.

6.1 The 'Optimal' Size of Government from a Macro Perspective

How big should government be? This question has fascinated economists for decades and of course there is no 'right' answer. But do governments have to spend as much money as they do today to score well on core objectives such as education, the rule of law or public infrastructure? Is it worth spending so much and paying high taxes, and take the risk of growing debt? How much more could we get from current spending in terms of public services, education, roads, security and social welfare, if only we did it more efficiently?

Unduly 'small' government leads to an under-provision of public goods and services and 'good' rules and regulations. Unduly 'big' government means more bureaucracy, more room for corruption and rent seeking, and a loss of freedom (Müller, 1986; Frey 1988). The objectives that governments try to achieve can become both complex and contradictory. It is then harder to see the strategy and the benefits while abuse increases (Tanzi, 2018a). High spending on existing programmes may also leave little room for tackling new challenges.

There are important external factors that influence the 'optimal' size of government. A small, open economy may want to have a bigger public sector with more safety nets than a large closed one so that the stabilising effect of government is larger. However, the opposite may also hold, because 'small' government means more competiveness via lower taxes. A country with an effective and less distortionary tax system can finance a bigger government at the same cost as another country might with a smaller government and a less efficient tax system (OECD, 2018b). Countries with well-functioning institutions and trust in government can afford a larger government than a country with weak institutions and a tendency to corruption and rent seeking. All this suggests that we should ask: how 'big' or 'small' should governments be to attain their core tasks?

There are a number of caveats for such an analysis, as already mentioned in Chapter 4. In some areas, private spending plays a significant role in addition to government and the choice of reference period may not be 'neutral' because external events (such as the financial crisis) may have a differentiated effect on countries and governments.

There is some literature on the 'optimal' size of the state (Afonso and Schuknecht, 2019). But again, given the considerations and caveats mentioned, these numbers should be seen as guidance rather than as 'truth'. Vito Tanzi and myself argued twenty years ago that 30–35% of GDP is enough, in some cases perhaps 40% (Tanzi and Schuknecht, 2000). This was a pragmatic and realistic objective. Pevcin (2004) has argued that in the past fifteen years the spending ratio of eight European countries (averaging around 50%) should have been 19% of GDP lower. Chobanov and Mladenova (2009) saw the 'optimum' at 25% of GDP in order to maximise economic growth in twenty-nine OECD countries.

Turning to our own analysis, our approach remains pragmatic rather than very technical. Recall the size of government across advanced economies in the ten-year period up to 2017 (see Figure 6.2). Chapter 4 argued that this was probably a reasonable horizon against which government

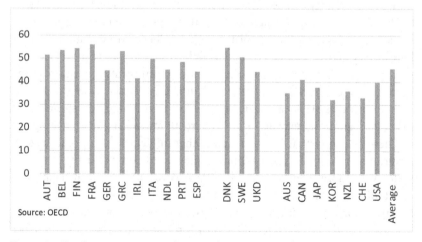

Figure 6.2 Total government spending, % of GDP, average 2008–2017.

performance and efficiency should be measured because it takes time for many programmes to affect outcomes. An administrative reform or a public investment programme will only slowly feed into better indicators for judiciary efficiency or infrastructure quality.

The total average over this period was 45% of GDP. Public spending in a number of 'small' government countries, notably Switzerland, Australia, New Zealand, Japan and the United States, averaged below 40% of GDP. Public expenditure in the United Kingdom and Ireland fell well below the 40% ratio towards the end of the period. Canada, Germany, the Netherlands and Spain are also in the group with near-average spending ratios. The other countries, including Southern Europeans, other Central-Western Europeans and the Nordics, averaged spending from near 50% to 56% of GDP.

When plotting the total expenditure data of countries against their performance indicators that were derived in Chapter 4, the results are intriguing (Figure 6.3). Three relatively small governments – Switzerland, Australia and Ireland – report the highest performance indicators. The other 'small' governments all perform above the average of 1 and so do a few other European countries. The United Kingdom, Finland and Denmark are pretty much on the average line, France is slightly below and the four Southern Europeans significantly below.

We did not include Singapore in Figure 6.3. This is a vibrant economy with public expenditure at 20% of GDP, which is even lower than in Switzerland or Ireland. It shows the present and future 'benchmark' set by low tax–low spending economies in Asia against which today's advanced countries will have to compete.

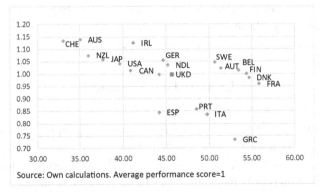

Source: Own calculations. Average performance score=1

Figure 6.3 Aggregate government performance and total spending, % of GDP, 2017.

This first exercise suggests that public expenditure could be much lower than it is today. Public expenditure in the 30–40% range correlates with a good if not top-level achievement of core government objectives. We also find that a number of the 'reform countries' of the 1980s and 1990s discussed in Chapter 5 (Australia, New Zealand, Ireland, Canada, United Kingdom) are in the well-performing group with low expenditure ratios. A few 'earlier reform countries' (the Netherlands, Belgium, the Nordics) are part of the well-performing group with average to high expenditure. A number of other 'big' government countries do poorly in this analysis.

6.2 Deriving the Potential for Expenditure Savings via Data Envelope Analysis

To bring an exploration of the 'optimal' size of the state beyond simple descriptive analysis, a number of economists started to apply so-called linear programming techniques. With these they examined a number of spending categories and their impact on performance indicators at the country and sub-national government level (Afonso and St Aubuyn, 2005; Afonso et al., 2005; Herrera and Pang, 2005; Sutherland et al., 2012; and a number of further studies by Afonso and his co-authors).

The idea is simple. If an expenditure input affects a certain performance indicator, we can plot countries' data along these two dimensions. The most efficient countries are those on the 'frontier' of expenditure and performance. The relative distance to the frontier in terms of expenditure and outcomes shows the degree of inefficiency of the countries that are not on it.

This so-called data envelope analysis (DEA) can also apply to a multidimensional space with several inputs and one (or several) outcomes, even though graphically and computationally it becomes more complicated. Moreover, the analysis does not argue that the countries on the frontier are in fact fully efficient. But lacking evidence that more efficiency is possible, it is prudent to assume that frontier countries are efficient.

DEA for Total Spending

Afonso and Kazemi (2017) undertook a DEA analysis for twenty OECD countries for the 2009–2013 period for the same type of performance and efficiency indicators that we used in Chapter 4. Figure 6.4 presents the results for total public spending and overall public sector performance. The production possibility frontier (PPF) is determined by just one country: Switzerland. It spent less and performed better than any other country.

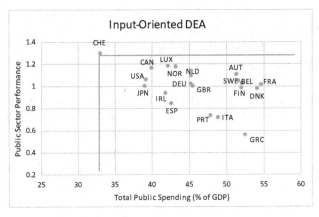

Figure 6.4 DEA model including all countries.

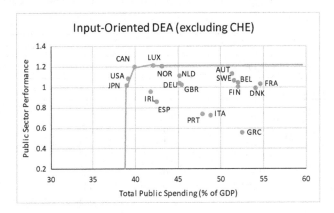

Figure 6.5 DEA model excluding Switzerland.

Canada, Luxembourg and Norway came close from an outcome perspective, although they spent more. The United States and Japan were closest to Switzerland from an input perspective (i.e. having the next lowest expenditure ratio) and Greece was furthest away from the frontier.

The finding of just one efficient country could suggest that Switzerland is an outlier that on its own does not provide much guidance for efficiency of input use relative to outputs. This argument is not very convincing, however, because there is no reason why other countries could not emulate the Swiss experience.

Nevertheless, for 'statistical reasons' a 'robustness check' suggests that we conduct the same analysis without Switzerland. This is shown in Figure 6.5. The PPF has shifted to the right as it is assumed that the Swiss output cannot be achieved by the other countries at the same level of inputs. Now the United States and Japan are on the frontier. Canada, Luxembourg and Norway are also on or very near it.

As mentioned, the relative distance to the frontier reflects the extent of a country's inefficiencies. The results including Switzerland are shown in Table 6.1. Column (1) reflects the possible input savings (while still reaching the same outcome). Column (3) shows the possible performance gains if the same level of spending had been applied in a fully efficient manner. The United States, with an input-oriented score of 0.85, spent about 15% more than necessary for its level of performance.

Table 6.1 *DEA results, 2009–2013*

	Output (performance score) – Input (total public expenditure)			
	including Switzerland			
	Input-oriented		Output-oriented	
	Score	Rank	Score	Rank
Country	(1)	(2)	(3)	(4)
Austria	0.65	14	0.854	5
Belgium	0.64	16	0.79	9
Canada	0.83	4	0.90	4
Denmark	0.62	19	0.75	15
Finland	0.64	16	0.76	14
France	0.61	20	0.79	10
Germany	0.74	9	0.79	10
Greece	0.63	18	0.43	20
Ireland	0.79	5	0.72	16
Italy	0.68	13	0.55	19
Japan	0.85	2	0.77	13
Luxembourg	0.79	5	0.92	2
Netherlands	0.74	9	0.84	6
Norway	0.77	8	0.91	3
Portugal	0.69	12	0.56	18
Spain	0.78	7	0.65	17
Sweden	0.64	15	0.81	8
Switzerland	1.00	1	1.00	1
UK	0.73	11	0.78	12
US	0.85	2	0.82	7
Mean	0.73		0.77	
Minimum	0.61		0.43	

Source: Afonso and Kazemi (2016)

The United States output socre of 0.82 suggests that it could have increased its performance by 18% if it had spent its money more efficiently.

When looking at input efficiency more broadly, countries on average spent 27% more than necessary to attain their performance (score of 0.73). Or they could have achieved a 23% better performance at the same level of spending if they had been on the frontier (score of 0.77). France (the biggest spender) could have saved 40% for the same performance; Greece (the poorest performer) could have done 57% better with the same amount of public money.

Another way of assessing relative efficiency is the ranking of countries (columns 2 and 4). Japan and the United States rank second on input efficiency, Luxembourg is second as regard outputs, very closely followed by Norway and Canada. The big European countries, Germany and the United Kingdom, are in the mid-field for both input and output efficiency.

What does this mean for the size of government? The findings from the DEA are very close to those from the descriptive analysis presented earlier. If the average savings potential is more than 25% and average total public expenditure about 45% of GDP, efficient countries would need to spend only 30–35% of GDP. France, at 56% of GDP, shows a savings potential of 40% which would also bring spending down into that range.

DEA of Other Performance Indicators

The DEA on overall performance can also be conducted for the sub-indicators of government efficiency. The summary results of Afonso and Kazemi (2017) appear in Table 6.2. The indicators include the opportunity indicators, administration quality, education, health and infrastructure.

The results are quite telling. Switzerland is on the efficiency frontier for public administration. Swiss public expenditure on this is very low (less than 12% of GDP) and the input score of 0.56 suggests that the other countries spent on average 44% too much (ca. 8% of GDP given average spending of about 20% of GDP) when looking at their administrative performance.

From the perspective of improving outcomes, countries should achieve a 19% (output score 0.81) higher performance for the amount of money they spent. In other words, they would have achieved an almost 20% better performance on corruption, red tape, etc. and almost 20% less on the shadow economy if they had been on the frontier. The minimum

Table 6.2 *Summary results across DEA models*

Inputs	Government consumption	Education expenditure	Health expenditure	Public investment
Outputs	Administration performance	Education performance	Health performance	Infrastructure performance
Countries on the frontier	Switzerland	Finland, Japan, Luxembourg, Netherlands	Ireland, Japan, Luxembourg, Switzerland	Germany, Switzerland
Average input scores	0.56	0.81	0.84	0.67
Average output scores	0.81	0.93	0.99	0.88
Minimum input scores	0.42	0.59	0.68	0.49
Minimum output scores	0.49	0.85	0.97	0.64
Total countries	20	20	20	20
Efficient countries	1	4	4	2

Source: Afonso and Kazemi (2017)

140

scores of less than 0.5 show that the least efficient country should have spent less than half, or done more than twice as well, to get to the frontier.

As regards education, four countries – Japan, Luxembourg, the Netherlands and Finland – are on the frontier. Differences across countries are smaller for this task of government: the average input inefficiency is less than 20% and output inefficiencies average less than 10%. This means that the savings potential in education could have been, for example, 1% of GDP on a total of 5%. Still the least efficient country could have saved over 40% of total education spending given its performance. From an output perspective, PISA scores could have improved by 6.6% or ca. 35 points without higher spending. This would have brought several countries from scores around or somewhat above average into the group of global top performers.

The savings potential for health is relatively similar to that for education according to DEA – 16% on average and 32% as a maximum. With an average spending of around 7.5% of GDP, average savings could amount to 1% of GDP. On the output side, additional spending can in fact do very little, at most 3%. Life expectancy and infant mortality, the two relevant indicators, are relatively similar across countries. The four most efficient countries include Ireland, Luxembourg, Switzerland and Japan.

Finally, DEA for public investment reveals two efficient countries, Germany and Switzerland, due to high performance coupled with relatively low spending. Average savings, given the existing infrastructure quality, could have been 33%, maximum savings about 50%. On an average spending ratio of 3% of GDP, this means about 1% of GDP of potential savings.

6.3 The Overall Savings Potential and the 'Optimum' Size of the State

What is the savings potential for governments that still want to attain good, if not top, outcomes? We follow the book's red thread of looking at opportunity indicators and Musgravian indicators.

Opportunity Indicators

As regards public administration, there does not seem a clear relationship between government real expenditure and performance; if anything it is slightly negative. Switzerland reports the highest performance and nearly the lowest spending, at 11.8% of GDP (Figure 6.6). The Swiss corruption score is 15% above average, red tape is 30% smaller and the judiciary

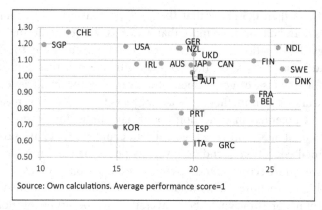

Figure 6.6 Administration performance and real expenditure, % of GDP, 2017.

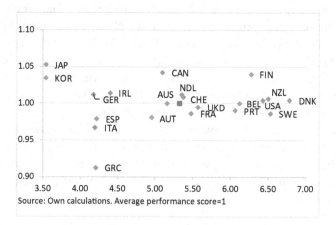

Figure 6.7 Education performance and education expenditure, % of GDP, 2017.

performs over 10% better. The size of the shadow economy in Switzerland is only about half the average. The United States and Ireland also show high scores with 'only' around 16% of GDP on public administration expenditure. Hence, compared to the average of over 20% of GDP and up to 26% in some countries, there could be a significant amount of savings under this category.

As regards education, there is again no visible correlation between public expenditure and education performance (Figure 6.7). Spending for the four best performers ranges from about 3.5% of GDP in South Korea and Japan to 6.5% in Finland. Canada, with a 5% ratio, is also fairly efficient. Therefore, on the whole, public spending in the 3.5–5% range should facilitate a top performance.

Japan's score of 528 is 26 points above average, Canada's comparative figure is slightly above 20 points and Singapore's is 50 points. By contrast, Greece scores 50 points below average, more than a full school year equivalent. This shows the enormous advantage of a good education system for some countries' citizens. Given that education performance is the best predictor of future growth, any shortfalls should be taken very seriously (Woessmann, 2016).

Turning to public health, the lowest spender, South Korea, also shows a relatively weak performance in terms of life expectancy and infant mortality (Figure 6.8). Finland and Japan report roughly the same performance while spending 6.8 and 8.5% of GDP, respectively. Finland's figure is still slightly below the average and does not feature a huge private health system. This suggests that it probably takes not more than 7% of GDP to attain a good public health system.

Infrastructure performance is another area where public spending – even when averaging 10 years data as we did – seems to show little correlation with infrastructure quality (Figure 6.9). Austria, Belgium, Germany, Japan and Sweden are high performers. However, their spending ratio differs enormously, ranging from 2.3 of GDP to almost twice that figure. This could be related to the fact that some countries have privatised much of their infrastructure provision, which seems to have been good for performance. In any case, these figures suggest that public infrastructure spending does not need to be above 2.5% of GDP compared to an average of over 3% in the 2010s. Economists who advise much higher public infrastructure spending should probably take a closer look at performance and the underlying micro structures.

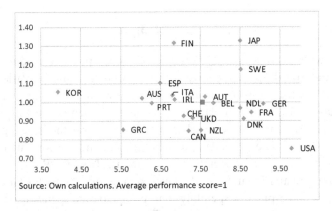

Figure 6.8 Health performance and health expenditure, % of GDP, 2017.

Value for Money

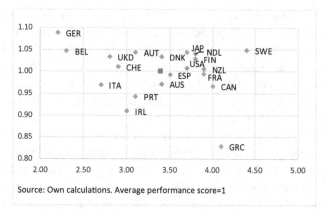

Figure 6.9 Infrastructure performance and public investment, % of GDP, 2017.

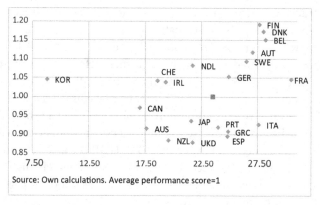

Figure 6.10 Income distribution and social expenditure, % of GDP, 2017.

Musgravian Indicators

Starting with income distribution, the relationship between Gini coefficients and social spending looks positive even though the variation is high. The Nordics, Belgium and Austria show the most equal income distribution (Figure 6.10). However, additional income equality seems to require very much more social spending. Therefore, the 'small' governments – Switzerland, Canada, Australia and Ireland – show higher efficiency scores with social spending of less than 20% of GDP.

Switzerland and Ireland report above-average equality, with a Gini index lower than 30 despite low spending. This points to high spending efficiency and probably also to the beneficial effect of strong labour markets and education systems on income distribution. The Netherlands is another country with a strong Gini (28.5) and below-average social spending of 21.7% of GDP. From this, we can conclude that social expenditure of around 20% of GDP can provide a very good level of income equality compared to an average of almost 24% for the past decade.

The key question is whether it is worth spending 8% of GDP (around 28% of GDP in the most egalitarian European countries versus around 20% of GDP) more for a modest gain in income distribution given that needs to be financed through higher taxes or lower spending elsewhere and may come at the price of higher unemployment. It is also important not to forget that these are small and relatively homogenous countries and their experience may not be easy to emulate.

This argument may apply even more strongly to Italy and France. The two countries feature similarly high social expenditure ratios as the Nordics. In France, income distribution is about the same as that in Switzerland, despite over 10% of GDP higher social expenditure. Italy even features amongst the most unequal advanced countries. At the other extreme, the United States has about the same level of social spending as Switzerland but the Gini coefficient is 25% worse.

Musgrave also proposed economic stabilisation as a core role of government. The stability of economic growth and the attainment of price stability over the past decade proxy economic stability (Figure 6.11). The 'small' government countries of Australia, Switzerland, the United States and New Zealand show the most stable economic performance, confirming the earlier macro picture that relatively low public spending does not conflict with stability, on the contrary in fact.

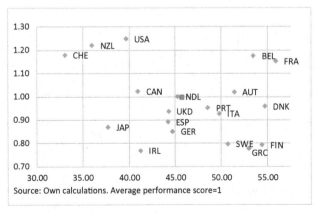

Figure 6.11 Economic stability and government spending, % of GDP, 2017.

The experience of the past decade shows that 'small' government could well be a plus for stability for a 'new' reason: these countries have a smaller risk of over-extended government and fiscal crisis so that there is less need for the type of ad hoc adjustment that some European countries had to go through: the European crisis countries feature in the group of less stable economies in Figure 6.9.

There are also two relatively stable countries with large public sectors, France and Belgium. Both countries managed to navigate the financial crisis with a relatively stable economic performance. This probably reflects the large automatic stabilisers in these countries, linked to the spending composition and stabilisation mechanisms (Fournier and Johansson, 2016), as well as these countries' avoiding fiscal crisis. This contrasts with the experience of Ireland where a small public sector did not help to prevent financial cum fiscal crisis and the resulting instability.

Finally, there is a strong negative correlation between the size of government and economic performance. This measure combines real economic growth, per capita GDP (purchasing power adjusted) and the unemployment rate (Figure 6.12). Switzerland and Australia come out on top, some of the European big government countries at the bottom. With many years of higher growth in 'small' government countries, the divergence of per capita GDP even increased since the 1990s (see Chapter 4).

The most remarkable and important difference from the perspective of economic performance but also inclusiveness is the much lower unemployment rate in the 'small' government countries. Some 'medium'-sized and 'big' governments featured very high unemployment rates even though

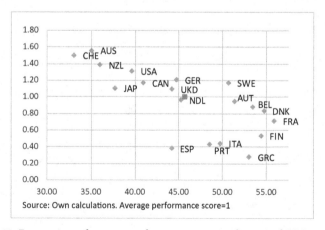

Figure 6.12 Economic performance and government spending, % of GDP, 2017.

the former crisis countries of Europe have made significant progress via expenditure reform (see Chapter 5).

The OECD has designed a novel way to look at the effect of public finances on output (Fournier and Johansson, 2016; OECD, 2018b). Based on simulations following panel analysis for the period since 1981, they analyse the effect of revenue, expenditure and the size and effectiveness of government on long-term per capita output. The findings are quite remarkable.

There are big differences in the growth implications of public expenditure (Figure 6.13). 'Small' governments tend to have a more positive effect than larger ones. However, Finland and Denmark are 'big' government 'outliers' where strong performance and effectiveness imply a positive contribution of expenditure to growth. By contrast, the same countries that did poorly in the earlier analysis also show a strongly negative contribution of the spending role of the state.

The OECD study also analyses the output effect across income quintiles, and found that the bottom quintile benefits most strongly in the Nordics (unsurprising), followed by the group of 'small' governments (more surprising). For the rest, the ranking does not change significantly.

A Mini Meta Analysis across Approaches

A mini meta analysis looks at all these approaches in a horizontal manner. It combines the top or top two performers of each approach (efficiency, performance, DEA and OECD analysis). Table 6.3 shows the results. Switzerland has the highest number of top scores followed by Australia. The United States, Japan, Germany, Finland and Canada also do well. A few other countries are listed as well. This shows that the ranking across countries and the strong performance and efficiency of 'small' governments is relatively robust across approaches.

6.4 The 'Optimal' Size of Government: A Synthesis

When putting the findings of the previous discussion together, one can well argue that public expenditure does not have to be above 30–35% or perhaps 40% of GDP for governments to do well in all categories, including income distribution. Absent any knowledge about a true 'optimum', we can refer to this range as a pragmatic 'optimum' for the size of government.

A number of countries within (or even below) that range, such as Switzerland, Australia and Ireland, have a healthy and inclusive economy. Singapore does very well on public expenditure at only 20% of GDP. Only

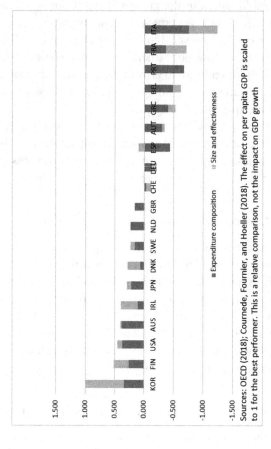

Figure 6.13 Per capita output and the size, composition and effectiveness of government expenditure.

Table 6.3 *Meta analysis on top scores*

	Total	Expenditure efficiency	Expenditure performance	DEA analysis	OECD
	Number of top scores				
Switzerland	7	4	1	2	
Australia	6	4	2		
US	4	1	1	1	1
Japan	3	1	2		
Germany	3	2	1		
Finland	2	1	1		
Canada	2	1		1	
Ireland	1	1			
Belgium	1	1			
UK	1				1
All others	0				

Source: Own calculations; Afonso and Kazemi (2017); Cournède, Fournier and Hoeller (2018)

as regards income distribution is there more to gain from the pain of higher taxes. Even the well-run and egalitarian Nordics show higher unemployment than the countries with 'small' public sectors.

A final 'exercise' identifies the savings potentials across spending categories in a slightly more granular manner to cross-check our discussion on aggregate figures. Naturally, any savings potential depends on many external and country-specific factors, but we derive some ball-park figures. Table 6.4 summarises the findings.

The highest savings potential is in the biggest expenditure categories. On public administrative spending (public consumption), savings could be as high as 8% of GDP compared to the average if Switzerland was the model. Following the United States and Ireland would still yield 4% of GDP in savings.

On education, Japan is the top performer and the lowest spender. But even following Canada would not mean that we have to spend more than 5% of GDP or so on public education to be top. This does, however, abstract from the real top performers in Asia such as Singapore.

On health, the model should be Finland and regarding public infrastructure, countries could learn from Austria and Germany (where the private sector plays a significant role).

Significant scope for savings lies in social expenditure but there the trade-offs are also worth considering. Switzerland, Ireland and the Netherlands

Table 6.4 *Synthesis on public spending, saving potential and 'optimal' government size*

% of GDP	Average spending, 2010s	Efficient spending levels with good performance	Savings potential compared to average	'Model' country
Public consumption	20.4	12–16	4–8	Switzerland, US, Ireland
Education	5.3	3.5–5	0–1.5	Japan, Canada
Health	7.6	6–7	0.5–1.5	Finland
Infrastructure	3.4	2–3	0.5–1	Austria, Germany
Social spending	23.3	Up to about 20	3–5	Switzerland, Ireland, Netherlands
Total savings[1]			8–15	
Total spending	45.7	30–35 or perhaps 40		Switzerland, Australia, Ireland, New Zealand

1. Sum of the five spending categories of previous lines.

manage a strong performance on income distribution with well below average spending. The 'small' government countries also show the strongest and most stable economic performance.

The two most efficient countries in Europe seem to be Switzerland and Ireland. Outside Europe, Australia and New Zealand come top. When you look at the 'big' countries, Canada, Japan and the United States combine good (but not top) performance with relatively low spending. Germany and the Netherlands, with an expenditure ratio slightly below average and a performance above it, could inspire countries that are far away from the 'top'.

6.5 Conclusion

There is significant scope for expenditure savings for many governments in the advanced economies. Governments do not need to spend more than 30–35% or perhaps 40% of GDP to do well and keep as much money as possible in the hands of their citizens. Some advanced economies such as Ireland and Singapore do well with even smaller states. We can call this the pragmatic 'optimal' size of government. Experience shows that this 'optimum' is not some pipe-dream number but is realistic and reachable for the advanced economies. For good reasons, the range has not changed much from twenty years ago (Tanzi and Schuknecht, 2000): the core tasks of government have not changed greatly and population ageing is mostly only just beginning to 'take off'.

There is a huge variation in performance and efficiency across countries and especially across 'bigger' governments: especially those with weak institutions and weak performance should roll back the role of the state. In some countries, such as the Nordics, with 'big' but well-functioning governments and strong policy programmes, more spending seems less costly in terms of taxes, growth and employment (OECD, 2018b; Tanzi, 2018b).

Whether the more equal income distribution is worth much higher spending is an open question: a differentiated approach and judgement is needed. The Nordic experience shows that strong institutional frameworks and good policies are necessary for 'big' government to be beneficial, but even the Nordic countries could continue to do well with reform and less public money.

The future thus has the potential for smaller and better government in many countries. Countries should pursue reforms of their institutions and policies, and international competition and peer learning should exert pressure in this direction. This is the clear lesson of Part II of this book, which this chapter concludes.

There are, however, major clouds on the horizon linked to the growing insurance role of government. Population ageing and global financial stability are important fiscal risks that are certain or likely to materialise. Part III discusses these risks.

PART III

FISCAL RISKS

7

Social Expenditure and the Risk
of 'Social Dominance'

*Unrestrained liberalism only makes the strong stronger and the weak weaker
and excludes the most excluded.*

Pope Francis

*The problem with socialism is that you eventually run out of other
people's money.*

Margaret Thatcher

Highlights

In the past decades, governments significantly expanded their 'insurance' role in the
economy. The 'all-insurance' state today is expected to cover almost all risks and
contingencies from social security, via protecting certain industries or the financial
sector to supporting demand and mitigating international crises.

Social expenditure reflects the most important 'insurance role' of government.
Social expenditure has been on a continuous upward trend for decades and absorbed
24% of GDP on average in 2016. Projections for the coming decades point to further
moderate increases in an optimistic scenario and very adverse dynamics in pessimistic
ones (Figure 7.1).

Large additional social expenditure increases would be hard to finance and would
crowd out other, productive spending. Such a world of 'social dominance' would not
be stable and sustainable. Fortunately, we have all the policy levers to prevent it.

7.1 The Main Risks for Government: Some Conceptual Issues

So far, we have discussed the evolving role of the state and public expenditure over the past 150 years in Part I and questions of 'value for money',
government reform and 'optimal' size in Part II. In this and Chapters 8 and
9 we will turn to trends and risks in the future. The main risks are linked to

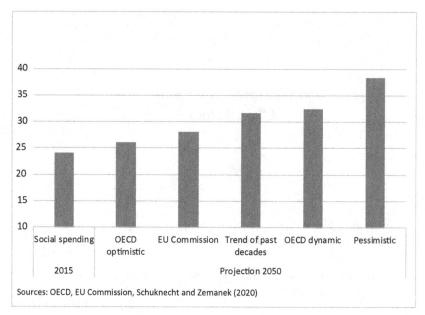

Figure 7.1 Social spending scenarios, % of GDP.

the insurance role of government and the resulting massive contingent and implicit liabilities in the social and financial sphere.

Recall that government expenditure commitments are of three types (Figure 7.2). The first type is budgetary liabilities that governments and parliaments agree upon; they fall due because of policy decisions. Governments have to pay interest on their debt and civil servants' salaries and they have to pay today's social security obligations such as pensions and health care.

The second type of commitments are contingent on certain events happening and so constitute fiscal risks. This includes the various insurance-type obligations of government. Future pensions and health benefits depend on people getting old and sick (which they naturally do). Expenditure on guarantees depend on whether the triggering event occurs (e.g. a public enterprise makes a loss on a project). These claims are also legal claims, whose potential magnitude is typically known in advance and a probability can be assigned to the event happening. Such liabilities are therefore reasonably predictable and measurable.

In some cases, the potential damage/liability may not be that easy to calculate despite the government's best efforts. How likely is it, for example, that an infrastructure project will fail if there are no geographical

Fiscal liabilities	1. Budgetary liabilities			
Fiscal risks from insurance-type events	2. Contingent liabilities			
	Measurable		Unmeasurable	
	3. Implicit liabilities			
	Measurable		Unmeasurable	
	Known	Unknown	Known	Unknown

Figure 7.2 Fiscal liabilities and fiscal risks.

or sectoral precedents? How likely is a major increase in unemployment due to a global crisis, as witnessed after 2007? Some health care costs are also hard to predict. Before March 2020, we did not know how a pandemic would enfold and would certainly not have expected it to be so damaging and costly. We can extrapolate from the past, but we do not really know. One could call these unmeasurable contingent liabilities.

The third category of commitments are the so-called implicit commitments. There is no legal claim behind them but they are still likely to fall on government and hence also constitute a risk. After a flood or a hurricane, governments tend to compensate the victims. When banks failed during the financial crisis, governments came to their rescue. When European governments were failing, the IMF, Eurozone governments and the ECB bailed them out. Governments did not have to do this but for political reasons or for fear of greater damage they did it anyway.

There are some differences between contingent and implicit claims. The magnitude of implicit liabilities and the probability of the event occurring is often not measurable. We have a pretty good idea about the probability and costs of a flood or a storm hitting our countries. But a financial crisis? And through which channel, and at what cost?

Many potential events with implicit liabilities are known, but not all of them. In principal, one could have expected fiscal problems in an incomplete currency union. But nobody seriously expected European governments to fail or whole banking systems to require financial support. And nobody wanted to think about it . . .

Looking forward, we can think about new, so far unknown, fiscal risks. For example, we know that private pension funds are often underfunded (Rauh, 2018; OECD, 2018c), but we do not know whether losses will ever materialise and fall on the public sector. In cases without precedent and prior knowledge, one should speak of uncertainty. But the border between risk and uncertainty is fluid in practice; we, therefore, stick to the broader use of the term 'fiscal risks', returning to questions of ignorance and uncertainty when warranted.

7.2 The Growing Insurance Role of Government

From Basic Safety Nets to an 'All-Round' Insurance View of the State

As we have seen in Chapters 1 and 2, in the nineteenth century, the fiscal role of government was very limited. It mainly consisted of paying for the provision of the rule of law and certain public goods, such as infrastructure, defence and (gradually) public education. The provision of social insurance, as furnished by the government rather than by churches or local communities, began on only a very limited scale in the late nineteenth century. By the Second World War, there was still not much more than basic public retirement, health and unemployment insurance, which had expanded to broadly universal basic 'safety nets' by the 1960s.

Since then, governments have taken on an ever-growing insurance role. Pension, health and unemployment insurance became more generous. Other forms of social assistance (e.g. child, family and disability-related benefits) emerged. Long-term care insurance became a relatively 'recent' addition to protect against the risk of disability associated with longevity. In the late 2010s, social insurance spending had grown to an average of almost one quarter of GDP and 50–60% of fiscal outlays in the advanced economies.

The public insurance role, however, goes much further (Schuknecht, 2013). Some governments provide de facto insurance against poverty and unemployment via public sector jobs or public works programmes. Governments insure corporations and even whole sectors against unfavourable market developments via temporary or permanent subsidies, tax credits or guarantees. More prominently, banks (and their clients) have had their assets 'guaranteed' in the global financial crisis.

With the assent of 'Keynesian' thinking, the role of public insurance began to include the stabilisation of aggregate demand more broadly. The so-called automatic stabilisers were the 'first line of defence' that had also been acknowledged by the classical economists: revenue fluctuated with the cycle while public expenditure remained relatively stable despite changing circumstances. 'Keynesian' activist, counter-cyclical policies that lowered spending in booms and raised it in downturns should further aim to stabilise demand.

This thinking also influenced the response of Western governments in the context of the global financial crisis, when countries undertook coordinated, stimulative measures to support demand across the globe (IMF, WEO, 2012). Unfortunately, some countries had already been too heavily indebted before the crisis, while others overdid the stimulus or found themselves with a huge bill from financial sector losses.

European fiscal crises then triggered international insurance: the IMF and European countries provided conditional financial support to Greece, Cyprus, Ireland, Portugal and Spain. Since 2009, central banks have also assumed a significant 'insurance' role by purchasing government and private assets so as to underpin stability.

Benefits and Risks from Public Insurance

From a conceptual perspective, insurance is one of the great achievements of the market economies. Insurance allows us to pool risk, to save and to smooth consumption over time. This opens up opportunities to increase income, growth and welfare. The main challenges of effective and efficient insurance are moral hazard and adverse selection: insurance can breed carelessness and attract bad risks. In the private sector, the risk of insurer bankruptcy and competition amongst insurers facilitates the monitoring of both behaviour and risk, and encourages appropriate pricing.

From this perspective, the role of government in insurance is both essential and problematic. Some social risks are difficult to insure in private markets, particularly if certain conditions such as affordability or universal coverage are a precondition. Others (such as stabilising aggregate demand or protecting economic sectors) are also difficult (and undesirable) to insure privately.

In the public finance literature, public insurance and the redistributive role of government are closely intertwined. The government provides social insurance to reduce poverty, longevity or health risks. The mismatch between those who receive and those who pay – mostly via taxes, but also via the redistributional design of social insurance contributions – is deliberate. The goal is to equalise income and benefits in society in favour of the poor, the elderly, children, and so on. But is government likely to provide the right type of insurance in the most efficient and incentive-compatible manner? The challenges for the good functioning of insurance markets apply perhaps even more strongly to governments than to the private sector. The provision of insurance may follow political motives, rewarding groups of voters or special interests. Politicians can provide 'favours' by not pricing risks properly and by not monitoring or penalising risk-increasing behaviour on the part of the insured.

The result can be a classic 'common pool' problem of too much and too inefficient public insurance. Everybody would be better off if public insurance were more contained and effective; but, equally, everybody has an incentive to seek the maximum in benefits. As a result, pension benefits are higher than what the actuarial value of contributions would suggest. The bill is picked up by future generations via explicit or implicit public debt. Health insurance benefits are largely granted independently of the lifestyle choice adopted, even though this can make the insurance system more costly. Governments initiate spending programmes in economic downturns even though these are often late, difficult to reverse and may benefit others than those who are suffering. Then politicians 'forget' about any countervailing consolidation in upswings, again at the expense of future tax payers. Farmers, the solar industry and coal mines receive sectoral support.

There is more. When the 'rich and greedy' bankers got public support after the financial crisis, 'normal' citizens and taxpayers became disenchanted. With every insurance 'claim' by one group (be it in the financial, corporate or social sphere), several others feel unhappy and demand their 'fair' share. Spiralling public insurance and promises cost more and more money without making many people any happier.

The combined fiscal costs of all these 'insurance schemes' carries the risk of unsustainability. Public spending may become unsustainable because spending grows too fast. If taxes rise or productive spending is crowded out, the capacity to service growing spending and debt declines. However, budgetary spending may not be the main problem. Banks, and even countries, may need 'public insurance' of unprecedented magnitude as they are 'too big' or 'too important' to fail. Banks and states may even be 'too big to save', either individually or through the compound effect of the various insurance claims in a 'systemic' event. In that case, claims either have to be reneged on by governments or have to be monetised by 'printing' money. Public insurance will then clearly have 'gone too far' (Schuknecht, 2013).

Economists call a situation of budgetary over-commitment that cannot be financed other than via the central bank 'fiscal dominance'. When the origin of over-commitment is ever-growing social expenditure, one can refer to it as 'social dominance' (Schuknecht and Zemanek, 2020). When financial sector problems are so large that the government cannot handle them, it is called 'financial dominance'. At some point, fiscal, social and financial dominance result in instability and misery: the adverse distributional effects tend to be strongest for the poor and middle classes who lose their jobs, hold limited wealth and cannot easily 'run'.

History is full of episodes where the over-use of resources and common pool problems have led to economic inefficiencies and, in some cases, disaster. Many of these episodes have been related to natural resources and their over-use. The failure of the first Viking settlement of Greenland in the middle ages or the decline of the Easter Island culture are stark examples brilliantly described by the paleo-anthropologist Jared Diamond (2005/2011). The German hyperinflation of the early 1920s following the monetisation of wartime debt is an example closer to home for advanced country economists.

The relevance of this issue to public finances is well known and various crises episodes are witness to it. Looking forward, record debt, continuing financial risks and the growing fiscal burdens of population ageing point to the next round of crisis if nothing is done. The containment of public insurance may, therefore, be an existential issue for the economic stability and prosperity of the advanced economies.

Needless to say, it is not the economic and political role of public insurance per se that is questioned here, and not all public expenditure can be explained by insurance provision. All types of public insurance can confer very important benefits; it is the risk of over-use, inefficiency and possible self-destruction that is problematic.

7.3 The Continuous Growth of Social Expenditure

The social expenditure commitments of the future are contingent liabilities. If we want to understand the fiscal risks from social expenditure in the future we have to understand the past, because the underlying

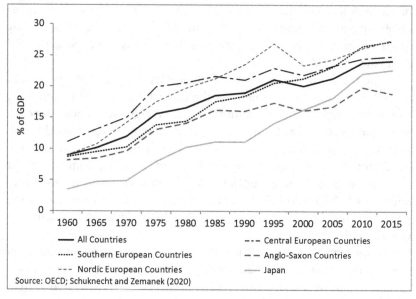

Figure 7.3 Social expenditure since 1960.

demography and policies have evolved over many decades. Recall that social expenditure, as defined by the OECD, includes pensions, health, long-term care, family and child benefits and unemployment spending as its main elements. Education is mostly not included (see Chapter 2).

Social expenditure has grown relentlessly over the past century at an average of 2% of GDP per decade from less than 1% of GDP in the late nineteenth century via 9% of GDP in 1960 to 24% of GDP in 2016. Figure 7.3 shows this trend for the past sixty years for different country groups.

The Central European countries had the biggest welfare state in the 1960s but they were only third in the second half of the 2010s. The Nordics spent most on social welfare as of the 1980s before the Southern European countries caught up with them. The Anglo-Saxon governments and Japan always had the smallest social expenditure ratios. Japan's starting point had been very low while spending was very dynamic throughout the period.

What drives social expenditure dynamics? Unsustainable dynamics could come from social spending being a superior good, so that people want to spend more the higher their incomes. Data for 1980 show that there was only very limited, positive correlation between social expenditure and per capita GDP at that time (as reflected in the very low R^2 value in Figure 7.4a). In the following thirty-five years, even this disappeared and

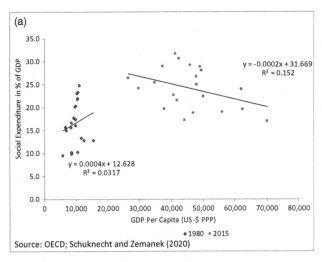

Figure 7.4a Social expenditure and per capita GDP.

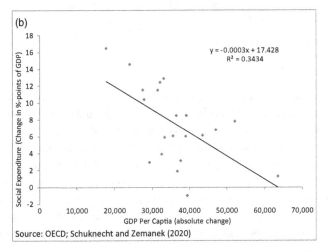

Figure 7.4b Change in social expenditure and per capita GDP, 1980–2015.

in 2015, if anything, the correlation had become slightly negative. In the meantime, the countries with the slowest income growth experienced the strongest increase in their social expenditure ratio (Figure 7.4b).

Several things may have happened. Lower growth could have implied more need for social spending, but can one argue on those grounds for a thirty-five-year period? There may have been 'catching-up' towards a common level of spending, but this argument is also refuted by the huge divergence of social spending ratios across countries. Finally, it is a possibility

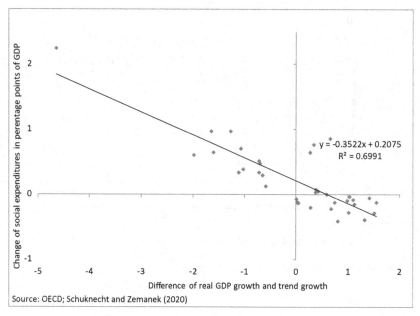

Figure 7.5 Social expenditure and the business cycle.

that higher social spending and spending growth may have undermined output growth (Fournier and Johansson, 2016). Be that as it may, the fact is that the 'superior good' hypothesis is not confirmed by the data.

Analysing the behaviour of social expenditure over the past four decades reveals some further interesting results. Figure 7.5 illustrates that social expenditure fluctuated with the economic cycle. It had gone up by about 1/3 of a per cent for each percentage point that real economic growth was below trend, and vice versa when growth was strong. This reflects the very important impact of 'automatic stabilisers' during both upswings and downturns.

More interesting is perhaps the finding that social expenditure increased by 0.2% of GDP on average in every single year, independent of upswing or downturn. This is suggested by the fact that the intercept of the regression line does not go through zero. The average annual increase seems small at first sight, but it corresponds to a 2% of GDP trend increase in social spending per decade. Over time, this has had huge effects.

A further explanation for the continuous increase in social spending can easily be dismissed. Unemployment related spending had a peak in the 1980s and 1990s, but by 2017 it had come down to the 1% average reported in the 1960s. Unemployment spending has therefore neither been an important contributor to social spending, nor has it been trending up.

Another possible explanation for the upward trend is political economy. Potrafke (2009) found social expenditure ratcheting up in the 1980s because left-wing governments raised spending while right-wing governments 'only' kept them constant; this holds even for Ronald Reagan and Margaret Thatcher. The 1990s were a more mixed period, with many reforms breaking the upward trend notably in the Nordics and Central European countries (Figure 7.3 and Chapter 5). After the financial crisis, social expenditure increased again under left-wing governments (Savage, 2018). Globalisation-related protection needs, however, did not significantly contribute to the upward trend in social spending (Ursprung, 2008).

The most obvious explanation for past social spending increases is population ageing, and again some simple data analysis is revealing (Figure 7.6). There is a strong correlation between ageing populations and rising social expenditure ratios. An increase of 1% in the old-age dependency ratio is accompanied by a 0.65% of GDP increase in social expenditure. Given that we expect further increases in the old-age dependency ratio by 20 percentage points or more in the next three decades, this already illustrates the gravity of the problem if past trends continue.

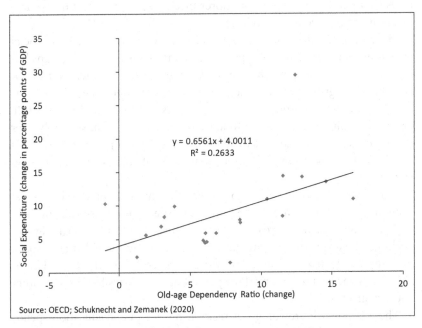

Figure 7.6 Social expenditure and population ageing, 1980–2015.

More sophisticated (econometric) analysis confirms the findings of the descriptive analysis (Schuknecht and Zemanek, 2020). There is an upward trend in social expenditure of roughly 0.2% of GDP per year and social spending rises and falls with the business cycle. Population ageing is a major determinant of social spending. Fortunately, the estimated impact is only 0.3% of GDP per percentage point of old-age dependency, but a 20% increase in thirty years would still mean 6% of GDP more spending – 2% per decade, just as in recent decades. The analysis also shows that higher deficits and debt only have a very limited constraining effect on social spending. This is rather concerning for the sustainability of public finances.

7.4 The Sustainability of Social Expenditure

Will social expenditure trends cause problems with fiscal stability and solvency in the future? The answer depends on whether past increases continue and how such increases are financed. Do spending dynamics slow down (good), do they result in higher deficits and debt (generally not good), do they crowd out other productive spending (also not good), do they cause cuts in unproductive spending (good) or do they induce higher taxes (not good if this results in poorer incentives to work and invest or if taxation limits have been reached).

The fact is that there have been big differences in the financing of social expenditure increases over the past forty years (Figure 7.7). All groups but Central Europe raised revenue, most strongly in the Southern European countries. All groups but Southern Europe experienced a decline in non-social spending. No group had higher deficits in 2017 than in 1980. Still, social expenditure as a share of total spending increased considerably over this period and exceeded 50% in all groups and 60% in Japan in 2016. This is a huge increase from little more than 33% of total spending in 1980 (Figure 7.8).

This does not yet allow us to answer the question of whether social spending crowds out other more productive spending. We start again with a descriptive analysis across country groups. There is a clear sign of declining investment and core administrative spending with rising social expenditure (Figures 7.9a and 7.9b; for details see Table 7.1). The relationship is strongest for Central Europe, but it is also visible for the other country groups.

There is no such crowding-out relationship for public education spending (Figure 7.9c). However, given growing school attendance and education

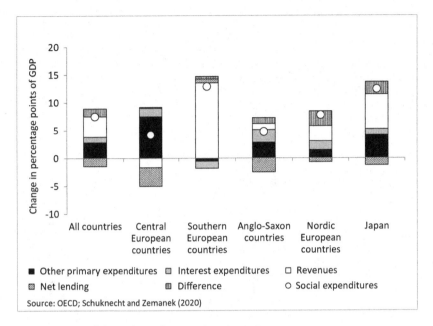

Figure 7.7 Social expenditure financing, 1980–2015.

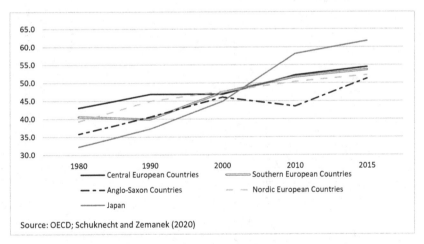

Figure 7.8 Growing share of social spending in total government spending.

requirements, the small increase from 4.8% to 5.4% of GDP over the 1980–2017 period may not have been enough compared to education 'needs' with proper prioritisation. Education performance is, however, not simply a matter of money, as Chapters 4 and 6 have shown.

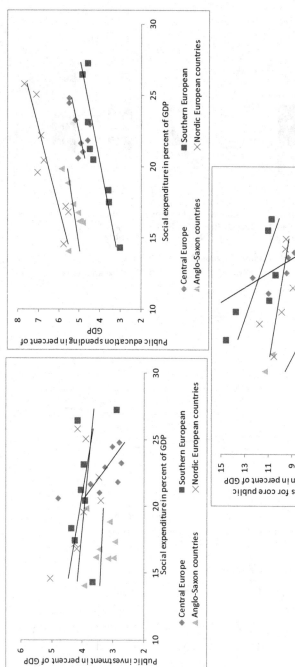

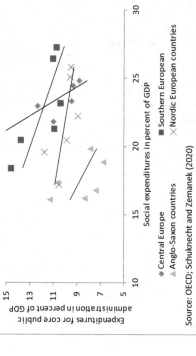

Figure 7.9 Social vs. other public expenditure.

Table 7.1 *Core public administration expenditure*

% of GDP	1995	2015	Change
			1995–2015
Australia	..	..	..
Austria	18.3	15.6	−2.6
Belgium	20.5	17.5	−3.0
Canada[1]	19.5	13.1	−6.4
Denmark	17.3	13.8	−3.5
Finland	19.9	16.0	−3.9
France	16.3	14.9	−1.4
Germany	20.8	11.7	−9.1
Greece	23.2	21.6	−1.6
Ireland	14.0	8.9	−5.1
Italy	21.8	15.0	−6.7
Japan[1]	9.9	9.5	−0.4
Netherlands	16.4	12.1	−4.3
New Zealand	..	..	..
Norway	15.0	12.4	−2.6
Portugal	16.4	16.0	−0.4
Spain	17.2	14.0	−3.2
Sweden	19.7	13.7	−6.0
Switzerland[1]	11.0	10.5	−0.5
UK	10.3	10.2	−0.1
US	13.1	10.8	−2.3
Average	16.9	13.5	−3.3

Source: OECD, Government expenditure by function database
1. Canada: 2006 instead of 2015; Japan: 2005 instead of 1995;
Switzerland: 2005 instead of 1995.

A more sophisticated technical analysis supports the claim of crowding out for public investment (Schuknecht and Zemanek, 2020). For core administrative spending, there seems to be a trend decline that is not linked to yearly social expenditure changes. For education, the evidence is inconclusive. Higher debt is correlated with less core public spending and higher deficits with less investment and less education. The relationship between social spending and public debt is, therefore, analysed next.

Social expenditure ratios and public debt are strongly correlated (Figure 7.10). This relationship is strongest for Southern Europe, where the doubling of social spending ratios since 1980 coincided with an increase in debt from 30% of GDP to well over 100% on average. The relationship is

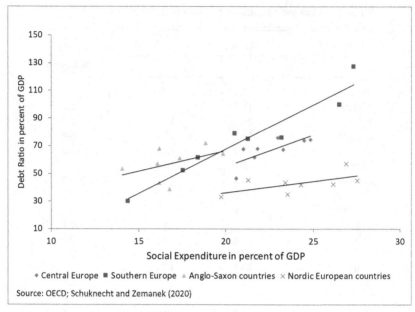

Figure 7.10 Social expenditure and public debt.
European Commission (2015).

weakest for the Nordic countries, but here declining spending also coincided with declining debt.

What will happen to social expenditure in the future? Evidence from the economic literature provide a tentative, though rather scary picture. When plotting the five-year spending average for the 1980–2015 period, the picture on the left of Figure 7.11 emerges. For 1980–2016, there is (again) a clear upward trend.

There are three approaches to looking at the future. The first approach is to simply extrapolate the trend. What held for forty and a hundred years may well also hold in the future. Average social expenditure would rise to 30% of GDP by 2050 – a figure that is only reached by one country (France) today. Countries with 'small' welfare states of less than 20% of GDP would be closer to 25% (a little above the 2016 average). The 'big spenders' would be around 35% of GDP.

There is a somewhat more positive scenario based on figures from the European Commission Ageing Report (European Commission, 2018), which suggests an increase by only ca. 3% of GDP for the European countries. This figure and the corresponding country estimates for 2050 are on the right of Figure 7.11. However, they may be somewhat too

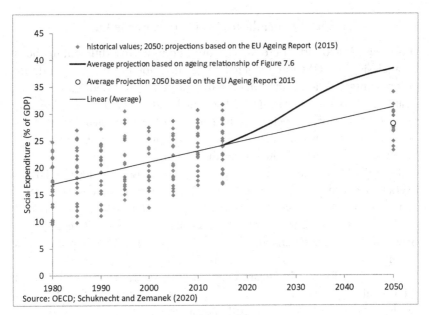

Figure 7.11 Social expenditure in the past and future.

favourable given some optimistic assumptions and the move to more generous policies in several countries in the late 2010s.

Finally, we can extrapolate the trends of recent decades by assuming
that the previous relationship between social spending and the old-age
dependency ratio continues into the future. A strong relationship would
imply a very significant, average increase of more than 10% of GDP. This is
reflected in the upper dotted line in Figure 7.11. The scenario may be too
pessimistic and the technical work already cited yielded a scenario near to a
broadly unchanged trend. But just as the European Commission scenario
may be optimistic, it is also worthwhile to 'stress-test' their projections
with a pessimistic one.

Technical analysis can also look at the implications of past developments
for the sustainability of social spending (Schuknecht and Zemanek, 2020).
The findings are not at all reassuring. Social expenditure rose almost 1.2
times (almost 20%) faster than GDP between 1980 and 2016. Social
expenditure rose 1.1 times as fast as total revenue and faster than primary
expenditure. The differences in growth rates also suggests that non-social
spending has been crowded out, as we have argued, and population ageing
is the main driver of social spending. A continuation of past behaviour
would thus clearly be unsustainable.

7.5 Social Expenditure Projections by the OECD

It is interesting to further cross-check our findings across different methods of analysis. The OECD conducted projections for the three expenditure components that are most relevant for future social spending: pensions, health and long-term care (see also OECD, 2017a, 2017b, 2017c). The projections compare expenditure in 2015 with that projected for 2050 (or 2060) based on prevailing policies and demographic projections. The results are quite consistent with our earlier discussion.

The OECD expected pension expenditure to increase by 1% of GDP on average between 2015 and 2050 (Table 7.2). However, there was a significant variance across countries: the figures for Ireland, Switzerland and South Korea showed the strongest increase. For France, Greece, Italy, Sweden, Australia, Japan and the United States the OECD projected a decline in their pension spending in the next three decades. By 2050, public pension spending would absorb between 4% (Australia) and near 15% of GDP (Italy, Austria, Greece). The huge variance reflects different benefit levels and different roles for private pensions.

There are, however, a number of caveats to these figures. First, in a few countries, pension benefits would fall to very low levels if these projections materialised. The question is then whether pension savings are politically realistic and sustainable. As mentioned earlier, a few countries announced reversals of parts of their earlier reforms so that higher expenditure paths are likely. There is therefore considerable political risk in the projections.

In addition, demographic projections have been notoriously poor in recent decades. Given shrinking working populations everywhere in the advanced economies and emerging countries, migration flows may improve the demographic outlook in some countries and worsen it in others. A vicious circle of emigration worsening the sustainability of pensions, thereby stoking further emigration, is possible.

Social expenditure projections see the greatest spending increase in public health (Table 7.3). But since health is particularly difficult to predict, there are two scenarios with more cost pressures and more cost containment. We do not know whether future longevity gains will mean longer lives in sickness or longer lives in good health. And we do not know whether we will realise the huge potential for expenditure savings from an improved organisation and digitalisation of the health sector and better incentives that are possible.

The cost containment scenario is relatively benign and public expenditure would 'only' increase by 1% of GDP on average in the advanced

Table 7.2 *Social expenditure projections for pensions*

% of GDP

	2015	2050	Change
Euro area			
Austria	13.4	14.6	1.2
Belgium	10.2	12.9	2.7
Finland	11.1	12.8	1.7
France	13.8	12.8	−1.0
Germany	10.1	12.5	2.4
Greece	16.2	14.4	−1.8
Ireland	4.9	10.0	5.1
Italy	16.3	14.8	−1.5
Netherlands	5.4	8.1	2.7
Portugal	14.0	14.4	0.4
Spain	11.4	12.3	0.9
Other Europe			
Denmark	8.0	7.5	−0.5
Sweden	7.7	7.2	−0.5
Switzerland	6.4	10.7	4.3
UK	6.1	8.1	2.0
Other advanced economies			
Australia	4.3	4.0	−0.3
Canada	4.6	6.9	2.3
Japan	10.2	9.5	−0.7
South Korea	2.6	6.3	3.7
New Zealand	5.1	7.2	2.1
Singapore	..	..	0.0
US	6.9	5.9	−1.0
Average[1]	9.3	10.3	1.0

Source: OECD
1. Unweighted, excluding Singapore and South Korea.

countries (Table 7.3). A number of countries would report spending increases around 3% as a maximum. Denmark, Sweden, Japan and notably the United States would be able to lower public spending on health. Spending levels would be rather homogenous, ranging from 7% to 9.3% of GDP.

The cost pressure scenario is less benign, as average spending would rise by almost 5% of GDP. Only the United States would expect a marginal decline under this scenario. Public health spending would exceed 10% of GDP in all countries and over 13% in France, German and the United States, a huge additional burden on public budgets.

Table 7.3 *Social expenditure projections for health*

	Average 2015	2060, cost pressure	2060, cost containment	Change Cost pressure	Change Cost containment
Euro area					
Austria	7.7	12.9	9.1	5.2	1.4
Belgium	7.9	11.6	7.7	3.7	−0.2
Finland	7.3	11.2	7.3	3.9	0.0
France	8.8	13.5	9.6	4.7	0.8
Germany	9.3	13.5	9.6	4.2	0.3
Greece	4.8	11.8	7.9	7.0	3.1
Ireland	5.3	11.9	8.0	6.6	2.7
Italy	6.7	12.6	8.7	5.9	2.0
Netherlands	8.4	12.7	8.8	4.3	0.4
Portugal	5.9	13.0	9.1	7.1	3.2
Spain	6.5	12.3	8.5	5.8	2.0
Other Europe					
Denmark	8.6	12.2	8.3	3.6	−0.3
Sweden	9.2	12.4	8.6	3.2	−0.6
Switzerland	7.5	12.2	8.3	4.7	0.8
UK	7.8	12.4	8.5	4.6	0.7
Other advanced economies					
Australia	6.4	12.0	8.1	5.6	1.7
Canada	7.3	12.2	8.3	4.9	1.0
Japan	9.1	12.5	8.6	3.4	−0.5
South Korea	4.2	10.9	7.0	6.7	2.8
New Zealand	7.4	12.7	8.8	5.3	1.4
Singapore	..	..	..	..	..
US	13.8	13.2	9.3	−0.6	−4.5
Average[1]	7.8	12.4	8.6	4.7	0.8

Source: OECD
1. Unweighted, excluding Singapore and South Korea.

Finally, there is long-term care spending, for which the same holds as for health. We have little experience and little foresight how ageing, income growth and changing societies will affect long-term care spending. Will more people reach the stage of Alzheimer's, one of the most expensive diseases, or will we find a cure for it, so that people need less care? Will we be able to develop 'Robocare' or will we reject this?

The OECD cost containment scenario points to virtually no change in long-term care costs (+0.2% of GDP) (Table 7.4). Countries such as Finland, Sweden and Japan would experience a significant decline. Countries

Table 7.4 *Social expenditure projections for long-term care*

	2015	2060, cost pressure	2060, cost containment	Change Cost pressure	Change Cost containment
Euro area					
Austria	..	2.2	1.8	2.2	1.8
Belgium	2.3	3.0	2.5	0.7	0.2
Finland	2.2	1.8	1.3	−0.4	−0.9
France	1.7	2.1	1.7	0.4	0.0
Germany	1.3	2.1	1.6	0.8	0.3
Greece	0.5	1.9	1.5	1.4	1.0
Ireland	1.4	1.3	1.2	−0.1	−0.2
Italy	0.7	1.9	1.5	1.2	0.8
Netherlands	3.7	3.7	3.1	0.0	−0.6
Portugal	0.5	1.4	0.9	0.9	0.4
Spain	0.8	2.0	1.6	1.2	0.8
Other Europe					
Denmark	2.5	3.3	2.8	0.8	0.3
Sweden	3.2	1.6	1.1	−1.6	−2.1
Switzerland	1.7	2.5	1.9	0.8	0.2
UK	1.5	1.8	1.4	0.3	−0.1
Other advanced economies					
Australia	1.2	1.4	0.8	0.2	−0.4
Canada	1.2	2.5	1.9	1.3	0.7
Japan	2.0	2.0	1.4	0.0	−0.6
South Korea	0.8	2.3	1.6	1.5	0.8
New Zealand	..	2.6	2.0	2.6	2.0
Singapore	..	..	..	..	..
US	0.5	1.3	1.0	0.8	0.5
Average[1]	1.6	2.1	1.7	0.7	0.2

Source: OECD
1. Unweighted, excluding Singapore and South Korea.

would be broadly in the 1–3% range by 2060. The cost pressure scenario also looks reasonably contained, with an average increase of 0.7% of GDP. But this is an almost 50% rise over the current level of 1.6% of GDP. The Netherlands had the highest spending ratio in 2015 and will continue to do so in 2060, at 3.7% of GDP.

Taking the impact of population ageing on all three components together, we arrive at a rather significant increase of 2% of GDP in the cost containment scenario and 6.4% if spending pressures materialise. An intermediate scenario would imply 4.2% of GDP in additional expenditure.

Expenditure increases for Ireland, South Korea and New Zealand would
be above 10% of GDP in the pressure scenario. In any case, and as stated,
raising revenue by 2–6% of GDP will not be easy, given that taxes are
already very high in most advanced countries.

Long-Term Projections under Different Assumptions and Policy Scenarios

It is in the nature of long-term projections to be very sensitive to assumptions and policy changes, as they have a long time to feed through the
system. This is particularly true for social expenditure and therefore all our
previous discussions should perhaps be taken with a large grain of salt.

There are a number of variables determining sustainability which policymakers can influence, or which may change due to outside forces. These
include the length of working lives and thus the number of years workers
contribute to earn their pension rights or the age at which they retire.
Fertility is important, particularly in pay-as-you-go systems, because
today's children pay tomorrow's pensions. The increase in life expectancy
is another key variable – the longer people live in retirement the higher the
cost increase if nothing else changes. Unemployment also makes a significant difference, while productivity does not, if pensions are closely linked
to wages.

The impact of different assumptions on these variables is in fact huge
over time. The German sustainability report (German Federal Ministry of
Finance, 2016) illustrates this very clearly (Figure 7.12). Under favourable
assumptions (and no change in revenue and other policies), Germany did

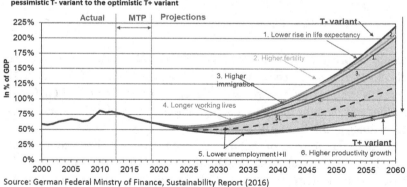

Source: German Federal Minstry of Finance, Sustainability Report (2016)

Figure 7.12 Sustainability of the German pension system under different assumptions.

not have any sustainability problem related to social spending. But with less favourable assumptions, the report predicted an explosion of debt towards the middle of the twenty-first century.

7.6 Conclusions

The strong social expenditure dynamics of the past coupled with population ageing constitute a major risk for the sustainability of public finances. Social expenditure has been growing at a rate of 2% of GDP per decade in the past forty and even a hundred years, and it might well continue to do so in the future.

There are also indications that social expenditure crowds out productive spending. This applies especially to investment but potentially also core administrative spending. Social expenditure is also strongly correlated with rising debt. We face these risks from rising social expenditure despite varying effects on income distribution and no correlation with trust, as shown in the Introduction.

The biggest risks arise from higher health expenditure. The figures for pensions and long-term care look somewhat less concerning in isolation, but every increase needs to be financed. The compound effects from rising expenditure in all three categories may be substantial even in an optimistic scenario given that expenditure and revenue are already very high and further revenue potential is virtually exhausted in many countries (Akgun et al., 2017).

The extrapolation of past trends or even more pessimistic dynamics would bring social expenditure to above 30% of GDP on average by the middle of the century. This is dangerous territory: it could provoke further crowding out of productive spending and a stoking of unsustainable debt. Such a scenario could be termed 'social dominance' and it could well lead to 'fiscal dominance', compromising macroeconomic and (ironically also) social stability.

The policy levers to deal with social spending-related fiscal risks are well known and we will return to them in more detail in Chapter 10. Structural reforms would enhance the growth and employment potential of economies and, thus, the sustainability of social security. Even fertility is not completely exogenous and could be boosted by appropriate policies. More can be said on health and long-term care: the fiscal risks are potentially huge, but we have all the tools to contain them.

Social spending is part of the growing 'insurance role' of government. This role has gone way beyond basic safety nets for the old, the unemployed and the sick. Today, governments are expected to insure the whole economy by stabilising aggregate demand, they are insuring other governments via international safety nets and they have ventured deeply into insuring the financial system. This latter risk is perhaps the most dangerous and difficult to measure and manage. Chapters 8 and 9 discuss the complicated domain of fiscal–financial risks and vulnerabilities.

8

Fiscal–Financial Risks 1

Interest Rate, Asset Markets and Real Economy Channels

The typical citizen would in political matters tend to yield to extra-rational or irrational prejudice and impulse . . . He will relax his usual moral standards as well and occasionally give in to dark urges which the conditions of private life help him to repress.

Joseph Schumpeter

Stable money and solid public finances are indispensable requisites for a free society.

Otmar Issing

Highlights

Financial sector developments pose the second important fiscal risk for the coming years and decades. It is important to both understand and map these risks, and this is the task of this chapter and Chapter 9.

Rising financing costs affect debt service expenditure, especially for countries with high debt and short-term financing. Asset price movements can constitute further major fiscal risks in a downturn. Adverse financial sector developments and negative confidence effects also burden public expenditure and finances via the real economy, and guarantees that fall due in 'bad' times can exacerbate this effect.

Debt has ratcheted up over consecutive economic and financial cycles in the past forty years, an effect particularly strong during the global financial crisis due to fiscal–financial linkages (Figure 8.1). Simulations show that the situation of several advanced countries is critical, given their lack of fiscal buffers for another big crisis.

8.1 A Fiscal–Financial Risk Map

In the global financial crisis that started in 2007, the advanced country governments experienced what had previously only occurred in developing

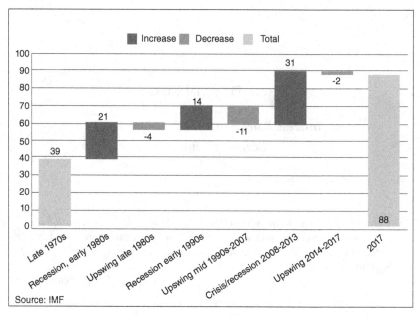

Figure 8.1 Debt dynamics since the late 1970s, % of GDP, advanced countries.

and emerging economies: huge bank bailout costs, abrupt and major increases in financing costs of government and even 'sudden stops' in market access. Public expenditure exploded and fiscal deficits in some cases worsened by over 10% of GDP in two or three years. Public debt ratios rose by 50% or even 100% of GDP.

These developments reflect linkages between public finances and financial developments. However, they are only the 'visible' parts of the fiscal–financial vulnerabilities 'iceberg' against which several governments have been shipwrecked. Apart from population ageing, these are the biggest challenges and risk for government finances looking forward.

So far, there is no systematic and comprehensive mapping and analysis of the transmission channels from the financial to the fiscal sphere and public expenditure. There are a number of studies on the fiscal costs of financial crisis. The IMF Autumn Fiscal Monitor (IMF, 2018) provides the most far-reaching framework for some of the channels as part of their government balance sheet assessment. The IMF Global Financial Stability Result (GFSR) (2018, 2019) discusses financial sector risks, but does not make the link to fiscal balances. Borio, Lombardi and Zampoli (2016), Borio et al. (2015) and his co-authors, the Bank of International Settlement

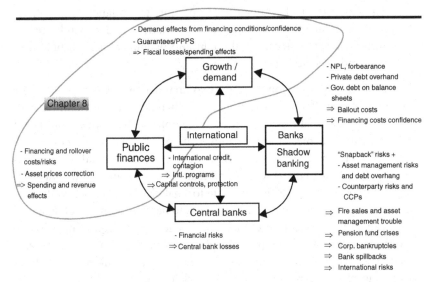

Figure 8.2 Fiscal–financial risk map.

(BIS, various issues) Eschenbach and Schuknecht (2004) and Morris and Schuknecht (2007) analysed some of the links between financial and fiscal vulnerabilities in an in-depth fashion. This and Chapter 9 present a fiscal–financial risk map (Schuknecht, 2019) and discuss what we know and do not know about the channels of transmission between the financial sector and public finances and prospective vulnerabilities (Figure 8.2).

Figure 8.2 shows five broad channels:

1. Fiscal variables are linked directly to financial developments via interest expenditure on public debt. There are also fiscal effects via asset markets and asset prices.

2. Financing conditions and financial sector effects on confidence affect fiscal variables via demand and growth. The financial environment also influences how far government guarantees fall due.

3. Financial losses in the banking and 'shadow' banking sectors can influence fiscal variables through the 'insurance' or 'bailout' channel. Here, we need to look beyond 'classic' bank bailouts and also focus on the risks in non-bank financing.

4. Central banks affect fiscal variables via the impact of monetary policies and financing conditions on the real economy. However, any financial losses from their much extended investment portfolios could also lead to fiscal costs.

5. The international transmission of foreign financial and fiscal
   problems can affect national public finances and expenditure via
   confidence, via international credit and bailouts and via capital flow
   and trade restrictions.

This chapter will focus on the first two channels and Chapter 9 on the
remaining three. Before starting, it is worth linking these channels with
the typology of fiscal risks presented in Chapter 7: budgetary, contingent
and implicit risks; measurable or unmeasurable; known or unknown.

Fiscal–financial risks are quite different from social expenditure risks as
regards their legal status and their measurability. We argued in Chapter 7
that most social spending risks are due to legal claims. They are contingent
on population ageing – and ageing is bound to happen. Some fiscal–financial
risks can also be contingent, such as changes in the financing costs of
government debt and the impact of higher interest rates. These risks are also
easily measurable. Much of the risk, however, such as bank recapitalisation
costs, is implicit and not based on a legal claim, and is hard to predict.

Most social spending risks are known, but this is less the case in the
financial sphere. Before 2009, the transmission of a 'housing bubble' to
public finances via the subprime and securities defaults burdening banks
was unknown, although we could have had our suspicions if we had thought
hard enough. We do not know where the next crisis will hit and we cannot
attach a probable price tag to it. But we should inform our 'guesses' as well
as possible.

Our risk map and analysis have three objectives. First, they should
provide a broad analytical and empirical overview. Second, they should
help us to focus on the risks of the future rather than on re-winning the
wars of the past. Third, they should build the case for strengthening resilience in both the financial and fiscal sphere.

8.2 Risks from Rising Financing Costs of Government

Financing Deficits and Debt

The first and most obvious channel by which financial developments can
affect public finances and expenditure is the cost of servicing the public
debt. The mechanism is simple. An increase in the interest rate affects
interest expenditure on public debt. The magnitude and timing of this
effect depend on the level of debt, on the profile of debt and the amount
that needs refinancing, and the deficit (which requires new financing).

Over time, a country with public debt of 100% of GDP will have to pay 1% of GDP more on debt service when interest rates rise by 1%. This is a huge amount given that total public investment in advanced countries is only about 3% of GDP on average. Of course, the opposite holds when interest rates come down. This effect, however, feeds through only over time. If the maturity structure of public debt is long and the deficit is not huge, the effect of changing financing costs is small. The effect is much larger if governments have issued mainly short-term debt and run large deficits.

On average, the advanced countries' financing needs per year (e.g. in 2018) were a little over 10% of GDP in the advanced countries, although on a weighted basis this share is higher at around 17% of GDP (Table 8.1, see also OECD, 2019d). The increasing maturity of the existing debt stock and relatively moderate deficits in most countries gradually brought down financing needs after 2010.

A country with a public debt of 100% of GDP and a 10% annual financing need would have to pay 0.1% more for debt service after one year and 0.2% after two years for each per cent interest rate increase. Even though it looks small, it is quite a significant amount of money if it requires financing via cuts in other programmes or tax increases.

For some countries, this effect is much greater. The governments of Belgium, Italy and the United States needed to finance roughly 20% of GDP in 2018 and for Japan this figure was over 40% of GDP. This implies that the one-year effect of 1% higher interest rates is 0.2% or even 0.4% per year. Or, putting it differently, it would take 2.5 years and 2% higher interest rates for Italy, Belgium and the United States to spend 1% more of GDP on debt service.

Such an increase is historically not a rare event. The US Federal Reserve raised rates by 2% between 2015 and the autumn of 2018. These calculations also do not take into account the fact that a number of countries have taken on board more short-term refinancing risk via central bank asset purchases (for more detail, see Chapter 9).

In the past two decades, most countries experienced important declines in the interest payments on government debt. Between 2000 and 2017, the decline averaged 1.7% of GDP. This is equivalent to more than half the average investment expenditure. On a cumulative basis, interest savings are quite impressive.

Interest savings, however, have been uneven. The countries that benefitted most were high-debt countries, such as Italy, and 'safe haven' countries, such as Germany and the United States. For Germany, the ten-year rate at

Table 8.1 *Gross financing needs, 2018*

% of GDP	Maturing debt	Deficit	Total financing need
Euro area			
Austria	5.9	0.3	6.2
Belgium	17.0	1.3	18.3
Finland	6.3	1.4	7.7
France	10.4	2.4	12.8
Germany	5.0	−1.5	3.5
Greece	..	..	..
Ireland	6.6	0.2	6.8
Italy	20.6	1.6	22.2
Netherlands	7.4	−0.6	6.8
Portugal	12.7	1.0	13.7
Spain	15.9	2.5	18.4
Other Europe			
Denmark	4.0	0.8	4.8
Sweden	4.1	−1.1	3.0
Switzerland	2.1	−0.4	1.7
UK	6.7	1.8	8.5
Other advanced economies			
Australia	1.6	1.7	3.3
Canada	8.5	0.8	9.3
Japan	37.2	3.4	40.6
South Korea	2.6	−2.0	0.6
New Zealand	1.4	−1.1	0.3
Singapore	..	..	..
US	18.7	5.3	24.0
Average[1]	10.1	1.0	11.2

Source: IMF Fiscal Monitor (Oct. 2018)
1. Unweighted, excluding Singapore and South Korea.

times was negative; the thirty-year rate came down from around 4% in 2007–2010 to less than 1% in mid-2016 before rising to slightly over 1% in 2018 and falling again.

The situation of some euro crisis countries was much more volatile. Until the eruption of the Greece crisis in 2009, the interest rates of all euro area debt evolved in tandem with those of Germany. Markets only charged a small mark up for higher deficits and debt (Bernoth, von Hagen and Schuknecht, 2012). This changed in the course of 2010 when the 'safe' countries rates started to come down and the spreads with highly indebted countries started to rise. In the global financial crisis, in a very short time

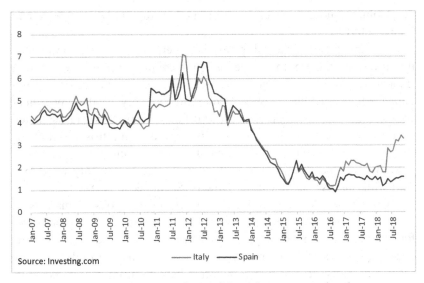

Source: Investing.com

Figure 8.3 Interest rates, ten-year Italian and Spanish government bonds.

span, debt-related spreads increased by a factor of 12 (Schuknecht, von Hagen and Wolswijk, 2011).

The risk or 'fragility' premium in European crisis countries reached several per cent in 2011–2012 (Figure 8.3). Ten-year rates in Spain and Italy, for example, jumped several per cent within a few months. They reached 6–7% before coming down after the summer of 2012 when reforms kicked in and the ECB reassured markets. Interest savings from lower interest rates were thus ultimately also very significant for these countries. The experiences of Greece and Cyprus were even more severe and rates on existing debt moved well into double-digit territory during their financial crisis.

Interest Risks and Market Turbulence

The fiscal risks from higher financing costs are particularly high and hard to predict in times of more general turbulence, such as during the global financial crisis. Markets (that is banks, investors, the public, . . .) may lose confidence in the government's ability to repay their debt, even if similar data and policy signals had invoked little reaction before. Interest rates will then increase very strongly and the weakest countries may lose access to financing altogether. This phenomenon is well known in emerging and developing economies under the term 'sudden stop' (Calvo, Izquierdo and Mejia, 2004).

Until the global financial crisis, however, there was no awareness that investors might not perceive industrial country debt as 'safe' and that 'sudden stops' could, therefore affect the advanced countries. It had not happened for decades – well beyond the memory of the investment community. The development of global financial markets had facilitated government debt financing over past decades. But, in retrospect, it seems also logical that public debt was safe only 'up to a point' and this 'point' is unknown: it depends on factors such as market size and history and it may shift with the 'risk sentiment' in markets (Schuknecht, 2018).

There are several reasons for sudden strong reactions of markets to rising debt, and we mention only three here. First, there are incentives for investors to follow their peers, the 'herd', so that one does not experience high losses while everybody else makes profits. Second, there are regulatory 'cliffs' beyond which investors have to disinvest. For example, a stock or a (government) bond that loses its investment grade rating is 'suddenly' no longer eligible for certain investment portfolios and central bank liquidity provision. Investors then need to sell while few buyers are around (fire sales of assets).

Third, new developments that were not on the 'financial radar' may also play a role. When markets 'unexpectedly' predicted much higher spending for bank bailouts in Spain in 2010–2011 and the public budget also developed less favourably than expected, confidence in government finances tanked. This contributed to much higher interest rates on Spanish bonds even when debt was (still) relatively low because market participants estimated the costs of the financial crisis to be very high and did not know how high they might be.

What are the risks in the future? Given the average G7 debt of 120% of GDP, a 1% average rate rise will over time raise interest spending by over 1% in this group. If rates rise by more, the risks can quickly become quite relevant. Moreover, it is important to know which will be the 'fragile' countries of the future that will potentially have to pay high and volatile risk premia on their debt service.

Fiscal risks from financing costs depend very much on the perceptions of political and economic risk. In spring 2018, a new Italian government promised more expansionary policies despite very high public debt. Subsequently, rates and risk premia increased significantly (again, see Figure 8.3). Ten-year rates hovered around 2% until spring 2018 before increasing by 1% to 1.5% (100–150 basis points in 'market speak'). Interest payments thus rose by 0.2–03% of GDP within a year. It is also noteworthy that Spain, which did not announce a change in the course of its fiscal policies and whose debt was not quite as high, did not have to pay higher risk premia.

8.3 Risks from Asset Prices and Guarantees

Fiscal Risks from Asset Markets and Boom–Bust Cycles

Fiscal risks can arise from the interaction between asset prices and fiscal variables and the transmission channel is 3-fold. First, and most prominently, rising asset prices can affect tax revenue. Higher house and equity prices make people feel wealthier; they can save less or realise some of their capital gains and increase their consumption. With rising consumption, indirect taxes such as VAT or sales taxes increase. Rising asset prices can also translate into higher personal and corporate income taxes through the taxation of capital gains. Transaction tax revenue on stocks or equity tend to increase with rising asset prices (Eschenbach and Schuknecht, 2004).

The impact of such revenue effects can be very significant, depending on the tax system and the magnitude of the asset price changes. Literature from the mid-2000s estimated such effects to be about 0.5% of GDP for every 10% change in equity and real estate prices for a number of European countries (Table 8.2 and Morris and Schuknecht, 2007). Hence, a 50% increase in asset prices can imply a change in revenue by 2% of GDP and more. Moreover, the effect is asymmetric for large changes in asset prices, with downturns leading to negative effects that are stronger than the corresponding improvement in an upturn (Eschenbach and Schuknecht, 2004).

The second effect of asset price increases on fiscal balances is on the expenditure side, and it is indirect. In the asset price booms of the early 2000s, governments experienced unexpected revenue windfalls as budgetary forecasting methods were not attuned to take into account the effect of asset price changes. As booms tended to last for a significant period, these windfalls occurred persistently for many years. Asset price booms also tended to coincide with prolonged periods of above-trend growth.

As a result, governments were tempted into raising both their projection of potential growth and their spending dynamics. When the boom ended, spending dynamics at first remained unchanged while growth and revenue dynamics reversed, leaving the countries with a higher expenditure and deficit ratio (Jaeger and Schuknecht, 2007). We illustrated this in Figure 1.4,

Table 8.2 *Asset price-related budget sensitivities, 1982–2005*

	Total[1]
Belgium	0.75
Finland	0.62
France	0.33
Germany	0.57
Ireland	0.62
Italy	0.45
Netherlands	0.55
Spain	0.79
Weighted average	0.53
Euro area aggregate	0.28

Source: Morris and Schuknecht (2007)
1. Total refers to the sum of the effect from a 10% stock and real estate price change on the budget balance via direct taxes on corporations/households, indirect taxes and transaction taxes.

where the 'boom' countries of Europe had raised expenditure dynamics well beyond sustainable levels in the early 2000s.

Third, a number of countries experienced a financial crisis when asset price booms reversed. In fact, this had already been true for some advanced countries, like the Nordics, in the 1980s and 1990s. However, the effects of the global financial crisis were often much stronger. We will discuss this in more depth in Chapter 9 when we look at the bank-budget transmission channel.

A significant amount of existing analysis concerned the boom–bust episodes of the 1980s and 1990s. The United Kingdom and Sweden experienced asset price booms in the late 1980s, followed by busts in the early 1990s (Table 8.3). In the 'boom' period, asset price effects from stock and real estate markets led to extra revenue of 2% and 3% of GDP, respectively, in the two countries. Strong growth further improved fiscal accounts via automatic stabilisers by a further 3% and 5% of GDP. Sweden also allowed public expenditure to increase rapidly during the boom.

The downturn came with a fiscal vengeance. The deficit in the United Kingdom increased by 8.9% of GDP and in Sweden by a staggering 16.8% in just three years. The effect from reversing asset prices was 3% and 6% of GDP as the revenue ratio declined in both countries. Falling real estate prices in particular had negative effects as they affected consumption and

Table 8.3 *Decomposition of the change in deficit, 1985–1993, United Kingdom and Sweden*

% of GDP	United Kingdom		Sweden	
Base year 1984	1985–1989	1990–1993	1985–1989	1990–1993
Total cumulative change in deficit	4.9	−8.9	7.9	−16.8
Expenditure		4.3		10.2
Revenue		−3.1		−4.4
Decompositon				
Non-asset price effect	2.9	−6	4.9	−8.2
Asset price effect	2	−2.9	3	−6.1
Thereof: stock price changes	1.8	0.8	2.4	−1.5
Real estate price changes	0.3	−3.7	0.6	−4.6

Source: Eschenbach and Schuknecht (2004)

income taxes through wealth effects, capital losses and a collapsing market. The expenditure ratio increased strongly as GDP shrank while expenditure continued to grow even more strongly.

The expenditure ratio rose by 4.3% of GDP in the case of the United Kingdom. Sweden experienced an increase in its expenditure ratio by 10.2% of GDP. The resulting total expenditure ratio of 68% of GDP in 1993 is probably the highest historic record ever for a market economy. Public debt exploded and the Swedish government had to pay large risk premia on its foreign currency debt.

The experience of some European countries during the global financial crisis was comparable. In Ireland, Spain and the United Kingdom, for example, expenditure ratios increased hugely while revenue ratios fell (Table 8.4) In Spain, the revenue ratio declined by a staggering 6% of GDP between 2007 and 2009 although policy-induced tax cuts were limited. This is indicative of the reversal of the very large revenue windfalls from the boom years. France, Germany and Italy, who had not experienced major asset price booms, saw their expenditure ratios rise as well. However, their revenue ratios did not fall.

The fiscal effects on revenue and expenditure from boom–bust episodes in asset markets are thus very significant. On the positive side, the crisis countries reformed their states and reduced public expenditure significantly, as we saw in Chapter 5. Boom–bust episodes can therefore have a positive long-term effect if the 'crisis is not wasted'.

Table 8.4 *Post-crisis expenditure and revenue developments, 2007–2009*

Change, % of GDP	Expenditure	Revenue
Ireland	11.1	−2.8
Spain	7.0	−6.1
UK	6.4	−1.2
France	4.6	−0.1
Germany	4.8	1.3
Italy	4.4	0.6

Source: OECD

Implications for the Future

What does this mean for the future fiscal risks from asset price booms and busts? In the late 2010s , there were some renewed signs of overheating in asset markets. However, the dynamics were weaker than before the global financial crisis, even though they often started from a higher level. Moreover, there was significant divergence across countries, so that the pattern was less clear than it had been in the early 2000s.

Comparing the dynamics of equity and real estate prices before the global crisis and in the late 2010s reveals some interesting findings (Table 8.5). Equity prices increased much faster than GDP between 1995 and 2007. Starting from 100 in 1995, equity prices averaged 340 in 2007 while GDP had only increased to 165 in the euro area and to 190 in the United States.

By contrast, the average aggregate increase in stock prices between 2007 and 2017 was only another 10% (to 367) with a deep intermittent slump by about 33%. A number of countries posted very strong increases after 2007. In Denmark, Sweden, Switzerland and the United States, equity indices stood 40–70% above their 2007 level.

The picture is similar for real estate prices. Property prices had also increased much faster than GDP and incomes between 1995 and 2007 on average. The period saw very dynamic property prices in the United Kingdom, Ireland and Spain (Table 8.6). Recall that it was these countries that also experienced the strongest asset price effects on fiscal variables. Many other countries including the United States also posted strong increases. Germany and Japan, by contrast, experienced no boom at all.

After 2007, many markets corrected, but by no means as much as they had increased in the boom, and corrections were steepest in Ireland and Spain. By 2010, property prices had fallen by almost 20% relative to GDP and continued to adjust in some countries. Real estate prices started to

Table 8.5 *Equity prices, 1995–2017*

	1995	2007	2010	2017	Change (%) 2007–2017
Euro area					
Austria	..	..	..	..	..
Belgium	100	354	215	338	−5
Finland	100	581	361	494	−15
France	100	326	216	321	−1
Germany	100	257	187	322	25
Greece	..	..	..	..	..
Ireland	100	433	145	340	−22
Italy	100	322	170	199	−38
Netherlands	100	277	180	272	−2
Portugal	..	..	..	..	..
Spain	100	551	364	349	−37
Other Europe					
Denmark	100	480	362	832	73
Sweden	100	413	346	603	46
Switzerland	100	393	308	544	38
UK	100	201	171	245	22
Other advanced economies					
Australia	100	305	228	285	−7
Canada	100	308	273	351	14
Japan	100	120	64	118	−2
South Korea	100	183	188	247	35
New Zealand	100	158	102	180	14
Singapore	..	..	..	..	..
US	100	273	210	452	66
Average[1]	100	338	229	367	10
Nominal GDP index:					
Euro area	100	165	171	199	21
US	100	190	198	255	35

Source: BIS
1. Unweighted, excluding South Korea and Singapore.

increase again after 2013 on the back of recovering economies and loose monetary policies.

In Germany and Switzerland, property prices took off and increased by 35–38% in the seven years to 2017. Sweden, Australia, Canada and New Zealand experienced an even stronger increase over this period. Property prices in 2017 were more than four times as high as in 1995 in Sweden, Australia and New Zealand. However, in the shadow of these 'outliers',

Table 8.6 *Residential property prices, 1995–2017*

	1995	2007	2010	2017	Change (%) 2007–2017
Euro area					
Austria	..	..	..	..	..
Belgium	100	217	233	269	24
Finland	100	230	247	269	17
France	100	242	240	250	3
Germany	100	92	95	125	35
Greece	..	..	..	..	..
Ireland	100	439	286	321	27
Italy	100	180	182	153	−15
Netherlands	100	274	263	267	−3
Portugal	..	..	..	..	..
Spain	100	323	293	242	−25
Other Europe					
Denmark	100	294	252	304	4
Sweden	100	264	297	465	76
Switzerland	100	114	131	158	38
UK	100	325	299	389	19
Other advanced economies					
Australia	100	260	315	445	71
Canada	100	214	229	357	67
Japan	100	65	62	68	6
South Korea	100	148	158	185	26
New Zealand	100	257	247	409	59
Singapore	..	..	..	..	..
US	100	227	172	241	6
Average[1]	100	236	226	278	21

Source: BIS
1. Average unweighted, excluding South Korea and Singapore.

many markets were dynamic and highly valued again in the late 2010s, especially relative to output and income dynamics.

Many analysts in the market and the official sector shared this analysis (see e.g. ESRB, 2016). The IMF (GFSR, 2018) spoke of rising medium-term risks. While markets were mostly less dynamic and, importantly, the US real estate market did not appear to be 'overheating' in 2017, increases in the 2010s often started from higher 'real' levels. The fiscal–financial risks from overvalued asset prices were therefore probably lower in the late 2010s than in 2007, but ultimately we will only find out later.

Can we estimate the likely budgetary risks from a potential correction of over-valued asset markets in the future? Yes, to some extent, and signs of revenue windfalls are, for example, clearly visible in Germany. However, there have been no updates of the studies from the 2000s. Doing such studies may also be more difficult than a decade ago: it is not clear what the right benchmark for future interest rates, equity and real estate prices should be, so it is also difficult to measure the potential for correction. Moreover, it is not clear whether the budgetary elasticities of asset price changes estimated for the 1980s and 1990s still apply. Asset price-related fiscal risks in the future are, therefore, likely, but hard to measure.

Based on the reported experience, a rough simulation of fiscal risks is possible. A 20% correction in asset markets and a 'normal' budgetary elasticity of 0.5% of GDP for every 10% asset price change, for example, would imply a fiscal risk of 1% of GDP for the deficit. Larger corrections with a renewed financial crisis would have much stronger effects.

Bond Market Risks

There is one additional asset market that may play a more important role in the future. With falling interest rates, bond prices have gone up and yields down. Holders of long-maturity government bonds had huge windfalls. A thirty-year German bond, for example, that was issued at 100 in 2007 at 4% interest was trading at 150 in late 2018 (Figure 8.4a). Some of the bond market windfalls may have resulted in capital gains taxes, some in more consumption as the 'bond boom' unfolded.

Source: Deutsche Finanzargentur, Emmission 1 Jan 2005, 4% Coupon

Figure 8.4a Germany: Price of thirty-year government bond.

'Snapback' risks from bond market corrections can arise, especially if at some point inflation and interest rates rise again and risk premia in the low-rated markets segments increase as well. Equilibrium interest rates may be lower in the late 2010s than a decade earlier; however, savings and investment patterns and equilibrium rates may reverse if disincentive effects from zero rates to savings materialise, and high savings cohorts in Europe and Asia retire and bolster the low-savings age groups.

Fiscal risks from the corporate bond market may have increased, and we will return to this issue in more depth in Chapter 9. The low-interest environment of the 2010s went hand in hand with very rapid growth of bond markets coupled with low average ratings, declining creditor protection and low risk spreads (OECD, 2019a). This boosted wealth and corporate profitability and, thereby, tax revenue, which, in turn, may reverse in any bond market downturn.

However, there are no studies of the fiscal implications of booms and busts in the bond market beyond the direct effect on financing costs. It is definitely worth more analysis but the experience of snapback risks and bond market crashes in the advanced countries may lie as far back as the 1970s. There are indirect behavioural risks for public expenditure, which we already saw materialising during the early 2000s boom. Germany, for example, decided to 'regularly' expand its non-interest expenditure in its multiyear budget plans after the financial crisis as interest expenditure came in lower than expected (Figure 8.4b).

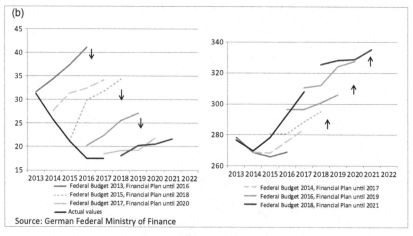

Figure 8.4b Germany: Interest payments and primary expenditure, billion Euro, successive budgets.

8.4 Fiscal Risks and the Real Economy

Automatic Stabilisers

There is a close link between fiscal variables and economic developments. First, real economy developments affect expenditure and revenue developments. Less growth means lower revenue from consumption and income taxes. Moreover, the budgetary inertia of spending when the economy booms or slows down stabilises the economy. Public spending and, thereby, demand, grows faster in a downturn than that of the private sector – the public spending ratio rises. The opposite holds in a downturn.

These are the fiscal effects of automatic stabilisers. Active counter-cyclical fiscal policies can reinforce the effect of automatic stabilisers if a government uses expansionary policies in a downturn or contractionary ones in an upswing. They do not affect long-term fiscal sustainability if applied symmetrically over the cycle.

The effect of automatic stabilisers is relatively well understood and measured. In most cases, it is broadly in line with the size of government. Hence, with government spending between 30% and 55% of GDP, the elasticities of budgets to economic changes are also mostly in the 0.3–0.5% range. In other words, a 1% growth slowdown raises the expenditure ratio and the deficit by 0.3–05.% of GDP. A long or deep recession with an output loss of 5% or 10% can have a correspondingly large effect on expenditure ratios, deficits and debt, although this should reverse in good times.

Financial Development, Real Economy and Fiscal Variables

There are reasons why real economy risks to budgets may be larger than expected due to financial linkages. First, strong domestic demand and methodological issues for calculating the output gap in boom times tend to misrepresent the cyclical and fiscal position of a booming country. In a boom, the output gap tends to be more positive than assessed in real time because temporarily high growth is mistaken as being permanent. Therefore, underlying fiscal positions (as measured, for example, by the cyclically adjusted balance) also tend to look better in real time than they really are ex post (Jaeger and Schuknecht, 2007; Schuknecht, 2010). This was the case after Lehman Brothers but also in earlier boom–bust phases. Borio, Disyatat and Juselius (2013) and Borio et al. (2016) have calculated financial cycle adjusted output gaps and fiscal balances (see also BIS, 2016).

Second, downturns triggered from the financing side can be quite strong and much stronger than deteriorating financing conditions alone would suggest. We know that unsustainable credit and asset price dynamics (amongst other factors) turned the Lehman Brothers bankruptcy into a greater economic crash than financing conditions alone would have suggested. Adverse 'confidence effects' on growth were very important. Financial sector problems, coupled with vulnerable public finances, provoked the European fiscal crisis and recession in the early 2010s while financing conditions for other countries remained favourable. However, we do not understand well if and when such 'non-linearities' set in and how strongly they affect the real economy and, thereby, public finances.

Third, in Europe, the economic boom with easy finance disguised problems in the real economy, especially competitiveness loss. This only became obvious in the crisis. Demand patterns financed easily from abroad in the boom were no longer sustainable. A seemingly healthy and sustainable fiscal position turned out to be more risky because the underlying economy was weaker than thought. This contributed significantly to the economic, fiscal and financial crisis in some European countries (Berti, Salto and Lequien, 2012).

A reasonably good indicator for the competitiveness problems that emerged in the euro area during the boom phase is unit labour costs in countries relative to the euro area average (Figure 8.5). Unit labour costs in the crisis countries increased much faster than the average of the euro area and, in particular, Germany. Between 1999 and 2007, the difference

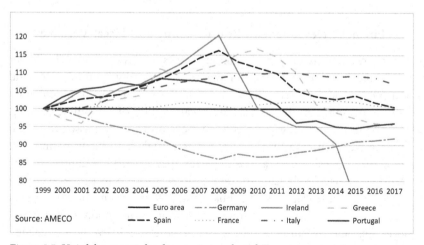

Figure 8.5 Unit labour cost developments in selected Euro area countries.

reached 20% or 30% in some cases. With the start of the crisis, however, a healthy rebalancing set in. Relative unit labour costs looked reasonably aligned again in 2018, except perhaps for Italy.

Fourth, and finally, there is a further little explored channel from financial developments to the real economy and, thereby, to public finances. Boom–bust cycles such as the global financial crisis and the preceding boom can undermine long-term growth prospects (Borio et al., 2015). In boom periods with rapid credit growth, labour and capital tend to migrate into the booming sectors. In Spain or Ireland, too many workers went into construction, which is a low-productivity sector by itself. The job opportunities there kept some young people from continuing their studies. In Ireland and the United Kingdom, the financial sector displayed similar patterns. When the boom ended, much capital and labour became redundant.

Moreover, forbearance and ultra-low interest rates arguably contributed to 'zombification' in the real and financial economy (White, 2017). Structural policy errors on the back of cheap money and low financing costs may have further brought down potential growth. There is clear evidence that the structural reform momentum in the advanced countries declined as the financial crisis subsided (OECD, 2019c). If government spending dynamics do not then adjust to the lower growth path, structural fiscal positions deteriorate.

Government Guarantees

Finally, we need to look at government guarantees when assessing fiscal–financial risks via the real economy channel. A project, for example, may have the backing of a government guarantee and no fiscal costs occur if the project goes well. Legal requirements typically assume that the risk of guarantees being called is very small. However, in extreme cases, especially when financial and economic conditions change strongly, this may happen.

Guarantees are sometimes quite untransparent. PPP contracts typically stipulate that the private providers will receive the revenue streams emanating from private investment as a return on their investment. However, in crisis times (or simply as a result of miscalculation) revenue streams can be much lower than expected. Many contracts then stipulate that the government will 'help' and pay for (part of) the difference. In other cases, projects have implicit guarantees because the government has to come to the rescue when private providers go under (or threaten to do so).

The level of implicit guarantees is not known, and hard to estimate. By contrast, the figures for explicit guarantees are often available and can be

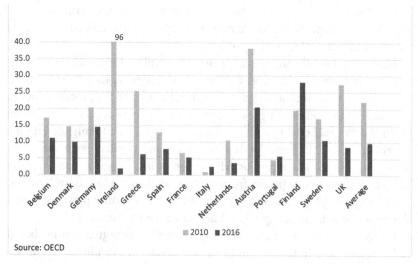

Figure 8.6 Government guarantees.

quite large (Figure 8.6). In 2010, near the height of the global financial crisis, guarantees averaged 20% of GDP in those advanced economies for which data are available. In Ireland, they reached almost 100% of GDP. By 2016, government guarantees had come down to half that level, below 10% of GDP; only Austria and Finland still reported figures above 20%. However, there has been no systematic assessment across countries on how many guarantees fell due in the context of the global financial crisis or earlier downturns.

8.5 Resilience or Fragility in Advanced Economies

Fiscal Buffers Post-crisis

What are the fiscal buffers and risks in the late 2010s? Many governments were in a much worse fiscal position than before the global financial crisis (Table 8.7). In 2007, Italy's debt stood at 100% of GDP while Japan reported 175%. By 2017, Italy's debt had increased to 132% of GDP, and that of Japan to 236%. The debt figures for the United States, France, the United Kingdom and Canada had increased roughly to the 90%–110% range. Only German public debt had reverted to pre-crisis levels.

G7 debt increased by almost 40% of GDP between 2007 and 2017, to reach 119% of GDP. This was about the same level as after the Second World War, with the difference that at that time populations were young

Table 8.7 *Fiscal buffers*

General Governmenl Deficit and Debt (% of GDP)

	2007		2017			
	Deficit	Debt	Deficit	Debt	Deficit	Debt
					Change (pp) 2007–2017	
US	−2.9	65	−4.6	108	−1.7	43
Japan	−3.2	175	−4.2	236	−1.0	61
Canada	1.8	67	−1.0	90	−2.8	23
UK	−2.6	42	−2.3	87	0.3	45
Germany	0.2	64	1.1	64	0.9	0
France	−2.5	64	−2.6	97	−0.1	33
Italy	−1.5	100	−1.9	132	−0.4	32
G7	−2.2	81	−3.4	119	−1.2	38

Source: Ameco

and growth high. Spain, Portugal, Belgium and Greece reported debt of near or above 100% of GDP as well.

Compounding the 'debt worry' were significant deficits – despite several years of recovery. In a number of countries, the fiscal deficits in 2017 were still near or above 3% of GDP and higher than in 2007 when debt levels were much lower. It makes a big difference to begin a recession with a 3% deficit or a balanced budget, as we will see below. Moreover, population ageing implies more spending pressure and a shrinking labour supply in the future.

Much lower interest rates and more credible safety nets than before the crisis are clearly a mitigating factor. Still, Italy's experience in the summer of 2018 – which were not crisis times – illustrates how quickly sentiment can shift, markets turn and crisis fears return when debt is high, deficits rise and growth prospects weaken.

The deficit–debt situation in the advanced countries in the late 2010s is not comforting. With deficits of 3% and debt levels of over 100% of GDP in good times, even a recession could become hazardous. Countries with their own monetary policies and a safe haven status have more, but not infinite, leeway: the euro area countries without their own monetary policies are at a disadvantage in this regard.

The ratings of government debt underpin these concerns. The ratings had improved gradually over the 1990s and early 2000s before deteriorating very rapidly (Figure 8.7). While such ratings should be 'early-warning'

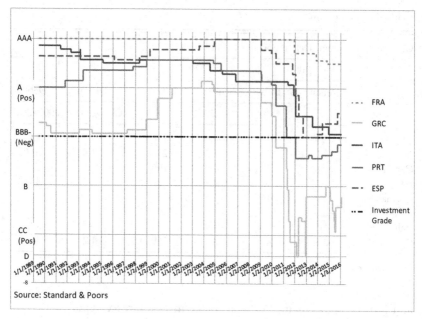

Figure 8.7 Rating history of selected European countries.

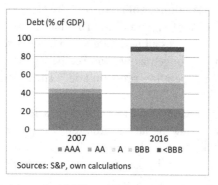

Figure 8.8 Euro area debt rating, 2007 vs. 2016.

indicators, in reality they reacted late. Markets therefore tend to be quite complacent and then react very strongly. In 2007, almost 66% of euro area debt was rated AAA (the best possible rating for debt) and much of the rest (Italy) was A. By 2016, only 25% was rated AAA and 40% at worse than A (Figure 8.8). The situation is similar when looking beyond Europe: Japan lost its AAA a long time ago and the United States lost it with Standard & Poor's in 2011 as well.

Simulations of Deficit and Debt Scenarios

What does this mean for fiscal buffers and 'optimal' deficits and debt? Of course, much depends on the country situation. Assume a country with 100% of GDP of public debt, an average interest rate of 3% on such debt, nominal growth of 3% per annum and a deficit of 3% of GDP in the first period (t0). This is not far from the situation of many advanced countries in the late 2010s. In this scenario, public debt would remain unchanged at 100% over the ten following periods t1 to t10 (Figure 8.9).

Alternatively, assume a balanced or nearly balanced budget (deficit of −1% to −0.5% of GDP in t0), the second scenario in Figure 8.9. The fiscal outlook would be much more resilient as debt would have gone down significantly by the tenth period. Still, it would take almost a decade for debt to fall from 100% to 80% of GDP. To get from a 3% deficit to only 1% without much output loss, consolidation needs to be well designed, and Chapter 5 provides ample historic evidence as to how this can be done successfully via expenditure reform.

In good times with low interest rates, both scenarios look reasonably benign. This changes with a significant downturn. Assume a one-year recession of −2% real economic growth followed by one year of stagnation as of the tenth period (t10) before a return to potential growth. Moreover, assume an expenditure stimulus or revenue decline of about 1.5% of GDP. As a result, the deficit would worsen by about 5% of GDP. This was broadly the (more benign) scenario of countries without a financial cum fiscal crisis in 2009/2010.

The implications of this scenario are very significant, depending on the starting point. If the starting point is a 3% deficit, the deficit would rise to

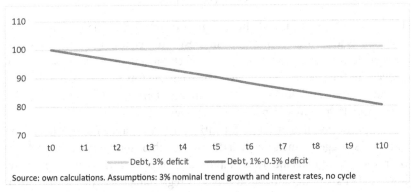

Source: own calculations. Assumptions: 3% nominal trend growth and interest rates, no cycle

Figure 8.9 Debt developments in 'good' times, % of GDP, two scenarios.

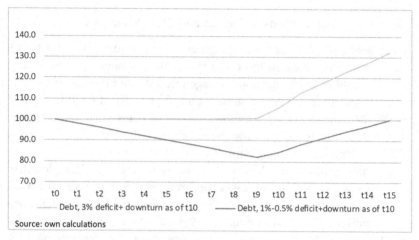

Figure 8.10 Debt developments with downturn, % of GDP, two scenarios.

8% of GDP in two years and the debt ratio from 100% to over 130% of GDP within five years (t15) (Figure 8.10). When the starting point is a nearly balanced budget, the deficit would only rise to 5%. With debt rising less and from a lower level of 80%, the debt ratio would 'only' rise back to the 100% of GDP ratio by t15, the same as before the downturn.

The simulation exercise illustrates that a balanced budget in good times tends to result in a reasonably safe level of public debt by the time a major downturn strikes. The simulation also illustrates the risk of debt ratcheting up over successive upswings and downturns if governments do not use the 'good times' for deficit and debt reduction.

8.6 Conclusion

This chapter has examined the first part of the fiscal–financial risk map. Fiscal costs and risks from higher interest rates, changing asset prices and markets and financial–real economy effects on public finances were very relevant in the past and are likely to be so in the future as well. Boom–bust episodes before and during the global financial crisis, but also earlier in the 1980s and 1990s, proved particularly 'expensive'.

The prevailing deficit and debt ratios in the advanced countries in the late 2010s suggest much lower fiscal buffers than ten years earlier. Moreover, the lack of consolidation in a number of advanced countries towards lower deficits and debt in 'good times' is regrettable (see for the euro area, Thygesen et al., 2018).

Simulation exercises show the vulnerability of countries when deficits remain high and debt reaches or exceeds 100% of GDP. Debt builds up quickly but its reduction is difficult and takes a long time, even under favourable conditions. In fact, only a few countries, such as Sweden, Finland, Germany and Ireland have managed a significant debt reduction since the 1990s, and that typically followed serious expenditure reduction and reform.

We will find that fiscal risks can be even greater and more uncertain when we look at further fiscal–financial linkages via banking and shadow banking, central banks and the international economy. This leads to the second part of the fiscal–financial risk map and to Chapter 9.

9

Fiscal–Financial Risks 2

Bank, Shadow Bank, Central Bank and International Channels

'Emergencies' have always been the pretext on which the safeguards of individual liberty have been eroded.

Friedrich August von Hayek

A big institution is 'too big' when there is an expectation that government will do whatever it takes to rescue that institution from failure.

Jerome Powell

Highlights

This chapter completes the discussion on fiscal–financial risks and looks at banks, shadow banks, central banks and international linkages.

Banks have increased their resilience considerably over the past decade, supported by the international regulatory agenda. However, global indebtedness has increased further and bank balance sheets are often loaded with risky public and private credit. Moreover, there are fiscal risks from market-based finance: highly priced, low-quality credit held partly by a run-prone asset management industry, an under-funded pension industry and large derivative clearing houses (Figure 9.1). Central banks face risks from large asset holdings. International credit is very high and could transmit problems across borders. International safety nets have grown but so have demands for international support.

Given record debt and debt increases and our lack of knowledge and experience of how fiscal–financial risks will unfold in the future, building resilience is of the highest priority. This vindicates constraints on deficits and debt such as the Maastricht limits and the regulatory agenda for the financial sector, and it provides a further argument for lean and efficient government.

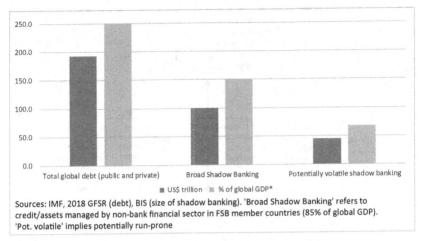

Sources: IMF, 2018 GFSR (debt), BIS (size of shadow banking). 'Broad Shadow Banking' refers to credit/assets managed by non-bank financial sector in FSB member countries (85% of global GDP). 'Pot. volatile' implies potentially run-prone

Figure 9.1 Total global debt and the role of shadow banking, 2017.

9.1 Fiscal Risks from the Banking Sector

Chapter 8 discussed the first part of the fiscal–financial risk map in the advanced countries. It included fiscal risks from higher interest rates, downturns in asset markets and the feed-through from the financial sector to public finances via the real economy. This chapter deals with the second part of the map, which includes the linkages from banks, shadow banks, central banks and the international economy to public finances (Figure 9.2). These linkages may impact on spending, deficits and debt via bank bailout costs, for example. However, there are potentially other, so far unfamiliar, ways. The literature is scarce, as are relevant experiences in the past. The discussion is, therefore, in part an exploration of what might happen rather than a discussion based on facts and experiences.

Costs and Determinants of Past Banking Crises

Banking crises have been the most severely debt-increasing events in the past, with the exception of wars (Bova et al., 2016). This held for the developing and emerging countries and, since the global financial crisis, for the advanced countries as well. In many countries, fiscal crises followed a financial crisis so that the countries needed international bailouts. Evidence on the global and earlier financial crises illustrate this claim (Table 9.1; see also Table 3.5 and Maurer and Grussenmeyer, 2015).

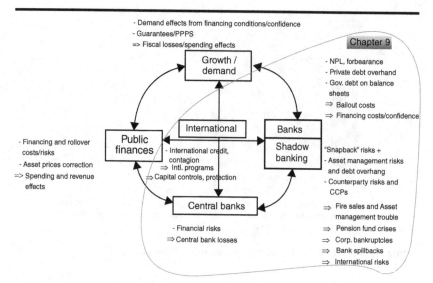

Figure 9.2 Fiscal–financial risk map.

Table 9.1 *Financial crisis support post-2009*

	Gross Impact (% of GDP)	Gross Impact in % of end 2009 Banking Assets	Recovery until 2014	Net Impact on Public Debt (% of GDP)
Austria	6.2	5.6	..	6.2
Belgium	7.2	8.9	3.3	4.0
Cyprus	20.0	..	0.0	20.0
Germany	12.3	10.4	4.4	7.9
Greece	34.9	33.1	8.1	26.7
Ireland	36.3	20.4	6.5	29.9
Netherlands	17.3	13.5	13.7	3.7
Slovenia	12.0	13.2	1.7	12.0
Spain	7.4	3.9	3.2	4.3
UK	11.6	5.9	4.7	6.9
US	4.3	6.4	4.8	−0.5
Average	7.4	..	5.0	2.5
Total US$ Billions	2,114		1,391	723

Source: IMF, Fiscal Monitor (April 2015)

The IMF reported that by early 2015, the fiscal costs of financial sector bailouts had increased government debt by 2 trillion dollars. Governments were able to recover 1.3 trillion of that amount, mostly in the United States, the United Kingdom and the Netherlands. Net losses of US$723 billion therefore largely fell on the euro area. Gross fiscal costs represented roughly 7% of GDP on average and up to 30% for Greece and Ireland. After 2014, significant further costs emerged in Greece and Italy.

When looking at costs relative to banking assets, there is slightly less divergence, as countries with large banking sectors (such as Ireland and the Netherlands) also reported higher costs. Fiscal costs ranged from 4% in the case of Spain to over 30% in Greece. This shows that in some countries total bank capital was de facto wiped out several times over.

The literature finds a number of determinants of a less and more costly crisis. Fiscal costs tend to be higher when countries have large banking sectors, when they rely on external funding, when debt in the private sector is high and when government guarantees prop up banks in crisis (Amaglobeli et al., 2015). Fiscal and economic costs tend to rise when banking crises mutate into fiscal crises (Laeven and Valencia, 2013). Fiscal costs also rise when governments permit blanket deposit guarantees, open-ended liquidity support, debtor bailouts and regulatory forbearance (Honohan and Klingebiel, 2003).

Borio, Contreras and Zampolli (2019) find that the fiscal costs of a banking crisis are significantly affected by the level and growth of credit to the private non-financial sector. Foreign exchange reserves (emerging economies) and higher bank capitalisation go hand in hand with lower public debt increases. De Mooij, Keen and Orihara (2014) and Langedijk et al. (2015) detected a positive correlation between debt biases in the tax system and the costs of financial crises.

Stronger institutions, good supervision and speedy reaction by governments rather than drawn-out, repeated interventions correlate with less costly crises (Honohan and Klingebiel, 2003; Amaglobeli et al., 2015; Bova et al., 2016). However, more fiscal support does not correlate with lower output losses, on the contrary (Detragiache and Ho, 2010).

Looking back at the global financial crisis, country experiences support these claims. The Irish crisis (large financial sector, debtor bailout, deposit guarantees, weak supervision) was particularly costly. Lack of creditor bail-in and weak supervision and forbearance worsened the crisis effects in other countries as well. Costs were more limited in the countries that reacted fast and determinedly, such as the United States and the United Kingdom.

Studies that looked into fiscal crisis determinants confirm the importance of strong public finances, financial sectors and real economies – the triangle of stability – for future crisis prevention. Most studies show that an unfavourable fiscal starting position following expansionary expenditure policies matters. Financial sector problems with strong credit growth and private debt migrating on to public balance sheets is then more likely to make a financial crisis also become a fiscal one. Moreover, an over-heating domestic economy, macroeconomic imbalances and competitiveness losses raise the risk of fiscal crisis when coming together with weak fiscal positions (Berti et al, 2012; Pamies Sumner and Berti, 2017; Cerovic et al., 2018; Mbaye, Moreno-Badia and Chae, 2018). Proactive consolidation reduces the probability of a fiscal crisis, as does strengthening institutions (Honda, Tapsoba and Issifou, 2018).

Higher Buffers and Remaining Risks

Fiscal risks from the banking sector have probably declined since the global financial crisis due to a number of regulatory measures that required banks to increase their buffers. All banks significantly increased their capital and contingent capital. As a result, they should be able to absorb significantly more losses than in the past. In Europe, capital ratios increased to about 15% on average in 2017 and above 20% in Ireland (Figure 9.3a). This is good news, although some observers have argued for further increases (Admati et al., 2013).

During the global crisis, banks also got into trouble because they did not hold enough subordinate debt, were short of liquidity and long-term funding was not secure. In all these areas, international regulation became stronger and implementation improved (FSB, 2019). By 2019, the banks had generally fulfilled the minimum capital, liquidity and funding requirements. Moreover, there was agreement on a minimum leverage ratio of

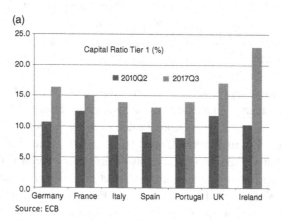

Figure 9.3a Bank capital in selected European countries.

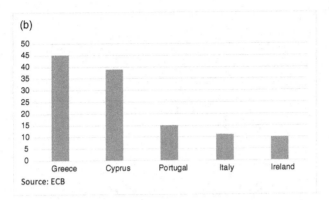

Source: ECB

Figure 9.3b Non-performing loans, % of total, December 2017.

capital relative to total assets (3% of assets) and on a minimum loss absorbing capacity (8% of assets). Banks had developed resolution plans so that failure would not plunge themselves and (through contagion) the banking system into chaos.

Looking forward, there were still important bank-related risks and vulnerabilities in the advanced countries in the late 2010s and a significant amount of non-performing loans on bank balance sheets (Figure 9.3b). In five European countries, these exceeded 10% of total loans; in two of them, they exceeded 33% of all loans. The fiscal relevance of non-performing loans became manifest in 2016–2018 when bail-in requirements were not applied to Italian and Cypriot banks and the government stepped in. The recapitalisation of the affected Cypriot bank cost over 10% of GDP, although banks had already received significant support in Cyprus' country programme earlier on.

Risks related to a possible snapback of interest rates could undo these positive developments via rising defaults and financing costs: the risk of banking problems from defaults is greater when the private sector is over-indebted. We only have a rule-of-thumb measure of over-indebtedness. The European Commission's scoreboard on economic imbalances identifies private debt in excess of 140% of GDP as 'risky'. Sectoral thresholds are at 80% and 60% of GDP for aggregate debt in the corporate and household sectors, respectively. These figures were derived from the crisis experience.

From this perspective, developments over the past decade were quite mixed. The countries most affected by the crisis saw some significant deleveraging. This was strongest in Spain, Ireland and the United States on the household side and in Spain, the United Kingdom and New Zealand on the corporate side (Figures 9.4a and 9.4b).

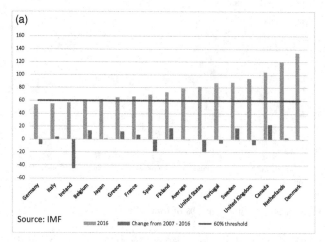

Figure 9.4a Household debt, % of GDP, 2007–2016.

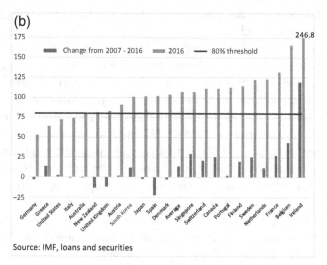

Figure 9.4b Non-financial corporate debt, % of GDP, 2007–2016.

Average household indebtedness, however, remained broadly unchanged and corporate debt even increased between 2007 and 2016 following a significant increase in leverage in the preceding decade (see also Table 9.2). Household debt in the advanced countries averaged 80.3% of GDP in 2016, 20% above the 'safe' threshold. Euro area countries mostly stayed near or below the 60% threshold; by contrast, most non-euro area countries were above it. Australia, Canada, Denmark, Switzerland plus the Netherlands reported household debt above 100% of GDP.

Table 9.2 *Household debt, all instruments*

% of GDP				Change pp	Overhang[1]
	2000	2007	2016	2007–2016	pp>60%
Euro area					
Austria	..	..	..	..	..
Belgium	41.2	47.5	60.9	13.4	0.9
Finland	33.9	55.7	72.9	17.3	12.9
France	45.5	59.1	66.2	7.1	6.2
Germany	71.6	61.5	53.6	−7.9	..
Greece	20.0	53.0	65.0	12.0	5.0
Ireland	..	101.5	56.3	−45.2	..
Italy	35.3	51.5	55.4	3.9	..
Netherlands	98.4	117.5	119.8	2.3	59.8
Portugal	69.6	93.3	87.2	−6.1	27.2
Spain	53.1	86.6	69.1	−17.5	9.1
Other Europe					
Denmark	95.5	134.0	133.5	−0.6	73.5
Sweden	48.5	71.0	88.3	17.3	28.3
Switzerland	105.4	107.4	..	..	..
UK	71.6	102.4	94.0	−8.4	34.0
Other advanced economies					
Australia	..	..	..	..	..
Canada	61.6	80.9	103.6	22.7	43.6
Japan	82.1	61.0	61.9	0.9	1.9
South Korea	..	..	95.6	95.6	35.6
New Zealand	..	..	..	..	..
Singapore	..	..	..	..	..
US	71.5	99.7	81.2	−18.5	21.2
Average[2]	62.8	81.4	80.3	−1.1	20.3

Source: IMF
1. Debt overhang only for countries with positive figure.
2. Unweighted, excluding South Korea and Singapore.

The development of corporate indebtedness has been more concerning over the past decade, especially in some countries. In 2016, corporate debt stood at 107% of GDP on average, almost 30% above the threshold of 80% and well above the 2007 level (Table 9.3). Leverage therefore grew at almost the same pace as before the crisis. The corporate debt overhang was strongest in Belgium, France and Ireland. Only seven countries still featured corporate debt below or near the 80% of GDP threshold in 2016; these included Germany, Greece, Italy and the United Kingdom in Europe, and Australia, New Zealand and the United States outside it.

Table 9.3 *Non-financial corporate debt, loans and debt securities*

% of GDP				Change pp	Overhang[1]
	2000	2007	2016	2007–2016	pp >80
	(1)	(2)	(3)	(4)	(5)
Euro Area					
Austria	82.6	88.8	90.9	2.0	10.9
Belgium	104.7	122.6	166.2	43.6	86.2
Finland	90.3	94.1	114.1	20.0	34.1
France	97.8	104.0	131.5	27.5	51.5
Germany	57.8	56.0	52.8	−3.2	..
Greece	39.1	50.5	63.9	13.4	..
Ireland	..	127.7	246.8	119.1	166.8
Italy	56.0	74.5	73.8	−0.7	..
Netherlands	128.9	111.3	123.0	11.8	43.0
Portugal	82.5	109.9	112.3	2.5	32.3
Spain	73.0	124.4	101.7	−22.7	21.7
Other Europe					
Denmark	69.7	106.5	104.1	−2.5	24.1
Sweden	105.6	97.0	122.2	25.2	42.2
Switzerland	86.1	90.2	111.4	21.3	31.4
UK	79.8	94.7	82.9	−11.9	2.9
Other advanced economies					
Australia	68.1	80.4	80.2	−0.2	0.2
Canada	86.9	85.9	111.4	25.5	31.4
Japan	119.7	103.0	101.2	−1.8	21.2
South Korea	91.3	88.6	100.4	11.8	20.4
New Zealand	82.0	94.7	81.7	−13.0	1.7
Singapore	80.5	77.9	107.0	29.1	27.0
US	63.9	69.7	72.2	2.5	..
Average[2]	82.6	93.7	107.0	13.3	..

Source: IMF
1. Debt overhang only for countries with positive figure.
2. Unweighted, excluding South Korea and Singapore.

These figures are interesting and important, but they do not lend themselves to easy calculation of banking or even fiscal risks. There are differences in tax systems such as mortgage-interest deductibility that can explain diverging debt levels and that result in different thresholds of sustainability for corporates and households. Interest rates in the late 2010s were significantly lower than ten years earlier. However, over-indebtedness could turn into renewed banking risks when conditions change.

Bank Exposure to Government Debt and the 'Doom Loop'

The biggest risk for many banks may not stem from their exposure to private debt but to highly indebted governments. There are three transmission channels: first, if government-financing costs rise, the market value of outstanding government debt falls. This creates an adverse balance sheet effect for all holders of such debt, including the banks. Second, when government financing costs rise, financing costs for the banking sector also tend to increase. This, in turn, means higher financing costs and less credit for the economy. In fact, there is a correlation between the rating and financing conditions of banks and their sovereign debt. This suggests that the value of implicit government guarantees to the banking system differs significantly across countries (CGFS, 2011).

Third, government debt also fulfils important banking functions, including liquidity provision, and collateral in payment systems, derivatives transactions and securities trading. Banks become weaker when government debt is downgraded or becomes less liquid. These three transmission channels can reinforce each other and give rise to a 'doom loop' between weak banks, weak governments and the real economy. Governments may then risk losing market access and need international assistance, as happened to Greece, Ireland, Portugal, Cyprus and Spain in the global financial crisis.

At the same time, government debt has important regulatory privileges: risk weighting and concentration limits do not apply to government debt. This plus higher returns encourages banks to hold low-rated government debt (BIS, 2017). There is also a strong home bias in the bank holdings of government debt.

The exposure of banks to government debt differs significantly across countries but it is often high and rising (Figure 9.5). There are two country groups with medium and high vulnerability, respectively. A first group with France, Canada and Belgium reported government debt not far from 100% of GDP and banks held about 20% of this debt in 2017. Valuation losses would have significant effects on bank balance sheets in these countries.

A second group of countries featured higher risks. Japan, Italy and Spain reported that banks held 30% of government debt, worth between 30% and 70% of GDP. Any (even moderate) loss of credibility, valuation and liquidity would probably undermine the health of bank balance sheets and the rating of banks, with adverse knock-on effects on private sector lending and the real economy.

Figure 9.5 also shows that the 'doom loop' potentially affects not just the banks: much of the rest of public debt was also in the hands of financial

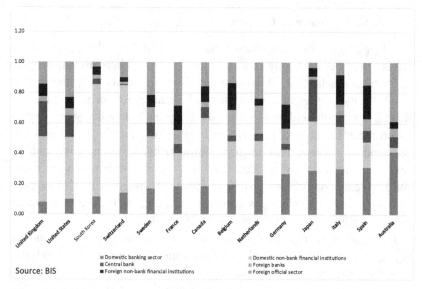

Figure 9.5 Holders of government debt, share by sector, 2016.

institutions. Domestic non-bank financial institutions held up to 75% of public debt. Central banks owned up to 25% of public debt, with the highest ratios in Japan and the United Kingdom. Foreign banks and non-bank financial institutions had up to 20% of all public debt on their balance sheets. In fact, this left surprisingly little public debt outside the financial sector.

The absolute numbers are also impressive. French banks held domestic official sector debt (government and central banks) worth around €1 trillion at end-2017. The corresponding figure for the United States was over 2 trillion. Italian public debt at nominal value rose from 100% of GDP or €1.8 trillion in 2007 to over 130% of GDP or €2.3 trillion by the middle of 2018. The exposure of banks – monetary financial institutions – to domestic official sector debt had increased to €763 billion (BIS Consolidated Banking Statistics).

It is also interesting to look at government debt in relation to the banks' capital and total assets. Recall that the banks should not lend more than the equivalent of 25% of their equity to single private debtors to avoid concentration risks. Moreover, private credit exposure is risk weighted so that low-rated exposures require more capital. These rules do not apply to government debt.

Government exposure by many banks is in fact much higher than the 25% private sector limit (Figure 9.6). Many banks had exposures well beyond their total capital, and peak exposures were as high as 500% or

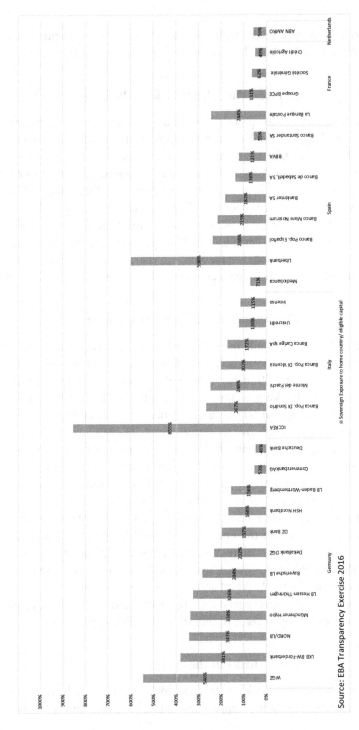

Source: EBA Transparency Exercise 2016

Figure 9.6 Net exposures of selected banks/banking groups to domestic general government debt in percentage of eligible capital, 2015.

800% in 2015. When a bank with a 500% exposure needs to write down its government debt holdings by 20%, in principal all its capital is gone.

9.2 Fiscal Risks from Shadow Banking

The financial crisis of the past decades in the advanced countries emanated from the banking system. However, in the global financial crisis, risks from shadow banking or non-bank, market-based finance also played a role. The banks had mistakenly thought that they had offloaded significant risk into special purpose vehicles. The bailout of the American International Group (AIG) (while Lehman Brothers was allowed to fail) was supposedly linked to huge risks from derivatives. Moreover, almost twenty years ago the failing hedge fund Long-Term Capital Management (LTCM) in the context of the Asian crisis suggested that contagion risk across asset managers was so important that it warranted a coordinated (private sector-led) bailout.

The Importance of Shadow Banking

The size of the non-bank financial sector has grown enormously and disproportionately in recent decades. Of the total global debt of US$ 200 trillion (or 250% of GDP) in 2017, about 50% or 100 trillion was part of the broader shadow banking sector. The BIS saw that half of that, US$ 50 trillion or 70% of global GDP, was potentially volatile and subject to run risks. This included collective investment vehicles (71%), non-bank financial entities engaging in loan provisions (7%) and market intermediaries depending on short-term funding (8% of the total). This is a huge amount of money and would create quite some market turbulence if it started 'moving' around in a significant and erratic manner.

In the context of the financial crisis, the G20 countries decided to strengthen regulation of the non-bank financial sector to increase buffers and make the industry more resilient. However, progress was mostly slower than in the banking area, except for life insurances. A first assessment took place by the FSB and showed less progress with the implementation of the regulatory agenda (FSB, 2019) and, consequently, more uncertainty as to the increase of buffers in this industry.

Risks in the 'Industry'

The risks in the non-bank financial sector emanate mainly from rising interest rates and spreads (snapback risks) in a high asset price, risk-taking and leveraged environment (ESRB, 2016). Low interest rates contributed to this environment and 'low (interest rates) for long' would provide a further boost (ESRB, 2016). There are a number of potential channels.

Automated trading and fickle investor behaviour can lead to sudden reversals of the risk sentiment and sharp changes in rates and asset prices. This, in turn, could stoke solvency and liquidity problems in the asset management industry. When certain assets turn bad, there is a significant risk of contagion. The bundling of assets in exchange-traded funds (ETFs) can result in the sell-off of all the assets in the Fund rather than only the affected ones. This could lead to firesales of assets spreading from companies to sectors, to countries and even to country groups.

Asset managers may not have enough liquidity, especially if markets dry up. The BIS (2018) and ESRB (2018b) described liquidity shortages and excessive leverage amongst the 'industry' as the main potential channels through which volatility could arise. The FSB (2018) pointed to a rising exposure to valuation losses in the 'industry' given more and more low-rated credit, and the BIS Quarterly Review (September 2018, March and September 2019) and OECD (2019f) discuss collateralised loan obligations where spreads were reminiscent of collateralised debt obligations that amplified the subprime crisis a decade earlier.

A number of liquidity management instruments have been designed to mitigate such risks. These include redemption fees, suspension of redemptions and redemptions in kind, gates or liquidity buffers to mention only a few. All European countries applied such instruments in 2018, but to varying degrees (ESRB, 2018a).

Regulation and ratings can reduce but also exacerbate snapback-related risks. Given 'cliff' effects between investment and non-investment grade assets, the volatility of prices and liquidity may be particularly strong in the BBB and BB segment of the market. If there is a wave of downgrades in the context of a recession, the BBB market may shrink and become less liquid. The high-yield market may not be able to absorb the increased supply of existing and newly downgraded debt and even freeze.

Some numbers underpin these concerns. The growing size but declining quality of market-based finance over the past decade is remarkable. Corporate bond finance doubled in size to US$ 13 trillion between 2008 and 2018. Half the market is in the United States, but China is growing most rapidly. The share of BBB bonds increased from about 30% to 54% (Figures 9.7a and 9.7b; OECD, 2019a). The share of AA–AAA issues fell from over 25% to just 10%. Moreover, the share of low covenant bonds with limited creditor protection grew strongly (OECD, 2019a, 2019f).

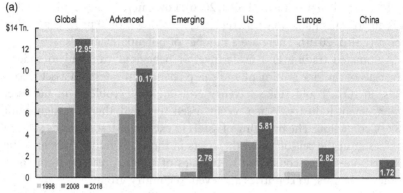

Source: Çelik, Demirtas and Isaaksson (2019)

Figure 9.7a Outstanding bonds issued by non-financial companies.

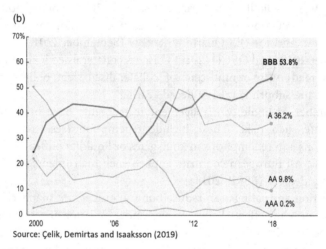

Source: Çelik, Demirtas and Isaaksson (2019)

Figure 9.7b Rating composition of investment grade corporate bonds.

Risky corporate bonds rated at BBB–B comprised, for example, 25% of investment by US funds (BIS, 2018). There must have been some risk-loving counterparts who took up all these issues.

Finally, asset managers also hold significant amounts of government debt. If such debt is of vulnerable governments with marginal ratings, the industry could stoke runs, volatility and sudden stops. Italian non-bank financial institutions held euro 450 billion of Italian government debt and non-residents held a total of 700 billion (though this included banks and other holders) (BIS, 2018). As mentioned before, the nervousness in financial markets in the summer of 2018 over Italian public debt was a stark reminder of this risk.

Shadow Banking Risks Turning into Fiscal Risks

Can we get a feel for the potential fiscal risks for governments from the inherent riskiness of the 'industry'? There is no methodology to derive concrete scenarios and measures of risk; nevertheless, four transmission channels from 'shadow banking' are worth looking at in more depth. The political economy bets seem strongly rigged against governments and their resolve to 'never make taxpayers pay again'.

First, pension funds and life insurances comprise a very large share of investments outside the banking system and pensions are a very sensitive issue. Rauh (2018) examined the pension funds of the United States, the United Kingdom, the Netherlands and Germany and argued that many are strongly under-funded (Table 9.4). Actuarial liabilities amounted to $10.7 trillion in 2015/2016 but market-based liabilities were 50% higher, at $15.8 trillion. In an adverse scenario, the European funds would face an even larger gap of an addditional $1.8 trillion. Risks are highest in the United States, with underfunding potentially at 25% or more of GDP (Rauh, 2018). The OECD (2019b) reports very large potential funding gaps as well.

The macroeconomic, fiscal and political relevance of pension funds becomes even clearer when looking at the global picture. The global pension fund assets in OECD countries amounted to US$ 27.5 trillion in 2018, or 53.3% of GDP. Pension funds in several advanced countries exceeded 100% of GDP and payouts reached up to 6% of GDP (Figure 9.8, see also Chapter 2 and OECD, 2018c, 2019e).

Table 9.4 *Situation of pension funds*

	Total liabilities			Adverse scenario
	Actuarial (billion)	Market	Gap	Additional gap
US Public (2015)	4,967	7,435	2,468	..
US Corporate (2016)	1,878	3,075	1,197	..
US Union (2015)	614	1,212	598	..
UK (2016)	1,825	2,566	741	1,411
Netherlands (2016)	1,257	1,339	82	348
Germany (2016)	171	210	39	61
Total (sum/average)	10,712	15,837	5,125	1,820

Source: Rauh (2018)

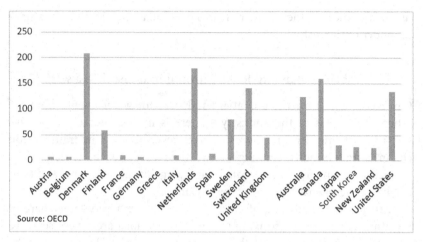

Figure 9.8 Assets in private pension plans, % of GDP.

In some countries, such as the United States, Canada and Switzerland, the private system is 'defined benefit', which means that benefits do not adjust to the returns of the pension fund. This keeps pension benefits predictable, but raises under-funding risks. Defined contribution systems (such as in the Netherlands) look more robust, as benefits adjust to returns of the pension funds. But there is also a big risk that in the case of a recession or crisis, falling pensions would stipulate calls for government assistance.

Risks for life insurers and pension funds could also arise via another channel. Customers may cancel private pension or life insurance contracts when interest rates rise rapidly as they try to get a better yield elsewhere. This could force asset managers to sell. If the interest rate rise coincides with risk-averseness in markets, such sales could turn into 'firesales' that undermine financial stability (Deutsche Bundesbank, 2019).

Second, asset managers could get into trouble. This should be no problem in principle – capitalism at work. In the past, bankrupt asset managers did not induce government rescues, although there are a few experiences with private bailouts such as LTCM in 2000 or some hedge fund defaults in the context of the global financial crisis. However, the industry is much larger today and the potential for causing turbulence through confidence effects and runs appears greater as well.

A confidence crisis in the volatile and risky parts of the market-based finance industry could undermine confidence in the more long-term-oriented segment such as life insurers. Problems of leveraged asset managers could spill over to banks (although internationally agreed constraints on lending to hedge funds should limit this problem). Particularly if systemic concerns emerge, e.g. via panic in the industry, or via spillovers to international markets, it is unlikely that governments would simply stand by.

Third, after the financial crisis, a significant share of derivative trading moved to centralised clearing platforms (CCPs) to prevent the bankruptcy of over-exposed banks in the future. Moreover, CCPs have a membership that aims to ensure that derivatives are maximally safe by requiring 'haircuts' to secure such trades. Loss-sharing formulas should distribute and dilute losses. Greater resilience of banks also reduces the risk of counterparty failure and, thereby, the risk of CCP losses.

However, we know little about how safe the system really is. Some government debt that constitutes safe and liquid collateral in 'normal' times may lose value and become illiquid in times of crisis. Winding down CCP services and implementing loss-sharing in a period of stress can hit weakened financial actors. The industry may still be prone to runs and panic given how big derivative exposures are. Government or central bank action may then be warranted (Cunliffe, 2018).

Fourth, the exposure of asset managers to low-rated company and government bonds is also an indirect source of fiscal risk. Financing for the low-rated corporate sector could dry up in the wake of risk-repricing and downgrades. This would spill back to the banking sector if banks extend loans or hold bonds of the same firms and industries (IMF, GFSR, 2018). A wave of bankruptcies could follow, and governments would find it hard to resist guarantees and bailouts to prevent widespread corporate failure. Alternatively, central banks could buy bonds and other assets for market stabilisation or take the risk on board via low-quality collateral. This would shift risks to central banks, as shown next in Section 9.3.

9.3 Central Banks and Fiscal Risks

A complete discussion of the fiscal–financial risk matrix must include central banks, but we cannot do more than touch on the topic. Central banks, just like any bank, can make losses on their investments. Losses become more likely when interest rates rise as this may lead to bankruptcies or debt restructurings. Central banks may also incur losses if they have to pay higher rates on their liabilities than they receive on their assets.

Many central banks have purchased medium-to-long-term government debt, the counterpart of which is deposits by banks with the central bank.

As long as the interest rate received on government debt (assets on the central bank balance sheet) is higher than the interest rate paid on deposits (liabilities), the central bank makes a profit. When short-term rates on deposits rise, the central bank will make a loss at some point.

Economically and from a consolidated balance sheet perspective, the central bank asset purchases have increased the short-term financing risk for governments. This is because the counterpart of the government debt purchased by central banks – bank deposits – are remunerated at the short term central bank rate which can change at any time. The positive effect of a long term-oriented maturity profile of government debt on refinancing risks is thus partly countervailed.

Central banks have capital to cover losses. Unlike commercial banks (and depending on statutes), central banks can normally not go bankrupt: they can print money and monetise losses. If that is not possible or not desirable, they can get capital from the government or can operate with negative equity – there are precedents for this. Losses can be 'parked' in special accounts to unwind over time.

The fiscal risks from central bank losses are not negligible. With various asset purchase programmes, balance sheets grew and the exposure to public and private debt increased. In many cases, the government debt central banks hold has become more risky (Figure 9.9). The market volume of central government debt securities outstanding in advanced countries increased from $30 trillion in 2009 to almost $40 trillion at the end of 2015. It increased rapidly further in subsequent years to over US$ 45 trillion in the OECD countries (OECD, 2019d).

Figure 9.9 shows the deterioration in government debt ratings between the late 1990s, when AAA predominated, and 2015, when AA+/A had become the 'new' normal. It also shows the important role that central banks had played as holders of government debt by 2015 (and beyond) and the large share of debt holdings that was not top-rated.

Central banks held more than 20% of advanced country government debt in mid-2018, or almost US$ 10 trillion (Figure 9.10). The most important holdings were with the Bank of Japan (3.9 trillion) and the US Federal Reserve (2.4 trillion). The central bank holdings of France, Italy, the United Kingdom, Switzerland and Germany were in the 400 billion– 600 billion range. The Bank of England and the Bank of Japan held the largest share of total government debt – 20–30%. The central banks of these two countries, plus Italy and Switzerland, also reported the largest exposure as a share of GDP. Swiss central bank debt holdings were mostly from foreign governments.

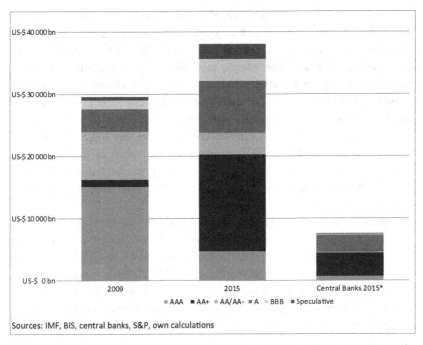

Figure 9.9 Market volume of central government debt securities by rating, advanced countries, 2009–2015.

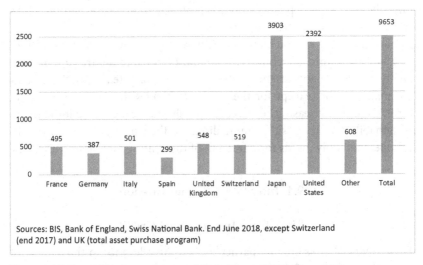

Figure 9.10 Central bank government debt holdings, US$ billion, 2018.

There is no quantitative analysis of fiscal–financial risks in the advanced countries via this channel, but some hypothetical calculations may illustrate them. Assume a central bank holds 20% of GDP of its own government's debt and the interest rate paid on bank deposits (liabilities) rises 1 percentage point above that received on government debt (assets). Losses would be 0.2% of GDP each year. This is not little and higher rate differentials would result in correspondingly large losses.

Japan is perhaps the most exposed country from this angle. The Bank of Japan held about 70% of GDP in government bonds in the late 2010s. Hence, the increase in costs for a corresponding amount of bank deposits with the Bank of Japan would be 0.7% of GDP for each percentage point of interest differential.

Restructurings of government debt would also be very costly. A 20% haircut on central bank holdings of public debt of 20% of GDP as in the example above would lead to central bank losses of 4% of GDP. Such losses would not be easy to absorb for the central bank and, therefore, would need to be included in the restructuring calculus. It is, hence, not surprising that central banks worry about such risks to their financial soundness and independence. It creates a trade off for central banks when they want to raise interest rates.

Durre and Pill (2011) examine how much government debt on the Eurosystem balance sheet could be 'retired' from Eurosystem profits (seigniorage) without jeopardising their financial health. Eurosystem holdings in 2018 fell into their range of about 1.5 trillion–2.5 trillion euros, with the range being highly dependent on assumptions. In any case, central banks can only 'retire' debt that way once.

'Normally', the central bank acquisition of government debt constitutes risk shifting within the country. It should be broadly neutral for sustainability when looking at the central bank consolidated with the rest of the public sector (except for the effect of changes in the maturity structure). Quantitative easing-related debt purchases are a positive for national sustainability if the risk is mutualised at the supra-national level. In Europe, that 'only' holds for a fraction of the central bank asset purchases.

9.4 International Transmission

Risks from International Credit

Fiscal financial risks attain a particularly strong relevance in the context of increasing global indebtedness coupled with deep financial interdependence.

Global public, private and total debt have all increased strongly since the turn of the millennium. This holds for the advanced, emerging and developing countries. At the end of 1998, total global debt stood at 192% of GDP (Figure 9.11; IMF, GFSR, 2018). Total debt added up to US$ 56 trillion, with over 90% incurred by the advanced economies (Figure 9.12).

By the end of 2007, when the global financial crisis was just beginning, global debt had increased to 217% of GDP, 25 percentage points more than

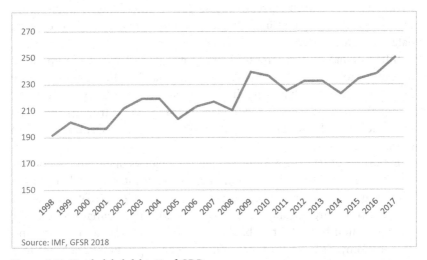

Source: IMF, GFSR 2018

Figure 9.11 Total global debt, % of GDP.

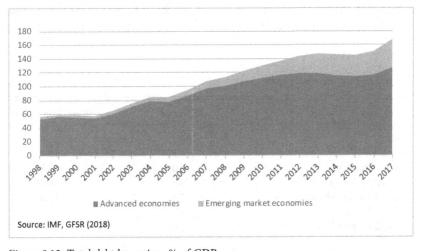

■ Advanced economies   ■ Emerging market economies

Source: IMF, GFSR (2018)

Figure 9.12 Total debt by region, % of GDP.

only nine years earlier. Indebtedness increased most strongly in the private sector of the advanced economies. Over the 2007–2017 period, total debt increased further and faster to 250% of GDP, with private debt rising rapidly in the emerging economies and public debt in the advanced countries. The emerging markets increased their share of debt to over US$ 40 trillion, or about 25% of global debt.

More total debt has gone hand in hand with more international credit. This includes exposure via bank lending and non-bank credit. Domestic borrowing in a foreign currency is also part of international credit, given the foreign currency and interest rate risk this implies. The BIS collected data on such exposure.

International credit is in fact huge (Table 9.5). Banks made up about 60% of the total of $30.7 trillion at the end of March 2018, via bank lending ($13.3 billion) or via banks holding international securities ($4.7 trillion). International debt securities not held by banks (12.8 trillion) made up the difference. Total international credit amounted to almost 40% of global GDP.

Exposures differ across countries, but such figures underpin the double-edged nature of international credit. It can serve as international insurance, spreading risks on many 'shoulders'. And it can exacerbate contagion in the case of large problems. There is significant potential for spillover from the non-bank to the banking sector. The related financial and real economy risks, in turn, can affect public expenditure and debt to a significant extent as happened in the global financial crisis. Cross-border losses were a large share of the total crisis costs in some countries with significant international asset positions, such as Germany. However, no systematic assessments on fiscal risks via this channel are available.

Table 9.5 *International credit*

	Trillion $	% of Global GDP
Total	30.7	37.6
Bank loans	13.3	16.3
Cross border	8.0	9.8
Local in foreign currency	5.3	6.4
International debt securities	17.5	21.3
Held by banks	4.7	5.7
Held by non-banks	12.8	15.6

Source: BIS Quarterly Review (September 2018)

International Safety Nets

International financial safety nets are the second channel worth discussing, because they aim to cushion the national fallout and the international transmission of a crisis. After the Second World War, the United States and other advanced countries created the IMF to deal with international financial tensions. The IMF works like an international financial insurance with the price being conditionality (plus interest and principal on IMF loans).

The IMF can lend up to roughly 1 trillion Special Drawing Rights (or SDRs, the IMF unit of account). This is equivalent to about US$ 1.5 trillion, of which around SDR 500 billion are own resources (so-called quotas). Almost SDR 200 billion constitute contingent multilateral borrowing and a little over SDR 300 billion are bilateral loans from member countries' central banks. In 2018/2019, the remaining 'firepower' of the IMF was about US$ 1 trillion, as part of its funds were tied up in existing programmes.

Europe created its own 'financial stability insurance' during the global financial crisis. The European mechanisms included the European Stability Mechanism (ESM), with a financing volume of more than €800 billion at their peak. Total financing for euro area countries since then was reduced to the ESM's €500 billion, with most of this as remaining 'firepower' in 2018/2019. ESM capital amounted to €704.8 billion, of which €80.5 billion had been paid in. Guarantees by euro area countries of €624.3 billion (or about 5.5% of 2018 euro area GDP) made up for the rest – and constituted contingent fiscal liabilities.

Table 9.6 *The size of IMF programmes*

		Amount Approved (Billion SDRs)	Amount Approved (% of GDP)[1]
Argentina	2018	40.7	11.2%
Greece	2012	23.8	14.9%
Portugal	2011	23.7	15.0%
Ireland	2010	19.5	13.7%
Greece	2010	26.4	13.8%
Argentina	2001	16.9	8.7%
South Korea	1997	15.5	3.8%
Thailand	1997	2.9	2.6%
Mexico	1995	12.1	4.9%

Sources: IMF Members' Financial Data, GDP from World Bank
1. GDP of respective country in indicated year.

From a global perspective, there were further regional financing arrangements and the financial crisis saw the emergence of some ad hoc mechanisms such as central bank swap lines.

The evolution of these frameworks and the magnitude of safety nets are important. But the increased size of the financial system and international credit also puts this into perspective. It is a fact that international financial support packages have increased significantly over the past two decades (Table 9.6). IMF programmes since the start of the global financial crisis exceeded 10% of GDP, even when excluding much higher regional support in the European countries (total support for Ireland and Portugal was around 40% of GDP and for Greece well over 100%). This compares with IMF programmes 'worth' 2–9% of GDP in the 1995–2001 period.

9.5 Quantifying Risks and Buffers

The global financial crisis revealed that we know too little about the potential channels of fiscal financial risks. Moreover, risk analysis typically focusses on fragments of the system and not the comprehensive picture. Consequently, the economic, financial and fiscal costs were much larger than anybody had expected or modelled. This was partly due to the lack of buffers in several parts of the system but also due to the multitude of channels and the compound effects on fiscal balances.

Sectoral Risk Analysis

In-depth quantitative analysis of the different transmission channels is patchy, as the discussion in Chapter 8 and the previous sections of this chapter showed. In principle, one should be able to attach a 'price tag' to various risks and vulnerabilities in the past and future: change in financing costs, asset price effects, automatic stabilisers, active policies, guarantees, bank and non-bank risks, potential central bank and international obligations.

We reported some of the price tags for the past. Asset price effects were up to several per cent of GDP per annum, financing costs increases can reach comparable magnitudes and so can real economy effects on public expenditure and finances. There are experiences with bank rescue costs ranging from a few to 30% of GDP.

However, from a forward-looking perspective, we do not have a good understanding of many of the risks, and how much they changed because of regulatory and economic developments over the past decade. We do not know the level of 'safe' private debt at the macro level and have to help ourselves with rule-of-thumb benchmarks such as those developed by the European Commission. The same holds for public debt and the limits of 'safe' bank exposure to public debt.

Analysing the risks from non-bank financing is even less easy, given the absence of precedents. If past experiences in banking are any guidance, the fiscal costs of a full-blown crisis could easily go into the trillions. In the best case of Spain, government costs were 4% of bank assets during the global financial crisis. Applied to a $50 trillion volatile shadow banking sector, this would imply a US$ 2 trillion burden for governments. A 4% burden from the global pension fund and life insurance industry would not be much lower. If the actual funding gaps reported here were any guidance, the potential for losses in this industry would be much larger, especially in crisis scenarios (see, e.g. Table 9.4). While this is pure speculation, the numbers illustrate the potential importance of such risks.

Compound Risks

Most importantly, we need to have a better understanding of the compound risks from fiscal–financial vulnerabilities. This, in turn, should inform the debate on 'optimal' or maximum 'safe' fiscal variables. Here, experiences with expenditure, deficit and debt increases in past financial crises could be an indicator of the fiscal buffers needed in the future. However, bailout costs alone are too narrow a gauge of crisis costs. It is more appropriate to look at the compound effect through all channels. Increases in the expenditure and deficit ratio by 5–10% of GDP within a few years – and more in some countries – illustrate the riskiness of high public expenditure ratios and deficits for fiscal stability and sustainability.

The change in the debt ratio is another reasonable proxy and warrants a more detailed analysis. Between 2007 and 2017, changes in debt levels were high in most countries and huge in the most affected ones (Figure 9.13). The Irish public debt ratio increased from about 25% to 120% of GDP, an increase of 95.7%. For Portugal and Spain, the increase exceeded 60% of GDP, for the United Kingdom it came close to 50% of GDP.

Note also that only Ireland managed to shrink public debt significantly after the crisis. Portuguese debt started to decline significantly as of 2017, but Spain and the United Kingdom (just as France and Italy) continued to report debt ratios near their post-crisis peak into 2019. This shows how difficult it is to bring down debt once it is up.

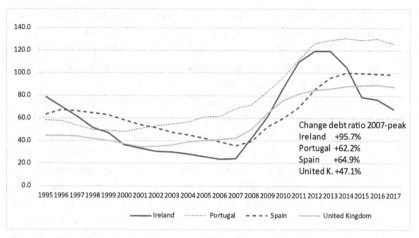

Figure 9.13 Public debt in Ireland, Portugal, Spain and the United Kingdom, % of GDP.

Borio et al. (2019) estimate econometrically the fiscal buffers that the advanced and emerging countries may need. They find that the debt ratio needs to be low enough to absorb a rise between 20% and 60% of GDP to avoid a fiscal crisis with 99% probability. These figures are lower than the debt increases experienced in the parts of Europe discussed here. They reflect the crises experiences over the past forty years which were mostly less costly. Hence, the range may even be conservative.

These figures and those from the global financial crisis give us a sense of how much of a fiscal buffer countries may need in the future. Monetary union members without their own monetary and exchange rate policies to facilitate adjustment experienced the highest debt increases. They may need larger buffers than others, although the United Kingdom's and Japan's debt increases of 45–60% of GDP are also telling.

With public debt ratios reaching 100% or even exceeding 200% of GDP, a number of countries may be just one major recession away from fiscal crisis. Recall the figures from Table 8.7. One can easily see that a repeat of the 2007–2017 experience would bring French and UK debt to 130%, US debt to 150%, that of Spain and Italy to 160% and that of Japan to about 300% of GDP.

It is true that larger buffers in financial systems and lower interest rates increase resilience and seem to permit lower fiscal buffers. At the same time, more public and overall debt globally, and the uncertain and unmeasurable risks in the financial system, increase vulnerability at both the national and international level. Safety nets are available for dealing with such situations; however, it is questionable whether they are sufficient to cover large countries. Moreover, it is unclear whether the advanced countries would get the necessary political support at home and abroad for the accompanying adjustment programmes in the future.

There is another, global, dimension to consider. On the basis of the figures in Table 9.6, we can make a rough calculation of the potential insurance role that the global financial safety net can play. With financing of US$ 1 trillion and an average IMF programme of 10–15% of GDP, the IMF can assist countries with a combined GDP of roughly US$7–10 trillion. This is not small, but in a total global GDP of about US$ 80 trillion it is also not that much. It implies that the world's major governments had better stay liquid and solvent, or else the established system will reach its limits. This is another, systemic argument in favour of building resilience and bringing down public debt.

9.6 Conclusions

This chapter has presented an account of fiscal–financial risks via banks, shadow banks, central banks and international linkages. The risks are likely to be significant, notably in the non-bank financial sector, while their extent, their transmission and their compound effects are uncertain.

Given this analysis, it is doubtful whether efforts to build buffers and reduce vulnerabilities have gone far enough. The IMF has repeatedly pointed to growing medium-term financial instability risks (IMF, GFSR, 2018; 2019). Moreover, population ageing and the political dominance of social expenditure have increased future budget pressures. Competitiveness and asset price disequilibria were probably lower in the late 2010s than a decade earlier, but so were growth prospects. Public and private debt was much higher, global financial safety nets were big but limited, and geopolitical challenges loomed larger than a decade earlier.

What does this mean for fiscal policies and 'optimal' public debt? What government deficit and debt ratios imply sustainable public finances with debt low enough to avoid a future fiscal crisis? Given debt increases of 40%, 60% or almost 100% of debt in the global crisis, the EU threshold of 60% may be a reasonable figure after all (Buck and Schuknecht, 2017; Schuknecht, 2018, 2019).

The IMF used to see a 60% threshold for the advanced countries and 40% for the emerging countries as a reasonably good proxy. Chapter 8 illustrated that broadly balanced budgets are a reasonable benchmark for 'good' times to gradually bring down debt. Moreover, the elimination of debt biases in tax systems is important to improve the incentives for financial soundness in the private sector (BIS Annual Report, 2019).

What do fiscal financial vulnerabilities imply for 'optimal' public expenditure? Spending ratios of near or above 50% of GDP are potentially not sustainable if they rise by a further 5% or 10% of GDP in a crisis. Low spending, low revenue and broadly balanced budgets (at least in good times) leave a lot more scope for orderly adjustment and a good chance for successful prevention. This is another reason for a lean and well-financed state with spending of around 30–35% or perhaps 40% of GDP, as discussed especially in Chapter 6.

These findings also suggest the need to strengthen financial sector resilience further, with emphasis on non-bank financing. This challenge was taken quite seriously in the G20 context in the post-crisis years. International rules and institutional agreements defined targets and processes to mitigate risks.

Finally, future crisis episodes may see governments seek short-term relief. Trade protection may aim to help domestic producers. Capital controls may prevent capital flight, as was done in the early 2010s in Greece and Cyprus. On the positive side, this facilitates private sector burden-sharing. On the negative side, it could increase uncertainty, volatility and capital flight more broadly. The World Trade Organisation (WTO) framework, the IMF's 'institutional view' and the OECD Code for the Liberalisation of Capital Accounts all aim at reducing the risk of disorderly trade and capital flow restrictions.

We will discuss the role of rules and institutional remedies to reduce risks and enhance resilience in more depth in Chapter 10.

PART IV

REMEDIES

10

Rules and Institutions

The very principle of constitutional government requires it to be assumed that political power will be abused to promote the particular purposes of the holder, not because it always is so, but because such is the natural tendency of things, to guard against which is the especial use of free institutions.

John Stuart Mill

Laws and institutions must go hand in hand with the progress of human kind.

Thomas Jefferson

Highlights

Rules and institutions are at the heart of effective and well-managed governments that focus on their core tasks. Sound rules and institutions constrain policy-makers and guide the expectations of citizens. This promotes trust, opportunities, prosperity and freedom. It prevents hubris and excessive expectations about what governments should and can do.

Sound rules and institutions constrain deficits, spending and debt. They govern the process of budget-making and implementation and ensure the effectiveness and efficiency of spending programmes. They also help constrain government activities relative to the private sector. Rules and institutions for the banking and shadow banking sectors protect government and citizens from the fiscal risks of financial crisis. The international institutional architecture underpins stability across both countries and continents.

Fiscal rules and institutions have gone through phases of support and decline and there has been more progress in the financial than in the fiscal sphere (Figure 10.1). We need to re-strengthen our rules and institutions to tackle successfully the challenges of the 'spending state' and keep government lean, efficient and sustainable.

Balanced budget as written or unwritten rule in peace time	Keynesian Activism	Renaissance of Rules	Renaissance of Activism
1870-1960	1960-1980	1980-2000	2000-2017

Figure 10.1 'Barometer' of support for fiscal rules.

10.1 The Reason for Rules

Governments and public spending have undoubtedly contributed enormously to the prosperity and well-being of people over the past 150 years. This holds particularly true for the period up to the 1960s when governments provided sound 'rules of the game' and a level playing field for well-functioning markets and developed the provision of essential public goods and services.

In the past fifty-sixty years, however, the growth of government has often gone well beyond what was necessary. The provision of goods and services became very costly. The peacetime 'rule' of balanced budgets was abandoned. The insurance function of government mutated to cover all aspects of life and the economy. As a result, governments often became much larger than the 30–35% or perhaps 40% of GDP needed to do a good job. And they built up high public debt.

With the global financial crisis, citizens in the advanced countries became visibly more concerned and polarised about the role of the state. Many people began to feel that the 'rules of the game' only applied to them while others got away with 'murder' as governments provided significant support to special interests and seemed to neglect core tasks such as security and good education. The financial and fiscal crises in Europe had huge costs and confronted governments and populations with stark choices to regain their stability.

Confronted with an expanding role of government, with threats to fiscal sustainability from high debt, population ageing and financial sector weakness and with the decline of rules-based policy-making, concerns about future economic prospects, stability and even individual freedom (that depends on rules and a level playing field) increased. Future bouts of financial instability and crisis could not only have potentially serious economic and fiscal costs but also further undermine trust in government, financial markets and our whole economic system (OECD, 2019f).

Mastering these challenges will require a rethink of the role of the state and a regime change in many of the advanced countries. We need to refocus on government's core functions. This means re-setting the 'rules of the game' and providing essential public goods and services. It means re-setting hard budget constraints, bringing down debt and reducing risks in the social and financial sphere. Governments also need to leave alone what is better left to the private sector (Kornai, 1986; Müller, 2003; Blankart, 2017).

Rules and institutions are the 'red thread' that can deal with the challenges identified in this book. This agenda is also almost 'commonplace' for the developing and emerging countries (Acemoglu and Robinson, 2012). How can we think that the advanced economies are any different?

This agenda is not necessarily popular at a time when most macroeconomists see the role of government as fine-tuning the economy and attaining a multitude of economic and social objectives (James, 2009). However, it is arguably this excessive faith in and demands on government that has led to the debt build up, the inefficiencies, the neglect of core tasks and 'rules of the game' and the over-commitment of governments. Hubris and disregard for economics and markets is a very old disease (Böhm-Bawerk, 1914; Issing, 2009).

Fortunately, there are success stories. A number of countries with 'small states', such as Switzerland, Ireland and Australia, are doing well. There have been many episodes of regime changes with successful reform of rules, institutions and expenditure policies both in Europe and outside it (see Chapters 4 and 5). The implementation of the regulatory agenda for the financial sector has also been progressing.

Fiscal Limits after the Financial Crisis

Has anything changed in the advanced countries that warrants a rethink of fiscal limits? Some economists do not see a public debt or spending problem, on the contrary. We have already touched on this and we will discuss the arguments in more depth in the concluding Chapter 11.

The previous chapters have provided strong arguments in favour of expenditure, deficit, and debt limits. Spending limits are almost self-evident. Without spending limits it is neither possible to control the size of the state nor its deficits and debt. However, for spending limits to be realistic and credible, it is important that policy programmes and commitments are consistent with them. Otherwise, spending is shifted off budget or bills remain unpaid.

A balanced budget brings down high public debt as experience shows, and it provides the room to react effectively to new challenges or in future crises. Existing rules require US states and European countries to balance their budgets – in Europe, over the budgetary cycle. This still seems to be a reasonable approach, as a minimum, in good times.

What is the appropriate public debt ceiling? The last crisis added almost 40% of GDP to G7 debt and even 60% or 100% of GDP to the most affected countries, as we saw in Chapter 9. Even if there is the firm intention not to use tax payers' money again to support the financial system, there may be good reasons for rapid (but not costless) clean-up operations in the future. The presence of sufficient deficit and debt buffers should reduce the risk of a financial crisis turning into a fiscal one (with the accompanying need for international support) in the future.

In Europe, a ceiling of 60% applies, and perhaps this is still a reasonable benchmark in a world of repeated financial crises. The large 'safe haven' countries, of course, can afford more debt (as long as they stay 'safe havens'). 'Small' countries with strong booms and large financial sectors may find the 60% ratio too high. This was the experience of Ireland and Spain after 2009. Andersson and Jonung (2019) proposed a 25% of GDP target for Sweden.

There are other reasons for a debt threshold in the vicinity of 60%. The stabilising role of public finances may suffer with debt above 75% of GDP and growth may fall with ratios above 80–100% (Sutherland et al., 2012; Checherita-Westphal, Hallett and Rother, 2014; OECD, 2015). There are thus good reasons to maintain hard budget constraints for governments.

10.2 Fiscal Rules and Sound Public Finances

Deficit and Debt Rules

If governments behaved in a welfare maximising manner, they would incur deficits in downturns and surpluses in upswings. They would design programmes in an optimal manner and only do what governments should do. However, governments in real life behave differently. Politicians seek re-election and support from special interest groups. Politicians also like to grant public insurance in the interests of industry, finance and social groups even if it is unaffordable and undesirable because the burden can often be passed to the future (or to others). In a monetary union, divergent developments and moral hazard may reinforce fiscal problems (see Müller, 2003 and OECD, 2015 for a detailed discussion).

To counter these behavioural disincentives, economists and governments have 'invented' fiscal rules that control public expenditure, deficits and debt. Historically, such rules tended to be very simple: balanced budgets had to prevail in peacetime so that debt would come down to low levels. As a result, public expenditure broadly followed revenue, and both developed in line with GDP.

In the 1960s and 1970s, fiscal rules fell by the wayside when the 'sky seemed to be the limit' of what governments could do. When reality hit and spending, deficits and debt expanded rapidly, rules were 'rediscovered' in the 1980s and 1990s. Rules evolved beyond nominal deficits and debt and included cyclical and structural considerations and, in some cases, public expenditure growth.

The OECD Budgeting Outlook (OECD, 2019b) presents key facts on fiscal rules and budgetary institutions in its 2018 survey. Twenty-eight countries featured fiscal rules to constrain expenditure, deficits and/or debt. Broadly balanced budgets as an operational target were still prominent, even though many quantitative and institutional nuances applied.

Most countries embedded fiscal rules and targets in their so-called medium-term economic frameworks whereby fiscal targets are to be consistent with forecasts of economic developments. This is very positive. But enforcement mechanisms were often weak, inconsistent or unclear. Only eleven countries reported automatic corrections of deviations from targets and only four of them foresaw automatic sanctions. In some countries, rules were simply not implemented (OECD, 2019b).

Fiscal rules probably exerted their strongest influence in the run up to EMU before 1999. The 2000s, however, witnessed a declining influence of rules that arguably contributed to the fiscal crisis in Europe in the early 2010s. In the late 2010s, more rules than ever exist, but their role in shaping policies has been mixed (see, OECD, 2015 or Heinemann, Moessinger and Yeter, 2018 for an analysis across a large number of studies).

Much of the literature argues that rules do constrain deficits somewhat so that debt would have been even higher otherwise. In Europe, the SGP has probably contributed to fewer episodes of high deficits (Caselli and Wingender, 2018). De facto, and due to limited compliance in good times, however, it worked in a pro-cyclical manner, with expansionary policies in booms and consolidation in downturns (Beetsma and Steclebout-Orseau, 2018). Most importantly, fiscal rules have not prevented the build-up of potentially unsustainable debt.

Europe's SGP is symptomatic of the difficulties in effectively constraining public finances. The SGP requires a broadly balanced budget and the prevention of 'excessive' deficits above 3% and debt above 60% of GDP. Our earlier analysis shows that these objectives are quite reasonable. Several reforms and complementary national rules in the so-called fiscal compact, however, did not improve the record of compliance. In the 1999–2017 period, four euro area countries broke the 3% threshold ten or more times and only two never did.

One should, however, not be dogmatic about compliance with fiscal rules in all circumstances. It would not have been reasonable to stick to balanced budgets or the 3% deficit limit during the global financial crisis, and the SGP provided this flexibility. At the same time, there is the risk that targets once missed are never reached again and exceptions become the rule. When fiscal adjustment is being delayed, there is a need for credible medium-term programmes to re-anchor expectations (Gaspar, Obstfeld and Sahay, 2016).

The malaise in the European Union can also be demonstrated by comparing fiscal targets with actual developments in Italy and France as examples (Figure 10.2). All the EU countries publish their fiscal targets for the next 3–5 years in so-called Stability Programmes in the spring and Draft Budgetary Plans in the autumn. Figure 10.2 shows the evolution of deficit and debt targets over the 2014–2017 vintages for the two countries. The reality was regularly very different from the plans and the targets were usually too optimistic. Despite repeated promises, deficits never reached 'safe' positions and debt did not decline. And it is the lack of compliance with rules and sound policies that make pro-cyclical policies more likely (Larch et al, 2020).

Expenditure Rules

One promising avenue to make fiscal rules more effective, keep debt reasonably low and governments lean is to have complementary rules on public expenditure. Expenditure should not grow faster than GDP. That keeps the expenditure ratio stable. If deficits and debt need to decline, expenditure growth should be slower. However, many countries in Europe used the 'good times' and revenue windfalls of the pre-crisis boom for very expansionary expenditure policies, when the presence of effective expenditure rules would have made a huge difference. Simulation results are quite telling in that regard (Hauptmeier, Sanchez-Funetes and Schuknecht, 2011).

Countries experienced an increase in expenditure ratios that was much higher than if they had followed an expenditure rule between 1999 and 2007. For France, Italy and Portugal expenditure ratios would have been up to 2% of GDP lower in 2007. For Spain, Greece and Ireland the simulation figures were even higher.

Public debt would have been much lower with rules-based expenditure policies at the outset of the global financial crisis in 2007 (Table 10.1). Public debt would have been 5% of GDP lower in France and Ireland, over

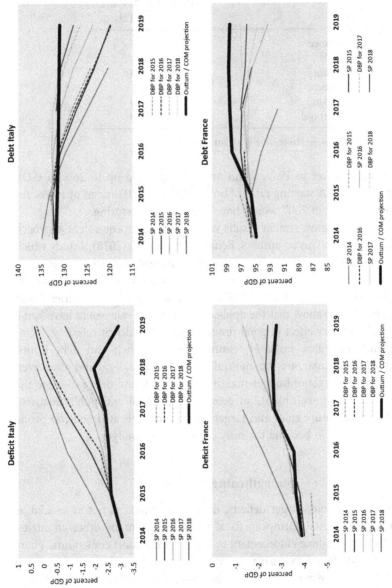

Sources: Ministries of Finance, Italy and France, Commission (Actual and Forecasts)
SP=Stability Programme (spring); DBP=Draft Budgetary Plan (autumn); Com=Commission

Figure 10.2 Fiscal performance over 2012–2018 stability programme vintages, Italy and France.

Table 10.1 *Simulated decline in debt ratio with expenditure rule, 1999–2007*

	Change in Debt Ratio (% of GDP)
France	−4.5
Italy	−10.1
Spain	−13.3
Greece	−26.2
Ireland	−4.9
Portugal	−11.9

Sources: Hauptmeier et al, 2011

10% of GDP lower in Italy, Spain and Portugal and up to 26% of GDP lower in Greece. A starting ratio of below 90% of GDP instead of 100%, for example, in Italy in 2007 would have been more reassuring.

Other studies show similar results when applying an equivalent approach to Hauptmeier and his co-authors. Bénassy-Quéré et al. (2018), a study which includes seven French and seven German economists, proposed an expenditure rule that would limit nominal public primary expenditure growth to nominal GDP with a downward adjustment for high-debt countries. Fuest and Gros (2019a) show that the application of such a rule would have had a greater disciplinary effect in good times compared to deficit rules.

Expenditure rules, however, cannot replace deficit and debt limits. Deficits, in particular, are the 'natural' administrative, legal and often even constitutional target of budget-making. The deficit and debt ratios are the bottom line for government, an economic, political and public focus of 'minds'. Expenditure rules and targets are too complicated and too prone to manipulation to become the only constraint on budgets.

Strengthening Governance

Whether fiscal rules target deficits, debt or spending is not as crucial as effective governance. European fiscal rules, just as many other countries' rules, lack the credible enforcement to create hard budget constraints. There is by now quite an extensive literature emphasising this point, starting with Kopits and Symansky (1998). The European rules' complexity renders enforcement even more difficult because it encourages exemption 'hunting' and certifies pseudo-compliance. By contrast, simplicity facilitates transparency and monitoring (Schuknecht, 2005).

The discussion in Europe since the early 2000s did not tackle governance challenges despite some good suggestions in the literature (Rother, Schuknecht and Stark, 2010; Schuknecht et al., 2011; Sinn 2014/2015). Beetsma and Steclebout-Orseau (2018) proposed freezing structural funds for deficit sinners in Europe and strengthening independent surveillance by outside national and European fiscal institutions. Von Hagen and Harden (1994), Hallerberg, Strauch and Von Hagen (2009) and OECD (2019b) suggest credible commitments as part of coalition agreements and strong finance ministers to overcome spending and deficit biases. In Germany, the 'Black Zero' slogan standing for a balanced budget was such a commitment during much of the 2010s: it was easy to understand and follow for both policymakers and the public.

A number of studies proposed enhancing financial market monitoring of public finances. Fuest and Heinemann (2017) proposed so-called accountability bonds, which would require governments to issue junior bonds when debt exceeds a certain threshold. Matthes and Rocholl (2018) argued for regulatory incentives to diversify the holding of government debt so that banks can reduce their exposure to the debt of just one government.

More orderly rules and processes for sovereign debt restructuring also aim to strengthen financial market monitoring via private sector bail-in and better incentives for government. Public debt restructuring regimes should include prolongation provisions when a country needs financial assistance, single-limb collective action clauses, provisions against hold-outs and a debt sustainability analysis (Weder di Mauro and Zettelmeyer, 2017; Andritzky, Christofzik and Feld, 2018; Zettelmeyer, 2018; Destais, Eidam and Heinemann, 2019).

Fiscal rules and market monitoring are all no real panacea, even bailout prohibitions at the constitutional level are not. In Europe, the 'no-bailout clause' of the European Treaties aimed to prevent over-indebtedness. When fiscal crisis struck anyhow, European countries agreed on conditional European and IMF financial support to balance solidarity and incentives. The United States experienced regional default in Puerto Rico in 2015/2017 and faced the same dilemma of destabilisation risks versus moral hazard (Chirinko, Chiu and Henderson, forthcoming).

10.3 Rules and Institutions and 'Value for Money'

Effective rules and institutions are not only essential for sound and sustainable public finances, they also contribute to the quality of public finances and 'value for money'. First, sound public finances are themselves 'good' for effective and efficient fiscal policies. Countries with unsound public finances often take recourse to ad hoc budgetary adjustments with cuts in investment (politically easy) rather than in bureaucracy (difficult). Excessive debt also often leads to high inflation and strongly falling public wages, which, in turn, stoke corruption, low-quality administration and a deterioration in the rules of law. Sound public finances are, therefore, essential for 'high-quality' public finances that provide 'value for money' and 'inclusiveness' to citizens.

Rules and institutions also advance government performance and the efficiency of policy programmes via better governance of the budget process. We mentioned the importance of medium term expenditure frameworks, which ensure consistency between budget plans and a realistic view of future economic prospects. Budget transparency and financial reporting increase the accountability of politicians and administrators, and this refers to both spending objectives and the envisaged outcomes of programmes.

In addition, the toolkit for strong budget institutions includes spending reviews, performance budgeting, fiscal risk analysis and independent fiscal watchdogs/institutions. In fact, the advanced economies undertook a large number of reforms in the 2010s to improve the institutional frameworks of budgeting (Figure 10.3).

Spending reviews have a strategic and a tactical objective. They help to enhance the efficiency of individual spending programmes and priorities

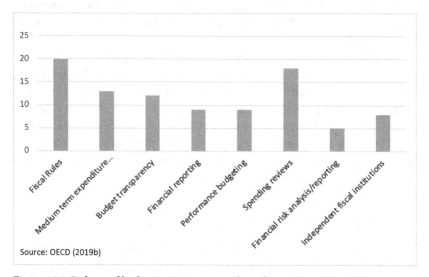

Source: OECD (2019b)

Figure 10.3 Reform of budget institutions, number of countries, 2014–2018.

across such programmes. Spending reviews tend to be successful when there is strong political commitment and 'ownership' by the administration; they must follow clear objectives and be well integrated in the budget process. Most importantly, implementation has to follow, and this should take place in an environment where performance counts and change is welcome. Moreover, there should be an ex post assessment of the impact they have had.

A large number of countries introduced spending reviews in the 2010s (Figure 10.4). The OECD (2019b) reports twenty countries that undertook such reviews in 2017, twice as many as a decade earlier. More than half of the reviews were broad-based or even comprehensive. In most cases, the reports largely or fully met their objectives, even though in some countries there was no ex post assessment (a significant weakness). Spending reviews were an important instrument underpinning reforms in the Nordics, the Netherlands and Canada. In Germany, spending reviews also aimed to underpin the achievement of the government's balanced budget target (Dönnebrink, Ebert and Schuknecht, 2019).

Many governments introduced performance budgeting to attain maximum value for money from their spending programmes. Performance budgeting tries to establish direct links between budget allocations and performance, to facilitate oversight by both Parliament and the public. However, there are important measurement problems (what exactly is the

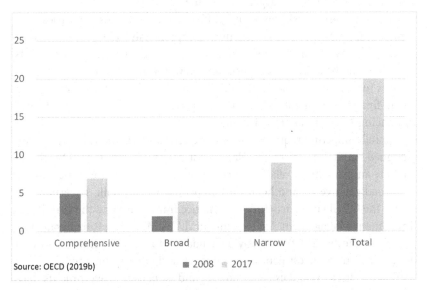

Source: OECD (2019b)   ■ 2008 ■ 2017

Figure 10.4 Prevalence of spending reviews, number of countries.

'outcome' of a teacher?). The OECD (2019b) therefore advises calling it 'performance-informed budgeting' instead. France's 'strategic dashboard' comes close to OECD best practice, while Chile, Canada and South Korea also provide 'good cases' to learn from.

Programme evaluation is the third element of budgetary institutions that attempts to promote expenditure efficiency. It typically includes an evaluation of a programme's design, efficiency and accountability. The positive impact of such evaluation is greatest for individual programmes. It is less suitable for strategic decisions at the ministry or government level. Again, Chile and Canada were model cases for programme evaluation according to the OECD analysis.

The rules on budget execution are particularly important to ensure compliance with budgetary targets and, thereby, hard budget constraints. At the same time, it is important that countries maintain some flexibility as regards re-allocation across priorities and carry-over across years. Adequate budgetary reporting complements budget execution by strengthening transparency and accountability, and so do the audits of public accounts.

Fiscal risk reporting is another important component of modern budgeting. Comprehensive risk reporting includes the identification, disclosure, analysis and management of fiscal risks. Ideally, fiscal risk scenarios and stress tests complement extensive reporting; this allows budget and policy makers to undertake adequate risk mitigation and management via the establishment of targets and buffers.

In reality, fiscal risk reporting differs strongly across countries. The United Kingdom published the most comprehensive data on the macro-economic environment, the financial sector, debt interest payments, spending and balance sheets. Germany, New Zealand and Sweden required buffers for any fiscal risks that could materialise. Given our discussion on fiscal–financial vulnerabilities, there is probably much scope for further enhancing fiscal (financial) risk analysis.

Capital budgeting requires particular attention. It should contain a well-designed capital investment plan. Cost-benefit analysis (CBA) should include an assessment relative to other investment priorities (and not just one road relative to another). OECD principles of public governance of PPPs, the OECD infrastructure governance framework and the IMF Public Investment Management Assessment (PIMA) (IMF, 2018; Ruiz Rivadeneira and Schuknecht, 2019) all provide guidance to governments on how to undertake public investment in an effective and efficient manner.

Finally, fiscal councils that advise and supervise governments have emerged in a number of countries, notably in Europe. The 'watchdog' role of fiscal councils works best when they are legally independent, when they have access to all relevant information, when they are involved with macroeconomic forecasts and when they conduct a timely and comprehensive monitoring of compliance with fiscal rules (Jankovics and Sherwood, 2017). The European Fiscal Board (EFB) and some European country boards are interesting examples (see, e.g. Thygessen et al., 2018).

It is important to see budget rules and institutions as a complex system of checks and balances. Still, rules and institutions cannot completely replace political commitment and the popular support of sound, high-quality fiscal policies. Rules and institutions also affect the size and efficiency of government. Weak budget processes encourage expenditure overruns and inefficiencies, thus undermining the principles of 'lean government' and 'value for money'.

10.4 Public Expenditure Programmes

If governments are to focus on core tasks, they should only undertake those activities for which there are compelling reasons to do so. That is the premise of market economies and underpins individual freedom. Many things that governments do today rightly belong in the public sector domain, but some others do not. The prerogative of a market economy should be that government and not the private sector needs to prove both its role and involvement. This principle is often forgotten today, but rules and institutions that limit government action and protect private property and markets can help.

There is broad consensus that government should (normally) not run enterprises, as the private sector can do so better. But it is sometimes not immediately obvious whether governments or the private sector should be responsible: this is, for example, the case in health and in education. No matter who does things, they should be done well and efficiently, and for that we need good rules and institutions. Public education needs good governance and so does private education. The same holds for health.

Public Consumption

Starting with public consumption or 'real' expenditure, much of what we said earlier in this chapter applies here. The key words for strong rules governing public consumption are 'strong budget preparation' and 'execution'. If applied properly, public consumption can be small: public consumption in Switzerland is only half as high as in some other countries and still provides a well-functioning rule of law and efficient public goods and services.

Many things that governments do under this heading the private sector could probably do better and cheaper. Running enterprises or banks is not a core function of government. Government can outsource more services to the private sector and many studies show that private providers mostly do them better and more cheaply. When there is a reason, government can regulate and finance private providers.

Education

Public education spending is mostly part of public consumption. It is perhaps the most important spending category because it determines a country's future growth and affects people's opportunities. Good early childhood, primary and secondary education in particular are great 'social equalisers' because they can provide everybody with a reasonably equal set of basic skills and opportunities in life, even when people come from a disadvantaged background.

Many different models of education funding and provision are used but there is no general finding that private education is better than public provision or vice versa. However, there are some principles for sound policy-making in both (OECD, 2017d, 2017e, 2018a). It is important to align roles and responsibilities so that people can do what they should do. Funding should be based on formulas that reflect reliable and clear data and criteria, with periodic reviews. The OECD also recommends multiannual planning with strategic targets and incentives for efficiency coupled with some flexibility. Evaluation and monitoring, audits and performance management should apply to budgets in general and to education in particular.

Public funding of private schools raises additional challenges. Private schools should be subject to the same regulation regarding tuition and admission as public schools to avoid any 'cherry picking' of students. Transparency and accountability in the use of public funds is essential. Good examples for the private provision–public funding model are the Netherlands, Belgium, Denmark and Estonia.

The closer the link between education and professional training the stronger the argument for private provision and financing so that firms get the skills they need. The case for private professional training and private tertiary education is stronger than for basic education. Private financing plays a significant role in vocational training, for example, in Germany and the Netherlands.

Investment

Public investment has tended to decrease over the past decades. Public invest-ment mostly builds and maintains the infrastructure of countries – roads, sewage, school buildings, etc. In the past, much of these were a public task because it was difficult to charge for their use, but technical progress has now significantly moved the boundary between public and private in infrastructure.

Many countries leave the building of their telecoms and energy networks to the private sector. In some countries, private enterprise builds and manages roads and railways via long-term concessions or quasi-private enterprises. Local roads and sewage, the classic examples of public infra-structure, may have gained 'marketability' as monitoring the movement of cars has become easier and people pay for sewage through their water bill. All infrastructure – public and private – requires good regulation to ensure an appropriate level of provision, 'fair' (instead of monopoly) pricing and a service in the public interest rather than in that of well-connected special interests. In fact, sound infrastructure governance is correlated with stronger productivity growth as schown by Demmou and Franco (2020).

PPPs now cover a range of intermediate approaches with more or less private provision and financing. The use of PPP models is widespread across countries but it covers only 5–10% of public investment (OECD, 2019b). PPP models can be the best way to build more infrastructure; however, there are important pitfalls. Providers may take advantage of less 'savvy' public administrations when it comes to the terms of PPP agree-ments. Such projects often involve guarantees, which may turn out to be very costly when poorly designed. We identified PPPs as a potentially important contingent liability of government in Chapter 9.

Social Expenditure: Health and Pensions

We have argued in Chapter 7 that social expenditure is a large and mostly predictable fiscal risk for most of the advanced countries. Social expend-iture may already crowd out other, more productive spending and it risks overstretching the financial capacities of many countries. It is therefore important to constrain social commitments to what is both feasible and necessary. Social insurance should focus on poverty reduction and basic social services. Huge savings are possible, as illustrated by the significant divergence of spending across countries and the reform experiences iden-tified in Chapters 4–6 of Part II.

Two categories of social spending make up the bulk of spending: health and pensions. The OECD estimates that health expenditure could 'easily' be 20% lower if expenditure programmes were efficient (OECD, 2017a). This would imply savings of 1.5% of GDP on total health spending of about 7.5% on average. This figure is broadly in line with the savings potential we identified in Chapter 6. Fewer hospitals, more generic drugs and fewer antibiotics are some of the concrete OECD recommendations.

The management of health expenditure programmes is again key. The buzzwords are the same as for other programmes: transparency and accountability, audits and anti-fraud measures and incentive-compatible remuneration systems. Desirable organisational changes include systematic discharge planning from hospitals, joint procurement by hospitals and better health data governance, to name only a few.

Health systems, however, differ hugely across countries, so that the reform needs also differ. Systems that rely on private finance are not systematically cheaper or better than their public 'brothers' and 'sisters'. The United States is the best example. Tax financed systems are not systematically better than contribution financed ones. There is only one tendency that is striking: mixed systems of tax and contribution-based finance tend to be more expensive than 'purer' ones. This may be because two financing sources soften the budget constraint towards more expensive health service provision (Dauns, Ebert and Schuknecht, 2015). Looking forward, the drivers of health service costs – incomes and technological progress – are very difficult both to anticipate and to control.

Pension expenditure is easier to anticipate, although the dynamics of income and demography are also less certain than economists would like us to believe. Rules-based policy-making is again essential. Public pension spending is particularly prone to political interference, given the growing share of voters in retirement. Pensions are very sensitive because the older people are, the less able they are to make up for income shortfalls through employment. Hence, trust in pension systems is very important for trust in both society and in government.

A good way to maintain sustainable, and thus trustworthy, public pension systems is via rules-based changes in key parameters. Linking retirement age to life expectancy or to a predetermined path is transparent, easy to understand and probably also seen as fair from an intergenerational perspective. Most countries feature rules-based adjustment of pension benefits via 'sustainability factors' and/or retirement age adjusting to longevity (Table 10.2). Independent, non-partisan assessment and advice and public involvement in a 'learning process' can help build public

Table 10.2 *Role of sustainability factors and retirement age in rules-based pension benefit adjustment*

Country	Sustainability factors	Retirement age
Austria	X	
Belgium		X
Denmark		X
Finland	NA	NA
France	X	X
Germany	X	X
Greece	X	X
Italy	X	X
Netherlands	NA	NA
Spain	X	X
Sweden	X	X
Switzerland	X	
UK	X	X
Australia	X	X
Canada	X	X
Japan	X	
South Korea	X	
New Zealand	X	
US	X	

Sources: Dauns, Ebert and Schuknecht (2015); OECD (2017c)

acceptance of reform (Parlevliet, 2017). Most of the advanced countries have private pension plans. Such plans complement public pensions and so alleviate public budgets and share some of the longevity risk with the private sector. Private pension plans play a strong role in several countries, though in others they play less of a role or their systems are still in the development phase. Further systemic reform across public and private pillars is worth considering in a number of countries: a greater reliance on private pensions is often possible even though this may also hold fiscal risks for government, as we saw in Chapter 9.

10.5 Rules to Mitigate Fiscal–Financial Risks

Rules for Banks and Shadow Banking

The governments of the advanced economies made huge mistakes before and during the global financial crisis. Before the crisis, financial regulation and supervision were inadequate, especially for banks but also in the shadow banking sector. During the crisis, governments took many decisions that turned out only to drive up fiscal costs. Starting with Ireland in 2009, they provided 'blanket' deposit guarantees and de facto open-ended liquidity support, engaged in regulatory forbearance and repeated bailouts of banks and debtors.

Lack of adequate rules and lack of implementation were at the heart of the problem. Given the global nature of financial markets, it was clear that rules had to be set internationally and then implemented nationally. As of 2009, the G20 and the FSB in cooperation with national rule-makers set about agreeing on and implementing an international regulatory agenda so that taxpayers 'would never have to pay again'.

Much progress was made in the following years. Agreement on the regulatory agenda was virtually complete and implementation was mostly strong by mid-2017 (Figure 10.5; FSB, 2018). Banks became much better capitalised even though six FSB member countries were still materially non-compliant with the agreed requirements. Countries with globally and domestically systemic banks introduced higher loss absorbency require-ments. The liquidity situation had generally become satisfactory. Some countries reported shortcomings in the leverage of banks and their long-term funding situation, but all countries had introduced compensation restrictions, notably as regards bonuses.

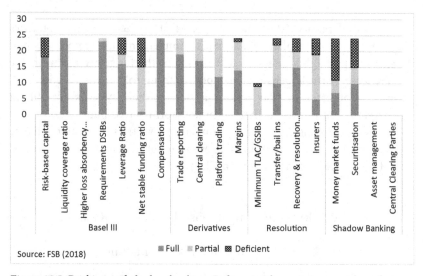

Source: FSB (2018)

Figure 10.5 Banking and shadow banking: Reform implementation, number of countries, 2017.

Another important area of international regulation was derivative markets. Excessive risk-taking on derivatives had almost brought down one of the biggest global banks (AIB) in 2009. Most countries had progressed with the reporting of trades, the clearing of trades through central platforms and the requirement of margins as security for trade. The size of the markets and the limited number of central platforms nonetheless leaves a significant unease over the ability to manage platform failure in the future (see Chapter 9).

Preventing disorderly bank failures was at the heart of the international resolution agenda. The agenda included requirements on bail-inable capital/debt. Banks and insurers had to design plans for their operation, recovery and resolution in case of trouble. The implementation of this part of the regulatory agenda was still in progress, and in some countries lagging, by mid-2017.

Europe implemented the international regulatory agenda as part of a broader move towards Banking Union and Capital Markets Union. The common European 'rule book' emphasised the importance of private sector bail-in and a liability cascade to minimise moral hazard for both politicians and the financial industry (Figure 10.6). Any costs of bank failure would fall on the private sector, starting with regular equity. Only late in this cascade would governments step in.

By 2019, there had been less progress on the implementation of the regulatory agenda for shadow banking/asset management and, consequently, more uncertainty as to the increase of buffers in this industry

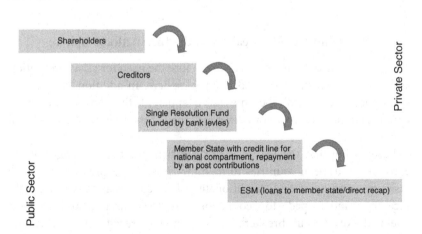

Figure 10.6 Banking union in the European Union: Liability cascade.

(FSB, 2019). The implementation of International Organisation of Securities Commissions (IOSCO) regulatory recommendations was well advanced in half of the twenty-four FSB countries, including the United States and China. Most countries had introduced a 'fair-value' approach for money-market fund portfolios. However, there was less progress in liquidity management, securitisation, risk-based capital requirements for equity in funds and large exposures. Work on securities financing transactions or SFTs (including haircuts on non-centrally cleared SFTs) was still at an early stage.

The privileged treatment of government debt on bank balance sheets continued. Exemptions from exposure limits, zero risk weights and preferential treatment as regards haircuts for liquidity purposes significantly impacted on bank behaviour and disadvantaged private financing. The Basel Committee, however, ended discussions on tackling this gross distortion (BIS, 2017; IMF, GFSR, 2018). Given the public debt situation in a number of countries and the balance sheets of many of their banks, this time bomb continues to tick.

Finally, it is worth spending a few words on the link between financial stability, fiscal risks and tax policy. There is some literature finding a link between tax policy that favours debt and increases the incidence and costs of financial crisis. Mortgage-interest deductibility encourages leverage of households. A favourable treatment of debt in corporate taxation is correlated with higher corporate debt (Wolswijk, 2009; de Mooij et al., 2014; Langedijk et al., 2015). Tax reform should eliminate such biases in the tax system, thereby complementing financial regulatory reform.

Rules and Circuit Breakers in the International Sphere

The global financial crisis brought to the fore the need for crisis prevention and resolution in the fiscal and financial sphere. In addition, the risks of international contagion became more apparent than ever. The international community therefore developed further the international financial architecture.

Recognising that the IMF was not sufficient for the challenges of the euro area, European countries formed the ESM, which provided financial assistance tied to strong conditionality. This combination set the right incentives and helped stop contagion and destabilisation and, thereby, operated like a 'circuit breaker'. It is important to recognise that this kind of 'international insurance' is a carefully designed, rules-based system.

There are other forms of circuit breakers. Standstills and prolongations in the case of sovereign debt crisis induce investors and debtors to reflect, negotiate and reform while 'the clock is on hold'. This can contain the exit of the private sector from public debt markets and, thereby, reduce the financing needs of international support programmes. However, well-balanced rules, as reflected for example in IMF financial access provisions, are essential to minimise moral hazard and potentially destabilising side effects.

Capital controls are another form of circuit breaker for financial markets, where excessive interconnection between markets can be destabilising (Stiglitz, 2018). Greece and Cyprus applied such controls in the 2010s to facilitate private sector bail-in. Again, a rules-based approach is essential or else one country's controls can lead to contagion, disorderly capital controls and even more volatility. The IMF's institutional view and the OECD codes on the liberalisation of capital flows provide a framework of transparency, consultation and restraint to maintain order in capital markets even in times of stress.

Many macro-prudential measures are 'soft' forms of capital controls. Such circuit breakers may be desirable in an environment of automated trading and volatile markets and prices. A number of instruments were already in use or available in this regard in Europe in the late 2010s and a predictable governance is essential (ESRB, 2018a).

Finally, the international system of trade rules reduces the risk of economic and financial turmoil via trade protectionism. It limits the use of such protectionism even in times of crisis and thus works as a circuit breaker against adverse political dynamics. It was a great achievement of international policy coordination that there was very little protectionism during and after the global financial crisis. In the Great Depression, by contrast, trade protection compounded the devastating effect of financial and fiscal crises across the globe.

10.6 Conclusion

Rules and institutions are key to keeping governments focussed on their core tasks and public expenditure sustainable and efficient. Constraining deficit, debt and spending dynamics via rules is particularly important. The existing constraints of broadly balanced budgets and 60% debt ceilings in Europe make a lot of sense, especially when considering the potentially huge fiscal costs of financial crisis.

In addition, budgetary rules and institutions can underpin sound fiscal policy-making. They can keep spending programmes focussed on core tasks and ensure value for money. Rules and institutions can also help avoid over-commitment, including in the social sphere, and prevent government from doing things that the private sector can do better.

Sound rules and institutions can also contain fiscal risks in the financial sphere. The G20/FSB regulatory agenda is important to make both bank and non-bank financial institutions more resilient. International financial safety nets based on conditionality, rules-based public debt restructuring and well-governed circuit breakers to foster macro-prudential and capital flow stability are also important to contain fiscal expenditure related to financial instability.

An economic order that delivers on core tasks and prevents instability ensures 'balance' in policy-making and preserves our (political and economic) freedom (Schäuble, 2019). Many countries reformed their rules, institutions and policy programmes and brought countries onto a better path for growth and well-being, and there has been much progress with the regulatory agenda for the financial system. But more needs to be done. Although rules and institutions are no panacea, they are the best way to deal with the challenges of modern states as regards public expenditure and fiscal risks.

11

Conclusions and Epilogue

The social market economy allows a responsible use of freedom within the framework of a market economy and it requires corrective elements outside the market – to avoid excesses.

Wolfgang Schäuble

11.1 Main Messages

There are four conclusions from this study worth re-emphasising. First, the role of government has evolved enormously over the past 150 years in today's advanced countries. Public expenditure in advanced countries has quadrupled from about 11% of GDP in the late nineteenth century to about 44% of GDP in 2017. In many ways, governments are doing a much better job today than in the past. They provide an institutional framework and essential public goods and services such as a well-functioning administration, security or education. These are at the basis of our freedom, opportunities and prosperity, and doing well on them builds trust with citizens. Public expenditure is an essential ingredient in this.

Second, and with so much more public spending, do citizens get adequate 'value for money'? This was broadly the case until about 1960 when public expenditure averaged near 30% of GDP. But there is more doubt about the spending growth beyond 40% or even 50% of GDP in the following decades.

Countries such as Switzerland, Ireland and Australia provide a good institutional framework and high-quality public goods and services with 'small' governments. These countries show that spending of 30–35% perhaps 40% of GDP should be enough to do well. One could call this a pragmatic 'optimum' size of government. However, these figures should not be viewed dogmatically: there are countries with 'bigger' governments that do well and there are even 'smaller' states that do so too.

Many governments have been spending too much compared to what they are delivering, while putting economic and financial stability at risk. Expenditure reform was the road to success for many of them in three reform waves in the 1980s, 1990s and 2010s (see also the great study by Alesina et al., 2019, on expenditure adjustment). There is nevertheless scope for much greater savings and reform.

Third, in many countries and perhaps more generally, the 'insurance' role of government has gone too far. Social insurance absorbs between 50% and 60% of public resources, and is only bound to rise further with population ageing. This risks leading to 'social dominance' where social spending is unsustainable and crowds out productive spending, such as investment.

There are also risks and vulnerabilities in the financial sector that we do not fully understand but that may well burden public finances significantly in the future. The financial sector has already received huge support in the global financial crisis and policy-makers still seem under the spell of those market developments ten years later. The global financial crisis raised public spending by up to 11% of GDP and public debt by 40%, 60% and even 100% of GDP, rising to levels close to those prevailing at the end of the Second World War: some countries may only be one major recession away from fiscal turmoil.

With such risks, a lean public sector, strict spending limits, broadly balanced budgets and a 60% of GDP public debt limit as required in Europe may not be that 'stupid' after all, especially in good times. 'Small', low-debt governments will be much more resilient to future crises than highly-indebted, 'big' governments.

At a time of record debt and spending, many governments are under pressure from public discontent and are at risk of promising even more spending and creating higher expectations than they can fulfil. It is not possible to satisfy all the calls for social, financial or industry support. The perception of 'all-round' insurance also undermines the spirit of individual responsibility and risk-taking, which are the essential ingredients of a dynamic market economy.

A number of economists have warned of high debt and mounting pressure on our monetary framework (Issing, 2019; Wolf, 2019). High debt and fiscal risks make it more difficult to deal adequately with 'new' challenges such as the environment and climate. They 'trap governments and reduce the policy space beyond fiscal policies more than we think. Over-indebted, we depend more and more on a continuing upswing which causes uncertainty, reduces confidence and at times even crises' (de Larosière, 2019).

What is the solution? There is no panacea, but this book argues in favour of rules-based policy-making and a refocussing of the state on its core tasks. Rules and institutions can help contain fiscal obligations. They can keep governments both focussed and efficient. Rules-based constraints on social security and the financial sector can help contain social and financial sector risks. Continued international coordination on financial regulation and safety nets is essential. This is the fourth message of this book.

We still seem to have lost both momentum and focus. Many if not all governments would benefit from re-setting their expenditure priorities on core tasks and rules-based policy-making. We should understand and anticipate better the essential challenges for our economies and explain better the need for change to our citizens.

A Holistic Approach to Government and Public Expenditure

These are orthodox messages. 'Orthodoxy' really means 'sound doctrine' or 'right opinion' and not 'backwardness', as some economists like to suggest. The messages reflect classical economic thinking following the tradition of great economists like Hume, Smith, Hayek, Buchanan and others. Classical economic thinking takes a holistic view of government and the economy, and we need a holistic view to deal with the challenges to the state today.

Orthodoxy should lead to orthopraxy, a 'rightness of action' or 'correct practice'. This book provides a lot of experience and advice. One of the greatest ortho-practitioners was perhaps Ludwig Erhard, the father of the German 'social market economy' model and 'Wirtschaftswunder' in the 1950s and 1960s. Erhard liberalised the economy after the Second World War. He re-focussed government on its core tasks, including social safety nets, while warning of excessive public regulation, spending and insurance. His 'Wohlstand für Alle', or 'Prosperity for All' (Erhard, 1957/ 2009) is still a very worthwhile read about how to reset a failed state and economy.

Other well-known reformers were the Conservatives Carl Bildt from Sweden and Margaret Thatcher from the United Kingdom, Labour Minister Roger Douglas from New Zealand and the Social Democrat Gerhard Schröder from Germany. These were controversial people in their time and often remain so until today. But their success in turning around depressed, moribund states and economies with comprehensive expenditure and structural reforms deserves recognition.

Ortho-practitioners – great reformers – knew that it is not enough to philosophise about well-functioning markets and government and then assume that the right things will happen. Policy-making over rules for the market and public goods and services is always subject to hard political struggles, even if tempered and ordered by a democratic process. Policy-makers need evidence on what works and they need to be accountable to do the right thing. The OECD and IMF provide much evidence on national and international good practice.

These messages also acknowledge the importance of more outcome-oriented thinking. Musgrave's focus on outcomes was a great achievement. It helped focus both the mind and the actions of policy-makers. Prosperity, economic stability and a reasonable income distribution that enhances social participation and equal opportunity are important outcomes. Citizens hold policy-makers and our market economies to account for outcomes. Therefore, it is outcomes, not spending, that matter for well-being and trust.

Musgravian indicators are more easily measurable than the functioning of markets which, in turn, creates a temptation. Outcomes like growth or GDP could create the illusion that this is all that matters, that the economy can be steered like a machine and that policy-makers will follow 'optimal' policies as advised by economists.

The Classical economists remind us that good outcomes are the result of a well-functioning market process and governments that do well on their core tasks. Rules constrain both politicians and private actors who are 'only' human. This creates an order that is not perfect, but it coordinates our many abilities and interests better than other economic models because it supports freedom, opportunities, prosperity and trust.

A Systemic Issue

There is probably a broad consensus on the improvements that government has brought and the need for 'value for money' raised by this book. There is probably also broad agreement on the core tasks of government underlying the 'social market economy model' and concerns about population ageing. There are, however, diverging views about the degree of the problems and the role of the state in solving them. The greatest differences are probably about the seriousness of future risks, notably from high spending, high debt and the financial sector.

Are public debt, high spending and fiscal risks really such important issues? If interest rates are lower than economic growth rates and additional expenditure results in significant additional growth, why should we worry

(Blanchard, 2019; New Monetary Theory)? Both claims are tempting, but do not convince.

The previous chapters provided ample evidence that excessive public debt and expenditure have often been at the source of crises. Looking forward, interest rates remain endogenous and they can rise rapidly when inflation rises, when policy errors occur, when risk sentiment changes or when disincentives and demographics start taking their toll on global savings. In some countries, interest rates are already higher than economic growth rates because of high debt and fiscal obligations (Fuest and Gros, 2019b).

Why can we not wait and bring down debt later? Experience shows (and our simulations confirm) that high debt is only brought down very slowly, even with balanced budgets. When it takes a decade or even a generation to bring debt back down to prudent levels, it may be too late to react when interest rates increase or new challenges arise.

Raising spending on productive categories seems to be a 'no-brainer' but it is not as easy as it sounds. Additional spending largely did not go into growth-enhancing uses in the past and is unlikely to do so in the future. The political economy is working strongly in favour of social spending and against investment.

Even if additional spending goes into education or infrastructure, there is no guarantee that the growth effects will be strong. Education perform-ance is uncorrelated with public spending and it did not improve where spending increased, as we saw in Chapter 4. Structural problems prevail, and such structural problems – e.g., long planning, environmental impact and public consultation processes – and not a lack of money also hold back infrastructure improvements in many countries. Structural reform could and should boost public and private investment in this regard.

If countries do manage to raise productive spending, debt-financing is not necessarily the first best option: re-prioritisation of spending is often the better alternative. There is enough unproductive spending with nega-tive multipliers to cut in most, if not all, countries. Tax reform can help raise growth and the financing potential of government. Relaxing the aggregate budget constraint and fiscal rules, by contrast, reduces incentives for both government efficiency and reform.

Some economists light-heartedly argue in favour of more public spend-ing to boost demand and inflation. Again, we should ask ourselves whether this is the best way to achieve the objective, given the potential side effects and risks. Many non-fiscal economists are unaware of how hard it is to turn around expenditure and debt dynamics, once set in motion (and special interests have got used to them). Budgets are as hard to manoeuvre as large tankers; we cannot simply switch public spending on and off 'like that'. Perhaps it would be better to improve the framework conditions for private investment (the 'rules of the game'!) and reform the tax system. This would get more 'bang for the buck' and a greater boost in confidence.

Finally, there is perhaps the hope that the debt-related 'day of reckoning' will never come. Central banks may deal with over-indebtedness via financial repression. Low interest rates in conjunction with moderate inflation may then reduce the real value of debt. Again, this is a gamble. What may fall by the wayside is our willingness and ability to adapt and reform, our innovativeness in the market and, of course, trust. If people perceive that this is the 'game', trust in both our governments and in our market economy will suffer.

A number of economists are advising us to take such a gamble. At a time of falling trust and growing protest movements within our countries, this seems both risky and short-sighted. It is also curious that anyone should advocate taking such risks when there is growing competition between our social market economy model and other models. To win these contests, we need to re-focus public expenditure and the role of the state on its core tasks: strong 'rules of the game' and high-quality, essential public goods and services. We will all benefit from a lean, efficient and sustainable state.

11.2 Epilogue

The COVID-19 Crisis and Public Expenditure

As this book was being prepared for print, the COVID-19 – better known as the Coronavirus – crisis broke out. This resulted in major disruptions of supply and demand, and major uncertainty about the magnitude and duration of the impact on the economy. Governments took rapid and drastic measures to contain the crisis, including confinement of countries' whole populations.

This reaction was a remarkable case of strong policy intervention to help restore confidence and underpin economic stability. It was appropriate and essential that governments and central banks introduced major, targeted fiscal, financial and monetary stimulus programmes to mitigate the human and economic costs of the crisis. The European Union also agreed on a major debt-financed support programme.

The fiscal cost and economic impact were far from clear at the time of writing this epilogue. First projections by the European Commission (2020) suggested a further major increase in expenditure ratios in 2020 that would partially reverse with the projected recovery in 2021. Expenditure ratios would increase by an average of over 7% of GDP in 2020 in the EU and the United Kingdom and even more in the United States. The highest expenditure ratios would reach almost 60% of GDP and even more in France. Deficits as a share of GDP would rise to double digits in a number of countries and average debt would increase by over 15% of GDP in Europe in just one year. These are huge figures and they do not include contingent fiscal risks from guarantees and central bank asset purchases. However, rather than focussing on the details, it is more important to take note of the patterns: in a severe crisis – be it financial or other – expenditure ratios, deficits and debt increase massively and very rapidly.

These patterns underpin the main messages of this book: First, we economists have great difficulties predicting the future and its challenges. Surprises and crises are certain to come at some point. Pandemics are on the list of challenges governments should be prepared for, as mentioned in Chapter 7. Expecting a pandemic to occur at some point is not very original. But the lack of preparation and the magnitude and speed of the Coronavirus crisis took everybody by surprise.

Second, the Coronavirus crisis underlines the importance of lean and efficient governments that deliver well on their core tasks, and thereby build trust (as per the Introduction). There was too much global complacency regarding the risk of pandemics, and health systems in several countries proved deficient. There may be other tasks that will also need more attention, while spending and debt are already high in many countries (Chapters 1–3). The money for new priorities could generally come from being more efficient. Most if not all countries have room for improvement here (as discussed in Chapters 4–6) so that, in fact, there would be no need for more spending in the aggregate. Government should become better, and not bigger!

Third, the crisis underlines the importance of fiscal risks from population ageing and the financial sphere. As the Coronavirus proved more dangerous for old and sick people than for the young, the human suffering and the financial costs were bound to be higher in ageing societies (Chapter 7). And the economic and fiscal fallout and uncertainty very quickly caused a reassessment of the fiscal–financial risks linking corporations, the financial sector and governments (Chapters 8 and 9). The global interdependence of financial markets also resulted in a quick transmission of risks. Credit spreads of highly indebted governments, companies and emerging economies shot up.

Fourth, the Coronavirus crisis underlines the need for sufficient buffers and resilience. This is all the more important when governments promise broad-based insurance from the associated risks. Already, the global financial crisis has been more costly because of the almost unlimited government insurance of the financial sector. It is very difficult to find the right balance between private and public liability for crisis costs.

Past crises teach us that prudence is of the essence for another reason. Debt that looks financeable and sustainable might turn out to be problematic under changed circumstances. National buffers with lean and efficient government are good as a precaution. International safety nets from central banks and international organisations like the IMF and the ESM can go a long way towards mitigating problems (and trigger reforms). But the room for manoeuvre of these players is also limited if they want to preserve their own integrity and reputation. Governments in many advanced countries did not do enough to rebuild fiscal resilience before the Coronavirus crisis.

Fifth, the crisis also underlines the importance of rules and institutions (Chapter 10). Resilience – with spending, deficit and debt buffers – is more likely to stay sufficiently large if countries generally follow the rules of sound fiscal policies. In exceptional circumstances, like in such a crisis, governments can then suspend the rules to stabilise economies and incomes while remaining credible and upholding the sustainability of public finances.

One thing is clear: the challenges for public spending and the role of the state will be greater than before this new crisis – and so too will the necessity of having an earnest debate on this. The social market economy is still our best chance for rebuilding resilience and securing the future.

Table of Data Sources

Data	Source	Available at
Fiscal data		
Selective historic data (see Tables)	Tanzi and Schuknecht (2000)	
Selective country data (see Tables and Figures)	European Commission, Ameco	https://ec.eurpa.eu
Public debt, unless otherwise specified	IMF Global Debt Database	https://IMF.org
Various spending, revenue, deficit and debt data	OECD	https://oecd.org
Spending data, Asia	IMF, WEO	https://IMF.org
Asset price related fiscal effects (Tables 8.2 and 8.3)	Morris and Schuknecht (2007); Eschenbach and Schuknecht (2004)	
German primary and interest expenditure, various vintages	German Federal Ministry of Finance	www.bundesfinanzministerium.de
Stability Programmes, Italy and France	Ministry of Finance, Italy and France	www.tresor.economie.fr; www.mef.gov.it
Selected expenditure categories		
Government consumption	OECD (National accounts unless otherwise specified)	https://data.oecd.org/gga/general-government-spending-by-destination.htm
Education	OECD	https://data.oecd.org/gga/general-government-spending.htm
Health	OECD	https://data.oecd.org/healthres/health-spending.htm
Public investment	OECD	https://data.oecd.org/gdp/investment-by-sector.htm
Social expenditure, health, pensions, long-term care	OECD	https://data.oecd.org/socialexp/social-spending.htm
Total spending	OECD	https://data.oecd.org/gga/general-government-spending.htm

Expenditure reform; expenditure and deficit reduction	Schuknecht and Tanzi (2005); Hauptmeier et al. (2014)	

Performance, institutions, real economy indicators

Rule of law and property rights (composite)	Fraser Institute	www.farserinstitute.org
Corruption	World Economic Forum: The World Competitiveness Index	http://reports.weforum.org/global-competitiveness-index-2017–2018/competitiveness-rankings/#series=GCI.A.01.01.02
Red tape	World Economic Forum: Global Competitiveness Index	http://reports.weforum.org/global-competitiveness-index-2017–2018/competitiveness-rankings/#series=EOSQ048
Quality of judiciary	World Economic Forum: Global Competitiveness Index	http://reports.weforum.org/global-competitiveness-index-2017–2018/competitiveness-rankings/#series=EOSQ144
Shadow economy	Medina and Schneider (2018)	www.imf.org/~/media/Files/Publications/WP/2018/wp1817.ashx
Secondary enrolment	OECD	https://data.oecd.org/eduatt/enrolment-rate.htm
PISA	OECD	www.oecd-ilibrary.org/education/data/oecd-education-statistics/pisa-programme-for-international-student-assessment_data-00365-en
Infant mortality	World Bank Development Indicators	https://data.worldbank.org/indicator/SP.DYN.IMRT.IN
Life expectancy	World Bank Development Indicators	https://data.worldbank.org/indicator/SP.DYN.LE00.IN

(continued)

Data	Source	Available at
Fiscal data		
Infrastructure quality	World Bank Logistics Performance Index (LPI)	https://lpi.worldbank.org/international/global?sort=desc&order=LPI%20Score#datatable
	Composite Infrastructure quality and governance Hertie School, for 2016	www.hertie-school.org/en/governancereport/govreport-indicators/
Income share, lowest 40%	World Bank Development Indicators	http://databank.worldbank.org/data/reports.aspx?source=2&Topic=11
Gini coefficient	OECD	https://oecd.org
Real economic growth	OECD, IMF	https://oecd.org; https://imf.org
Unemployment rate	OECD	https://data.oecd.org/unemp/unemployment-rate.htm
DEA analysis	Afonso and Kazemi (2017)	
Expenditure and growth	Cournède et al. (2018)	
Unit labour costs	EU Commission, AMECO	https://ec.eurpa.eu
Budget institutions, spending reviews	OECD (2019b)	https://oecd.org
Surveys on social expenditure and equality	European Science Foundation	https://europeansocialsurvey.org
Ageing-related Indicators		
Private Pension Benefits	OECD (2017c)	https://oecd.org
Health expenditure system financing	OECD Health Statistics (2017)	https://oecd.org
Old-age dependency ratio	UN World Population Prospects	https://population.uin.org/wpp
Age-related expenditure	European Commission Ageing Report (2015); IMF	https://ec.eurpa.eu
Debt-sustainability, Germany	German Federal Ministry of Finance	www.bundesfinanzministerium.de
Ageing-related figures in Chapter 7	Schuknecht and Zemanek (2020)	

Capital Tier One	European Central Bank	www.ecb.europa.eu
Non-performing loans	European Central Bank	www.ecb.europa.eu
Financial data		
Government gross financing needs	IMF, Fiscal Monitor (October 2018)	https://IMF.org
Equity and real estate prices	BIS	https://BIS.org
Global debt	IMF Global Financial Stability Report (2018)	https://IMF.org
Size of shadow banking	BIS	https://BIS.org
Household and NFC debt	BIS	https://BIS.org
Holders of government debt by sector/percentage of assets, Italy	BIS	https://BIS.org
Exposure of banks to government debt (% of capital)	European Banking Authority, Transparency Exercise, 2016	www.eba.europa.eu
Pension fund solvency	Rauh (2018)	
Corporate bond markets, size, ratings	Çelik, Demirtaş and Isaksson (2019)	www.oecd.org/corporate/Corporate-Bond-Markets-in-a-Time-of-Unconventional-Monetary-Policy.htm.
Assets in private pension plans	OECD (2018c)	https://oecd.org
Central Bank government debt holdings	BIS, Bank of England, Swiss National Bank	https://bis.org; www.bankofengland.co.uk; www.snb.ch
International credit	BIS Quarterly Review, September 2018	https://BIS.org
Ratings of government debt	Standard & Poor's (S&P)	www.standardandpoors.com
Financial crisis support in the past	Laeven and Valencia (2008)	
Fiscal costs of global financial crisis	IMF Fiscal Monitor (2015)	https://IMF.org
IMF programmes, size	IMF, Members' Financial Data	https://IMF.org
FSB reform implementation	FSB (2018)	https://FSB.org

(continued)

(continued)

Data	Source	Available at
Fiscal data		
Banking union, liability cascade	German Federal Ministry of Finance	www.bundesfinanzministerium.de
Italy ten-year bond yields	Investing.com, Historical Data	www.investing.com/rates-bonds/italy-10-year-bond-yield-historical-data
Spain ten-year bond yields	Investing.com, Historical Data	www.investing.com/rates-bonds/spain-10-year-bond-yield-historical-data
Germany thirty-year bond yields	Deutsche Finanzagentur	www.deutsche-finanzagentur.de
Government guarantees	OECD	https://oecd.org
Quotes		
Joseph Schumpeter (Ch 1), David Hume (Ch 3), John Stuart Mill (Ch 10)	Blankart (2017)	
Edmund Burke (Introduction), Aristotle (Ch 4), John Stuart Mill (Ch 6), Joseph Schumpeter (Ch 8)	Müller (2003)	
Wolfgang Schäuble	Schäuble (2019)	Frankfurter Allgemeine Zeitung, 17 January 2019 (own translation)
All others	Brainyquote (2019)	www.brainyquote.com

Bibliography

Acemoglu, D. and J. A. Robinson (2012) *Why Nations Fail: The Origins of Power, Prosperity and Poverty*. Chicago: Crown Publishing Group.

Admati, A. R., P. M. DeMarzo, M. Hellwig and P. Pfleiderer (2013) Fallacies, Irrelevant Facts, and Myths in the Discussion of Capital Regulation: Why Bank Equity Is Not Expensive. Stanford Business School Working Paper 2065.

Afonso, A. and M. St Aubyn (2005) Non-Parametric Approaches to Education and Health Efficiency in OECD Countries. *Journal of Applied Economics*, VIII(2): 227–246.

Afonso, A. and M. Kazemi (2017) Assessing Public Spending Efficiency in 20 OECD Countries. In B. Boekemeier and A. Greiner (eds.), *Inequality and Finance in Macroeconomics*. Cham: Springer: 7–42.

Afonso, A. and L. Schuknecht (2019) How 'Big' Should Government Be? EconPol Working Paper 23/2019.

Afonso, A., L. Schuknecht and V. Tanzi (2005) Public Sector Efficiency: An International Comparison. *Public Choice*, 123(3–4): 312–347.

Afonso, A., J. Tovar Jalles and A. Venancio (2019) Taxation and Public Spending Efficiency: An International Comparison. EconPol Working Paper 25/2019.

Akgun, O., D. Bartolini and B. Cournède (2017) The Capacity of Governments to Raise Taxes. OECD Economics Department Working Papers 1407.

Alesina, A. (1995) Fiscal Expansions and Fiscal Adjustments in OECD Countries. *Economic Policy*, 21: 205–208.

  (1996) Fiscal Adjustments in OECD Countries: Composition and Macroeconomic Effects. IMF Working Paper 96nO.

Alesina, A. and S. Ardagna (2010) Large Changes in Fiscal Policy: Taxes versus Spending. In R. Brown (ed.), *Tax Policy and the Economy*. Chicago: University of Chicago Press, 24: 235–268.

  (2013) The Design of Fiscal Adjustments. *Tax Policy and the Economy*, 27: 19–68.

Alesina, A., I. Angeloni and L. Schuknecht (2005) What Does the European Union Do? *Public Choice*, 123: 275–319.

Alesina, A., C. Favero and F. Giavazzi (2019) *Austerity: When It Works and When It Doesn't*. Princeton, NJ: Princeton University Press.

Amaglobeli, D., N. End, M. Jarmuzek and G. Palomba (2015) From Systemic Banking Crises to Fiscal Costs: Risk Factors. International Monetary Fund Working Paper 15/166.

Andersson, F. and L. Jonung (2019) The Swedish Fiscal Framework – The Most Successful One in the EU? Lund University Department of Economics Working Paper 2019:6.

Andritzky, J. D., I. Christofzik and L. Feld (2018) Sovereign Debt Restructuring in the Euro Area? In J. Andritzky and J. Rocholl (eds.), *Towards a More Resilient Euro Area: Ideas from the 'Future Europe' Forum.* Brussels: CEPS: 31–40.

Beetsma, R. and E. Steclebout-Orseau (2018) European Fiscal Rules and Governance, Quo Vadis? In J. Andritzky and J. Rocholl (eds.), *Towards a More Resilient Euro Area: Ideas from the 'Future Europe' Forum.* Brussels: CEPS: 21–28.

Bénassy-Quéré, A., M. Brunnermeier, H. Enderlein, E. Farhi, M. Fratzscher, C. Fuest, P.-O. Gourinchas, P. Martin, J. Pisani-Ferry, H. Rey, I. Schnabel, N. Véron, B. Weder di Mauro and J. Zettelmeyer (2018) Reconciling Risk Sharing with Market Discipline: A Constructive Approach to Euro Area Reform. *CEPR Policy Insight*, 91.

Bernoth, K., J. von Hagen and L. Schuknecht (2012) Sovereign Risk Premiums in the European Government Bond Market. *Journal of International Money and Finance*, 31: 975–995.

Berti, K., M. Salto and M. Lequien (2012) An Early-Detection Index of Fiscal Stress for EU Countries. European Commission Economic Papers 475.

BIS (Bank for International Settlement) (various issues: September 2018, March 2019; September 2019) Quarterly Review. Basel.

(2016, 2018, 2019) Annual Report. Basel.

(2017) The Regulatory Treatment of Sovereign Exposures. Discussion Paper. Basel.

Blanchard, O. (2019) Public Debt and Low Interest Rates. PIIE Working Paper 19-4.

Blanchard, O. and D. Leigh (2014) Learning about Fiscal Multipliers from Growth Forecast Errors. *IMF Economic Review*, 62(2): 179–212.

Blankart, C. B. (2017) *Öffentliche Finanzen in der Demokratie*, 9th ed. Munich: Vahlen.

Böhm-Bawerk, E. von (1914) Macht oder Ökonomisches Gesetz? Zeitschrift für Volkswirtschaft. *Sozialpolitik und Verwaltung*, 23: 205–271.

Borio, C., J. Contreras and F. Zampolli (2019) *Banking Crises: Implications for Fiscal Sustainability.* Basel: BIS Mimeo.

Borio, C., P. Disyatat and M. Juselius (2013) Rethinking Potential Output: Embedding Information About the Financial Cycle. BIS Working Papers 404. Basel.

Borio, C., E. Kharroubi, C. Upper and F. Zampolli (2015) Labour Reallocation and Productivity Dynamics: Financial Causes, Real Consequences. BIS Working Papers 534. Basel.

Borio, C., M. Lombardi, and F. Zampolli (2016) Fiscal Sustainability and the Financial Cycle. BIS Working Paper 552. Basel.

Bova, E., M. Ruiz-Arranz, F. Toscani and H. Elif Ture (2016) The Fiscal Costs of Contingent Liabilities: A New Dataset. IMF Working Paper 16/14.

Brainyquote (2019) Various Quotes. www.brainyquote.com.

Brennan, G. and J. M. Buchanan (1985) *The Reason of Rules: Constitutional Political Economy.* Cambridge: Cambridge University Press.

Buchanan, J. M. (1975) *The Limits of Liberty: Between Anarchy and Leviathan*. Chicago: University of Chicago Press.

Buchanan, J. M. and G. Tullock (1962) *The Calculus of Consent: Logical Foundations of Constitutional Democracy*. Ann Arbor: University of Michigan Press.

Buck, F. and L. Schuknecht (2017) Fiscal Soundness and the Triangle of Stability. *Credit and Capital Markets*, 50(2): 171–187.

Calvo, G. A., A. Izquierdo and L. F. Mejia (2004) On the Empirics of Sudden Stops: The Relevance of Balance Sheet Effects. NBER Working Paper 10520.

Caselli, F. and P. Wingender (2018) Bunching at 3 Percent: The Maastricht Fiscal Criterion and Government Deficits. IMF Working Paper 18/182.

Çelik, S., G. Demirtaş and M. Isaksson (2019) *Corporate Bond Markets in a Time of Unconventional Monetary Policy*. Paris: OECD Capital Market Series.

Cerovic, S., K. Gerling, A. Hodge and P. Medas (2018) Predicting Fiscal Crisis. IMF Working Paper WP/18/181.

CGFS (Committee on the Global Financial System) (2011) The Impact of Sovereign Credit Risk on Bank Funding Conditions. CGFS Papers, 43. Basel.

Checherita-Westphal, C., A. H. Hallett and P. Rother (2014) Fiscal Sustainability Using Growth Maximising Debt Targets. *Applied Economics*, 46(6): 638–647.

Chirinko, R., R. Chiu and S. Henderson (forthcoming) *What Went Wrong? The Puerto Rican Debt Crisis, the 'Treasury Put' and the Failure of Market Discipline*. Institute of Monetary and Economic Studies/Bank of Japan Working Paper.

Chobanov, D. and A. Mladenova (2009) What Is the Optimum Size of Government. Institute for Market Economics.

Coase, R. H. (1960) The Problem of Social Cost. *Journal of Law and Economics*, 3: 1–44.

Cogan, J., T. Cwik, J. Taylor and V. Wieland (2010) New Keynesian versus Old Keynesian Government Spending Multipliers. *Journal of Economic Dynamics and Control*, 34: 281–295.

Collier, P. (2018) *The Future of Capitalism*. London: Penguin.

Cournède, B., J.-M. Fournier and P. Hoeller (2018) Public Finance Structure and Inclusive Growth. OECD Economic Policy Papers 25.

Cunliffe, J (2018) *Central Clearing and Resolution – Learning Some of the Lessons of Lehmann*. Speech given at FIA International Derivatives Expo, London.

Dauns, M., W. Ebert and L. Schuknecht (2015) *Paying for the Future: Working Systems for Pensions and Healthcare*. London: Politeia.

Demmou, L. and G. Franco (2020) Do Sound Infrastructure Governance and Regulation Affect Productivity Growth? New Insights from Firm Level Data. OECD Economics Department Working Paper 1609.

De Larosière, J. (2019) Nous sommes entrés dans une ère ou la dette dirige nos économies. Les Echos, 22 June.

De Mooij, R., M. Keen and M. Orihara (2014) Taxation, Bank Leverage and Financial Crises. In R. de Mooji and G. Nicodeme (eds.), *Taxation and Regulation of the Financial Sector*. Cambridge, MA: MIT Press: 229–253.

Destais, C., F. Eidam and F. Heinemann (2019) The Design of a Sovereign Debt Restructuring Mechanism for the Euro Area: Choices and Trade-Offs. EconPol Europe Policy Report 11/2019.

Detragiache, E. and G. Ho (2010) Responding to Banking Crises: Lessons from Cross-Country Evidence. IMF WP 10/18.

Deutsche Bundesbank (2019) Finanzstabilitätsbericht (Financial Stability Report). Frankfurt.

Diamond, J. (2005/2011) *Collapse.* New York: Viking Press.

Doennebrink, E., W. Ebert and L. Schuknecht (2019) Gute Evidenz für wirksame Finanzpolitik. In C. Buch and R. Riphahn (eds.), *Evaluierung von Finanzmarktreformen: Lehren aus den Politikfeldern Arbeits-markt, Gesundheit und Familie.* Leopoldina-Forum Nr. 1. Halle: Leopoldina-Forum: 83–94.

Dreher, A., J. E. Sturm and H. W. Ursprung (2008) The Impact of Globalisation on the Composition of Government Expenditures: Evidence from Panel Data. *Public Choice,* 134(3): 263–292.

Durre, A. and H. Pill (2011) *Non-Standard Monetary Policy Measures, Monetary Financing and the Price Level.* Frankfurt: Mimeo.

EEAG (European Economic Advisory Group) (2019) *EEAG Report on the European Economy.* Munich: CESifo.

Erhard, L. (1957/2009) *Wohlstand für Alle.* Köln: Anaconda. [In English: *Prosperity for All.* New York: Frederik Plaeger.]

Eschenbach, F. and L. Schuknecht (2004) Budgetary Risks from Real Estate and Stock Markets. *Economic Policy,* 19(39): 313–346.

ESRB (European Systemic Risk Board) (2016) *Macroprudential Policy Issues Arising from Low Interest Rates and Structural Changes in the EU Financial System.* November. Frankfurt: ESRB.

(2018a) Recommendation of the European Systemic Risk Board of 7 December 2017 on Liquidity and Leverage Risks in Investment Funds. Frankfurt. February.

(2018b) EU Shadow Banking Monitoring Report 3/2018. European System of Financial Supervision.

European Commission (2015) The 2015 Ageing Report: Economic Budgetary Projections for the 28 European Member States (2013–2060). Brussels: European Commission.

(2018) Ageing Report: Economic and Budgetary Projections. European Commission Institutional Paper 079. Brussels: European Commission.

(2020) European Economic Forecast Spring 2020. Brussels: European Commission.

Eusepi, G. and E. Cerioni (1989) *Constitutional Constraints on Government: The Impact of Article 81 of the Italian Constitution.* Paper presented at the European Public Choice Society Meeting, Linz.

Fournier, J. M. (2016) The Positive Effect of Public Investment on Potential Growth. OECD Economics Department Working Papers 1347.

Fournier, J. M. and A. Johansson (2016) The Effect of the Size and the Mix of Public Spending on Growth and Inequality. OECD Economics Department Working Papers 1344.

Frey, B. (1988) Explaining the Growth of Government: International Perspectives. In J. A. Lybeck and M. Henrekson (eds.), *Explaining the Growth of Government.* Amsterdam: North-Holland: 21–28.

Friedman, M. and R. Friedman (1980) *Free to Choose.* Boston, MA: Harcourt.

FSB (Financial Stability Board) (2018) Global Shadow Banking Monitoring Report 2017. Basel.

(2019) Implementation and Effects of the G20 Financial Regulatory Reform. 4th Annual Report. Basel.

Fuest, C. and D. Gros (2019a) Applying Nominal Expenditure Rules in the Euro Area. EconPol Policy Brief 15/2019.

(2019b) Government Debt in Times of Low Interest Rates: The Case of Europe. EconPol Europe Policy Brief 16/2019.

Fuest, C. and F. Heinemann (2017) Accountability Bonds – Reconciling Fiscal Policy Based on Market Discipline with Financial Stability. EconPol Policy Brief 3, November.

Galbraith, J. K. (1958) *The Affluent Society*. Boston, MA: Houghton Mifflin.

Gaspar, V., M. Obstfeld and R. Sahay (2016) Macroeconomic Management When Policy Space Is Constrained: A Comprehensive, Consistent, and Coordinated Approach to Economic Policy. IMF Staff Discussion Note SDN/16/09.

German Federal Ministry of Finance (2016) *Fourth Report on the Sustainability of Public Finances*. Berlin.

Giavazzi, F. and M. Pagano (1990) Can Severe Fiscal Contractions Be Expansionary? In O. Blanchard and S. Fischer (eds.), *NBER Macroeconomics Annual*. Cambridge: MA: MIT Press: 75–110.

Gordon, R. J. (2016) *The Rise and Fall of American Growth: The U.S. Standard of Living Since the Civil War*, Princeton, NJ: Princeton University Press.

Górnicka, L., C. Kamps, G. Köster and N. Leiner-Killinger (2018) Learning About Fiscal Multipliers During the European Sovereign Debt Crisis: Evidence from A Quasi-Natural Experiment. ECB Working Paper 2154.

Hallerberg, M., R. Strauch and J. Von Hagen (2009) *Fiscal Governance in Europe*. Cambridge: Cambridge University Press.

Hank, R. (2012) *Die Pleiterepublik: Wie der Schuldenstaat Uns Entmündigt und Wie Wir Uns Befreien Können*. Munich: Blessing Verlag.

Hanushek, E., M. Piopiunik and S. Wiederhold (2019) The Value of Smarter Teachers: International Evidence on Teacher Cognitive Skills and Student Performance. *Journal of Human Resources*, 54(4): 857–899.

Hanushek, E. and L. Woessmann (2015) *The Knowledge Capital of Nations*. Cambridge, MA: MIT Press.

Hauptmeier, S., M. Heipertz and L. Schuknecht (2007) Expenditure Reform in Industrialised Countries: A Case-Study Approach. *Fiscal Studies*, 28(3): 293–343.

Hauptmeier, S., A. J. Sanchez-Fuentes and L. Schuknecht (2011) Towards Expenditure Rules and Fiscal Sanity in the Euro Area. *Journal of Policy Modelling*, 33(4): 597–617.

(2014) Mastering the Fiscal Crisis: The Role of Ambitious Expenditure Reform. Unpublished manuscript.

Hayek, F. A. von (1960) *The Constitution of Liberty*. Chicago: University of Chicago Press.

Heinemann, F., M. D. Moessinger and M. Yeter (2018) Do Fiscal Rules Constrain Fiscal Policy? A Meta-Regression-Analysis. *European Journal of Political Economy*, 51: 69–92.

Herrera, S. and G. Pang (2005) Efficiency of Public Spending in Developing Countries: An Efficiency Frontier Approach. World Bank Policy Research Working Paper 3645.

Hobbes, T. (1651) *Leviathan*. London: Penguin.

Honda, J., R. Tapsoba and I. Issifou (2018) When Do We Repair the Roof? Insights from Responses to Fiscal Crisis Early Warning Signals. International Monetary Fund Working Paper 18/77.

Honohan, P. and D. Klingebiel (2003) The Fiscal Cost of Implications of an Accommodating Approach to Banking Crises. *Journal of Banking & Finance*, 27(8): 1539–1560.

IMF (International Monetary Fund) (2018) *Public Investment Management Assessment – Review and Update*. Washington, DC: International Monetary Fund.

(various issues) *Fiscal Monitor*. Washington, DC: International Monetary Fund.

GFSR/Global Financial Stability Report. Washington, DC: International Monetary Fund.

WEO/World Economic Outlook. Washington, DC: International Monetary Fund.

Ilzetzki, E., E. G. Mendoza and C. Végh (2010) How Big (Small) Are Fiscal Multipliers? NBER Working Paper 16479.

Issing, O. (2009) Politischer Wille oder Ökonomisches Gesetz? Einige Anmerkungen zu einem grossen Thema. CFS Working Paper Series 2009: 24.

(2019) Bei jedem Schnupfen ein Antibiotikum. *Handelsblatt*, 2 August 2019.

Jaeger, A. and L. Schuknecht (2007) Boom–Bust Phases in Asset Prices and Fiscal Policy Behaviour. *Emerging Markets Finance and Trade*, 43(6): 45–66.

James, H. (2009) The Financial Crisis and the Disciplinary Challenge of Natural Law. *Zeitschrift für Staats- und Europawissenschaften (ZSE) / Journal for Comparative Government and European Policy*, 7(3/4): 436–449.

Jankovics, L. and M. Sherwood (2017) Independent Fiscal Institutions in the EU Member States: The Early Years. EC Discussion Paper 067.

Johansson, A. (2016) Public Finance, Economic Growth and Inequality. OECD Economics Department Working Papers 1346.

Jonung, L., M. Tujula and L. Schuknecht (2009) The Boom–Bust Cycle in Finland and Sweden 1984–95 in an International Perspective. In L. Jonung, J. Kiander and P. Vartia (eds.), *The Crisis of the 1990s in Finland and Sweden: The Nordic experience of Financial Liberalization*. Cheltenham: Edward Elgar: 183–201.

Keynes, J. M. (1926) *The End of Laissez-Faire*. London: Hogarth Press.

(1936) *The General Theory of Employment, Interest, and Money*. San Diego: Harcourt Brace Jovanovich.

König, N. and L. Schuknecht (2019) The Role of Government and Trust in the Market Economy. In W. Heusel and J. P. Rageade (eds.), *The Authority of EU Law – Do We Still Believe in It?* New York: Springer.

Kopits, G. and S. Symansky (1998) Fiscal Policy Rules, IMF Occasional Paper 162. Washington, DC.

Kornai, J. (1986) The Soft Budget Constraint. *Kyklos*, 39: 3–30.

Laeven, L. A. and F. V. Valencia (2008) Systemic Banking Crises: A New Database. IMF Working Paper 08/224: 1–78.

(2013) Systemic Banking Crises Database. *IMF Economic Review*, 61(2): 225–270.

Langedijk, S., G. Nicodeme, A. Pagano and A. Rossi (2015) Debt Bias in Corporate Income Taxation and the Costs of Banking Crises. CEPR Discussion Papers 10616.

Larch, M, E. Orseau, and W. van der Wielen (2020) Do EU Fiscal Rules Support or Hinder Counter-Cyclical Fiscal Policy? European Commission: JRC Technical Reports.

Matthes, D. and J. Rocholl (2018) A Eurozone Basket as a Stabiliser for the Euro Area. In J. Andritzky and J. Rocholl (eds.), *Towards a More Resilient Euro Area: Ideas from the 'Future Europe' Forum*. Brussels: CEPS: 69–76.

Maurer, H. and P. Grussenmeyer (2015) Financial Assistance Measures in the Euro Area from 2008 to 2013: Statistical Framework and Fiscal Impact. ECB Statistics Paper Series 7/2015.

Mazzucato, M. (2013) *The Entrepreneurial State*. London: Anthem Press.

Mbaye, S., M. Moreno Badia and K. Chae (2018) Bailing Out the People? When Private Debt Becomes Public. IMF Working Paper 18/141.

Medina, L. and F. Schneider (2018) Shadow Economies Around the World: What Did We Learn Over the Past 20 Years? IMF Working Paper 1817.

Morris, R. and L. Schuknecht (2007) Structural Balances and Revenue Windfalls: The Role of Asset Prices Revisited. European Central Bank Working Paper 737.

Moser, P. (1994) Constitutional Protection of Economic Rights: The Swiss and U.S. Experience in Comparison. *Constitutional Political Economy*, 5: 61–69.

Müller, D. C. (1986) *The Growth of Government: A Public Choice Perspective, DM/86/33*. Washington, DC: International Monetary Fund.

(2003) *Public Choice III*. Cambridge: Cambridge University Press.

Musgrave, R. A. (1959) *The Theory of Public Finance: A Study in Public Economy*. New York: McGraw-Hill.

OECD (2015) Prudent Debt Targets and Fiscal Frameworks. OECD Economic Policy Paper 15.

(2017a) *Tackling Wasteful Spending in Health*. Paris: OECD.

(2017b) *Health at a Glance*. Paris: OECD.

(2017c) *Pensions at a Glance*. Paris: OECD.

(2017d) *School Choice and School Vouchers: An OECD Perspective*. Paris: OECD.

(2017e) *The Funding of School Education: Connecting Resources and Learning*. Paris: OECD.

(2018a) *Education at a Glance*. Paris: OECD.

(2018b) Public Finance Structure and Inclusive Growth. OECD Economic Policy Paper 25.

(2018c) *Pension Markets in Focus*. Paris: OECD.

(2019a) *Corporate Bond Markets in a Time of Monetary Policy Transition*. Paris: OECD.

(2019b) *Budgeting Outlook*. Paris: OECD.

(2019c) *Going for Growth*. Paris: OECD.

(2019d) *OECD Sovereign Borrowing Outlook*. Paris: OECD.

(2019e) *OECD Global Pension Statistics*. Paris: OECD.

(2019f) *OECD Business and Finance Outlook*. Paris: OECD.

Olson, M. (1982) *The Rise and Decline of Nations: Economic Growth, Stagflation and Social Rigidities*. New Haven, CT: Yale University Press.

Pamies Sumner, S. and K. Berti (2017) A Complementary Tool to Monitor Fiscal Stress in European Economies. European Commission Discussion Paper 049.

Parlevliet, J. (2017) What Drives Public Acceptance of Reforms? Longitudinal Evidence from a Dutch Pension Reform. *Public Choice*, 173(1–2): 1–23.

Peacock, A. and J. Wiseman (1961) *The Growth of Public Expenditure in the United Kingdom*. Princeton, NJ: Princeton University Press.

Perotti, R. (1998) The Political Economy of Fiscal Consolidations. *Scandinavian Journal of Economics (Sweden)*, 100(1): 367–404.

Pevcin, P. (2004) *Does Optimal Spending Size of Government Exist?* Paper presented at the European Group of Public Administration Conference, 1–4 September, Ljubljana.

Pigou, A. C. (1920) *The Economics of Welfare.* London: Macmillan.

(1928) *A Study in Public Finance.* London: Macmillan.

Potrafke, N. (2009) Did Globalization Restrict Partisan Politics? Empirical Evaluation of Social Expenditures In a Panel of OECD Countries. *Public Choice*, 140: 105–124.

(2018) The Globalisation–Welfare State Nexus: Evidence from Asia. *World Economy*, 42(3): 959–974.

Ramey, V. (2019) Ten Years after the Financial Crisis: What Have We Learned from the Renaissance in Fiscal Research? *Journal of Economic Perspectives*, 33(2): 89–114.

Rauh, J. (2018) *Fiscal Implications of Pension Underfunding.* Stanford University and Hoover. Unpublished manuscript.

Rodrik, D. (1998) Why Do More Open Economies Have Bigger Governments? *Journal of Political Economy*, 106(5): 997–1032.

Rother, P., L. Schuknecht and J. Stark (2010) The Benefits of Fiscal Consolidation in Uncharted Waters.. European Central Bank Occasional Paper 121.

Ruiz Rivadeneira, A. M. and L. Schuknecht (2019) Ensuring Effective Governance of Public Private Partnerships, *Journal of Infrastructure Policy and Development*, 3(2), DOI: http://dx.doi.org/10.24294/jipd.v3i2.1148.

Savage, L. (2018) The Politics of Social Spending after the Great Recession: The Return of Partisan Policy Making. *Governance*, 32(1): 1–19.

Schäuble, W. (2019) Die Balance halten. *Frankfurter Allgemeine Zeitung.* 17 January.

Schleicher, A. (2018) *World Class: How to Build a 21st Century School System.* Paris: OECD Publishing,

Schleicher, A. and L. Schuknecht (2019) Bildung, Ausbildung, Fortbildung: Herausforderungen aus Internationaler Perspektive. *ifo Schnelldienst*, 72(15): 20–35.

Schuknecht, L. (2005) Stability and Growth Pact: Issues and Lessons from Political Economy. *International Economics and Economic Policy*, 2: 65–89.

(2010) Fiscal Activism in Booms, Busts and Beyond. *Revista de Economia y Estadistica*, 3: 105–139.

(2013) Has Public Insurance Gone Too Far? CESifo Working Paper Series 4217.

(2018) The Supply of Safe Assets and Fiscal Policy. *Intereconomics*, 53(2): 94–100.

(2019) Fiscal–Financial Vulnerabilities. SAFE White Paper 62. Frankfurt.

Schuknecht, L. and V. Tanzi (2005) *Reforming Public Spending: Great Gain, Little Pain.* London: Politeia.

Schuknecht, L. and Zemanek, H. (2020) Social Dominance. *Public Choice*, DOI 10.1007/s11127-020-00814-5.

Schuknecht, L., P. Moutot, P. Rother and J. Stark (2011) The Stability and Growth Pact: Crisis and Reform. European Central Bank Occasional Paper 129.

Schuknecht, L., J. von Hagen and G. Wolswijk (2011) Government Bond Risk Premiums in the EU Revisited. *European Journal of Political Economy*, 27(1): 36–43.

Schulze, G. and H. W. Ursprung (1999) Globalisation of the Economy and the Nation State. *World Economy*, 22(3): 295–352.

Schwartz, G., M. Fouad, T. Hansen and G. Verdier (eds.) (forthcoming) *Strengthening Infrastructure Governance – From Aspiration to Action.* Washington DC: IMF.

Simpson, D. (2013) *The Rediscovery of Classical Economics: Adaptation, Complexity and Growth.* Cheltenham: Edward Elgar.

Sinn, H. W. (1997) The Selection Principle and Market Failure in Systems Competition. *Journal of Public Economics*, 66(2): 247–274.

(2014/2015) *The Euro Trap*. Oxford: Oxford University Press.

Smith, A. (1937) *An Inquiry into the Nature and Causes of the Wealth of Nations*. New York: The Modern Library.

Stiglitz, J. (2018) *Lessons from the Financial Crisis and Their Implications for Global Economic Policy*. New York: Columbia Academic Commons.

Sutherland, D., P. Hoeller, R. Merola and V. Ziemann (2012) Debt and Macroeconomic Stability. OECD Economics Department Working Papers 1003.

Tanzi, V. (1998) Fundamental Determinants of Inequality and the Role of Government. IMF Working Paper 98/178.

(2018a) *Welfare Systems and Their Complexity*. Paper presented at Congress of the International Institute of Public Finance, Tampere.

(2018b) Rethinking Keynesianism 10 Years after the Global Crisis. *Acta Oeconomica*, 68(S2): 127–139.

(2018c) The Limits of Stabilisation Policies. *Acta Oeconomica*, 69(S1): 141–151.

Tanzi, V. and L. Schuknecht (1997a) Reconsidering the Fiscal Role of Government: The International Perspective. *American Economic Review*, 87(2): 164–168.

(1997b) Reforming Government: An Overview over the Recent Experience. *European Journal of Political Economy*, 13(3): 395–417.

(2000) *Public Spending in the 20th Century – A Global Perspective*. Cambridge: Cambridge University Press.

Thygesen, N., R. Beetsma, M. Bordignon, S. Duchêne and M. Sczurek (2018) *Assessment of the Fiscal Stance Appropriate to the Euro Area in 2019*. Brussels: European Fiscal Board.

United Nations (2015) *World Population Prospects. The 2015 Revision*. New York: United Nations.

Ursprung, H. W. (2008) Globalization and the Welfare State. In S. N. Durlauf and L. E. Blume (eds.), *The New Palgrave Dictionary of Economics*, 2nd ed. London: Palgrave Macmillan.

Von Hagen, J. and I. Harden (1994) National Budget Processes and Fiscal Performance. *European Economy Reports and Studies*, 3: 311–418.

Weder di Mauro, B. and J. Zettelmeyer (2017) The New Global Financial Safety Net: Struggling for Coherent Governance in a Multipolar World. In *Essays on International Finance*, 4. Ontario: Centre for International Governance Innovation (CIGI).

White, W. (2017) Conducting Monetary Policy in a Complex, Adaptive Economy: Past Mistakes and Future Possibilities. *Credit and Capital Markets*, 50(2): 213–235.

Woessmann, L. (2016) The Importance of School Systems: Evidence from International Differences in Student Achievement. *Journal of Economic Perspectives*, 30(3): 3–32.

Wolf, M. (2019) *Escaping the Trap: Secular Stagnation, Monetary Policy and Financial Fragility*. 46th OeNBEconomics Conference, Vienna.

Wolswijk, G. (2009) Fiscal Aspects of Housing in Europe. In P. Arestis, P. Mooslechner and K. Wagner (eds.), *Housing Market Challenges in Europe and the United States*. New York: Palgrave Macmillan: 158–177.

Zettelmeyer, J. (2018) Managing Deep Debt Crises in the Euro Area: Towards a Feasible Regime. *Global Policy*, 9(1): 70–79.

Index

Printed in the United States
By Bookmasters